The Council of Heresy

See where they squat behind the escarpment
Ignorant of metre, of faction and schism,
Destined by favourless Fortune to be the true
Heirs of the Kingdom.

—Anthony Thwaite
'Letters of Synesius' Letter VI

Also by Andrew Duncan:

Poetry
In a German Hotel
Cut Memories and False Commands
Sound Surface
Alien Skies
Pauper Estate
Switching and Main Exchange
Anxiety before Entering a Room, new and selected poems
Surveillance and Compliance
Skeleton Looking at Chinese Pictures
The Imaginary in Geometry
Savage Survivals (amid modern suavity)

Criticism
The Poetry Scene in the Nineties (internet only)
Centre and Periphery in Modern British Poetry
The Failure of Conservatism in Modern British Poetry
Origins of the Underground
Fulfilling the Silent Rules (forthcoming)

As editor:
Don't Stop Me Talking (with Tim Allen)
Angel Exhaust (magazine: 1992–98 and 2005–   )
Joseph Macleod: *Cyclic Serial Zeniths from the Flux*

The Council of Heresy

—A Primer of Poetry in a Balkanised Terrain—

Andrew Duncan

Shearsman Books
Exeter

Published in the United Kingdom in 2009 by
Shearsman Books Ltd
58 Velwell Road
Exeter EX4 4LD

ISBN 978-1-84861-007-1
First Edition

Cover: 'A storm approaches Clavel Tower, Dorset' © 2006 by Blackbeck
Photographic.

Acknowledgements
Some of the essays appeared in earlier versions as follows: 'Goodbye to Eric
Mottram' was published in *Angel Exhaust*; 'The past as damage: Tom Raworth'
was published in different form in *Angel Exhaust*; 'The mythical history of
Northumbria: Barry MacSweeney' was published in *Salzburg Poetry Review*; 'In
the House of the Shaman' was published in *Angel Exhaust*; 'Siren Furnaces Blow
Infirm Metals' was published in the *CCCP Review*; 'From oracle to dialectic: Kelvin
Corcoran' was published in *Salzburg Poetry Review*; part of 'Deep Politics' was
published by Shearsman online at www.shearsman.com.
For quotations made in the essays, we are grateful to the following: Allen
Fisher, Tony Lopez, D.S. Marriott and Maggie O'Sullivan for permission to quote
from their published poems; Brian Keeble, literary executor for the Estate of
Kathleen Raine, for permission to quote from Kathleen Raine's out-of-print or
unpublished writings; Golgonooza Press (U.K.) and Counterpoint Press (U.S.A.) for
permission to reprint work from *The Collected Poems of Kathleen Raine*, copyright ©
2001 by Kathleen Raine; Enitharmon Press for permission to quote from Anthony
Thwaite's *Collected Poems*; Anthony Thwaite for permission to quote extracts from
the poem 'The Pine Processionary' from his collection *Inscriptions*—this poem
was commissioned as a film commentary by BBC2 for *Horizon*; Faber & Faber,
London, and Farrar, Straus & Giroux, New York, for permission to quote from
All Day Permanent Red by Christopher Logue; Anvil Press Poetry for permission to
quote from the poems 'Coloured Mansion 1474', 'Doctrines', 'Who Left the Door
Open' and 'She Passes Through the Poem', published in *Throw Out the Life Line
/ Lay Out the Corse: Poems, 1965–85* (Anvil Press Poetry, London, 1983); Bloodaxe
Books for permission to quote from two poems contained in Barry MacSweeney's
Wolf Tongue: Selected Poems 1965–2000 (Bloodaxe Books, Tarset, 2000), and also to
the Estate of Barry MacSweeney for permission to quote both from that volume,
and from uncollected work; Carcanet Press for permission to quote two poems by
Tom Raworth from *Collected Poems* (Carcanet Press, Manchester, 2003).

Contents

The Council of Heresy

Introduction

How do we grasp incomprehension? It slides away from us as we advance towards it, and winks out of view at the instant that we shed light on it. All the same the task of a prose work about poetry, such as this one, is to move into the area of maximum incomprehension and try to reduce it. Evidently the act of reading a poem is not always attended by understanding. There is a sort of sound like the sound of a needle skidding across a gramophone record which points to a failed literary experience. What seems to make it skid is a fluff-ball made up of the obscurity of the poet, the lack of cultural experience of the ordinary reader, and the malice of poetry world insiders distracted by jealousy and pre-existing alliances. To dissolve this complex, we need to apply diverse techniques at the same time. We will try to construct an overall map which puts poets in relation to each other, to discuss special and recent literary techniques or verbal games, to expound certain unusual theories about the universe used by some poets, as well as describing the work of a dozen individual poets.

The present work is, inevitably, a mile-long span spanning a two-mile river and is part of a series of six books on the period 1960–97 which have tried to track the radical expansion of scope of British poetry. The recurring theme of this volume is depolarisation. My preference would be for hostility to decrease, and for certain inherited feuds to end in a truth and reconciliation process. The idea of orthodoxy is present as an ideal, a state which you can reach once disinformation has been swept away. We are trying also to conduct an argument about heresy and whether radical originality is destructive of a shared literary culture or the greatest achievement of 20th-century literature.

Much of the information available around the scene is the product of malice. The issue may be less of Baroque obscurity in elaborate texts than of acts of disinformation by conservative cultural managers tangled up in alliances with other cultural managers. Where two people want exactly the same thing, they may be deadly rivals. In fact, fighting with someone may be evidence that you are similar to them. Poetic malice is not vitally dependent on differences of any kind, including political and stylistic ones. I have chosen not to discuss it because I think it is very well understood already. I feel in a good position to explain one faction to another. This volume is an attempt to set down the knowledge of expert readers, but also to expose the shadow knowledge, and to encourage a new era of openness and forgiveness.

The first non-heretical proposal is that poetry is born in cliques but is truly successful only when the poet's rivals admit that it is good. I set out as everyone's rival, with the ambition that the poets should recognise the descriptions as fair even when they feel themselves underrated. A second orthodox rule has to do with the difference between what is within a poet's fiat and what is not. The intention of the poem is a voluntary act by the poet, in an essentially arbitrary regime. Intention is as free as tyranny. The value of a poem is, though, something which other people have a vote on. A poem exists in a geography of successively less internal and more exterior zones. There is a question of ownership here, traced by finely shifting boundaries. The path of externalisation is difficult but is crucial to writing, may indeed be the principal part of the writer's task. Another rule we have to insist on is that a meaning which is inadequately externalised is not truly a poem, although it may include words and represent a lump of subjectivity. Obscurity is not pure autonomy. A poet can be the prime witness of what they want but they are not a privileged witness to issues belonging to a shared realm: for example, whether they are original, whether they are obscure, who they are similar to. The last one invokes much disagreement. Poets want almost more than anything else to be compared to other poets, but only the ones they choose. The ones they wish to resemble may not at all be the ones they resemble. The poet Luis Cernuda said that what people dislike about you may be the most significant thing about you, the thing you can least afford to lose. So also for poets who they resemble is crucial.

The equipment of orthodoxy must include the value of the descriptive terms with which we describe the poets, to be supported by definitions which the informed community would agree on. It's clear that other poets are the most accurate reference points and that comparison is more evocative than words like classical, rhetorical, pop, anti-classical, sensitive, etc. So the problem of establishing poetic groupings is on the direct path to making maps that tell you where you are. Some groupings are on the

Map pages at the end of the book. The construction of a map which dares to put poets near to the poets they are near to is bound to arouse outrage at the same time that it helps with rational discussion of disagreements. The project is to establish a set of shared artistic facts about the period, not to continue warfare.

Much of the hostility towards the very idea of a common map comes from a history of treating poets as groups—i.e. writing them off as groups. Justice requires an examination of the behaviour of individuals. This makes the process slow. The "information universe" of poetry includes the vital knowledge about several hundred individuals as a minimum. We can only look at a few in this session. I only have time to write about each poet once. This volume includes poets I haven't written about before. The cultural process involves thousands of people besides me, so I do not have to collect every grain of truth.

We are trying to develop classifiers based on modern practice and not on the 18th Century or Ancient Greece. Old classifiers fail because the inherited genres have collapsed, and for the last half century or so poets have had to invent procedures as well as think up poems. Misunderstanding is possible, and this is another area where we try to help the reader. The information is right there in the text, but preconceptions lock it out. Areas where explanation can help include the procedures for reading a poem; the context of it; and the ideas about lifestyle and politics on which the poem depends. If we explain the procedures, readers can interpret the primary evidence (the texts) for themselves. For poets who use procedures which we can describe either as similar to everyday speech or as similar to 19th century poetry, there is nothing to explain.

Another line of approach is to describe unshared intellectual backgrounds. Much of the book is doing that. The utility of this may be limited to a few poets. This kind of support covers agreed fantasies as well as simply beliefs: many poets write about shamanism, but this is a legitimated temporary identity rather than a proposition about how the universe works. This whole area can also be considered as heresy. (I wonder if it is true that some fantasies can be considered as not legitimate.)

Being released from wrong ideas is a liberation like any other. It is the nature of our brains to be beset by errors, much as plants are disposed to be beset by hungry parasites. Shedding wrong ideas brings a sensation of health, unity, and freedom. A Council of Heresy might be a process which frees us from bad ideas. I am not interested in putting a cracked pedestal under every crackpot. I believe that there is going to be an orthodox position and this is what I am trying to develop. The idea is a database which everyone agrees on, and which dozens of critics write and populate. But in our society originality is orthodoxy and the poets who fulfil this imperative most fully arouse disagreement. Conjecture is orthodoxy, experiment is orthodoxy, stylization is orthodoxy. Critique of our political system is orthodox. We all have a notion of artistic failure but it is hard to make that notion explicit.

Most of the information of which poetry is made consists of information about people. This information is about free actions but is subject to validation. The key idea in a body of poetic work may be the poet's idea of him—or herself. It follows that the heresies we are concerned with will often be poets' false ideas about themselves. Other data objects are opinions held about a poet by other people. So in fact a large share of the heresies to be adjudicated will be opinions about poets. There is a real chance of uncovering truth here, as the opinions are often based on malice and ignorance. The case would be heard at the Tribunal of Conceit, or the Assizes of Malice and Belittling. We are able to discover the poet's work as direct evidence. Indeed, the poems of poets have a function of making a case.

I have said much less about the lifestyle issues—the area where poetry surrenders to real life, or takes it over. Looking back, most people are glad that the UK did not become a Marxist republic, as some people actively expected in the 1970s. Not every alienated gesture is still interesting today. Yet the threat of the audience being 1,000 miles ahead of them inspired all factions in poetry to go beyond the secure artistic routine and reach a higher level. A literary critic is writing from shared memory, captured in print, and not from within a society we can't live in—or texts that never got written. I am writing about repeatable procedures of reading, and about texts which actually exist and can be retrieved. I was going to say that the upsurge of radical criticism created the levels of mutual alienation.

But that is not quite true—the level of frustration with a conservative English society created the radicalism. Strangely, one of the things we may have to get in touch with, looking back at the recent past, is the level of frustration. The papers submitted to the tribunal will include not only the writings of the poets but also evidence about the society they are rejecting and about their conjectures. The hearing is not going to make much of whatever is incomprehensible, perverse, vengeful, aleatory, which creates an empty space and is then unable to give it features. On the other hand, surely it would grant the classic poets of the 1970s the status they deserve. One possible meaning of a Council of Heresy might be a court which allows due process to occur before reaching a verdict. This might include allowing a thousand people to vote on each decision.

I had doubts about separating politics (ideas about how society ought to work) and lifestyle (images of people living in a certain way, the poet or others). Are these two different things or not? A proportion of poems refer to the state of being of a group of people, we think of that group as we read the poem, and our assessment of the poem is partly an assessment of that group. If a poem contains ideas about the future, we may have to wait 30 years before assessing whether those ideas were good. The problem of evaluating serious poetry is not greatly simpler than the problem of assessing what life in Britain is like. Clearly the council will reach decisions slowly. Simply living our lives as human beings qualifies us to assess what life is like. We can judge whether political ideas are true or false. We are allowed to look at the worlds they refer to. Even poems about a self are not merely self-referential: poets can make right or wrong bets about who to be. I have kept away from this whole area because it is too complicated. If you write boring poetry it quite probably is because your life-style is boring. That is simple, I suppose.

The Council could also be a vast jirga where all the heresies meet and argue their case. I haven't made my mind up. I envisage a Charlatans' Market where Iamblichus, Marx and Lévi-Strauss all have a stall, and we stroll by watching them plying their patter and muffing their miracles. Sun-worshippers, pre-Adamites, post-processualists, Gnostics, nonists, Fifth Monarchy men, Althusserians, sacrators of Basilidian talismans, sound poets, spells for the ears of headless demons . . .

NOTES

Books frequently referred to in this volume are abbreviated as follows: DSMT: *Don't Start Me Talking*, ed. Tim Allen and Andrew Duncan (Cambridge: Salt, 2006); Marvels, *Marvels of Lambeth, interviews with Allen Fisher*, edited Andrew Duncan (Cambridge: Salt, in preparation); FCon, *The Failure of Conservatism in Modern British Poetry* (Cambridge: Salt, 2003); Scene, *The Poetry Scene in the 90s* (published on the Internet at www.pinko.org); Origins, *Origins of the Underground* (Cambridge: Salt, 2008); Silent Rules, *Fulfilling the Silent Rules* (Cambridge: Salt, in preparation).

The Balkan Landscape, *or* Multipolar Order

We spoke of bad knowledge—of scurrilous versions of poets, not based on study of their works, shapes sculpted by the plastic force of malice rather than by DNA. You may well say that rivalry is inherent in poetry and that finally, where you have hundreds of poets you have hundreds of kilograms of raw rivalry. I would not set out to disprove this. The poetry scene has been essentially stable in the 35 years I have been involved in it. Nonetheless, the flagrant conflicts that existed in the 1970s are now depolarising, because the positions are obsolete and because the people who occupied them are either different people or actually dead. Even if new demarcation lines are coming into being, the ones I grew up with are dissolving and acts of reconciliation can now take place. We can make an innocent space even if the guilty acts are still in memory.

We worship originality and admire people who break the rules more than almost anything. How then could there be a heresy? Raymond Garlick wrote:

> Poetry is communication
> If there's need for elucidation
> The poem fails to that degree.
>   ('Notes for an Autobiography')[1]

As the Welsh poet suggests, the answer is that there are features which are at the gateway before you reach the thoughts of the poem and if these are badly managed the whole process fails and we would then say that the theory underlying it is wrong. That is, where the poet lacks insight into the reader and the information conveyed before and in the poem we can call this heresy. That is, ignorance produces a pattern of ideas, coherent enough to produce a book, which because wrong we define as heretical. For example, in *Odes*[2] by Barry MacSweeney the text is obscure and impossible to retrieve for most of its length. This obscurity shows a canon of literature, namely that we want to understand what we read. Where this obscurity is systematic we can speak of a heresy.

The information available around a text is so rich and various that we have difficulty capturing it. We have to envisage a human starting at birth with complete ignorance and learning a language and then artistic and behavioural codes of many sorts and grasping the specialised languages of modern art and then failing in one specific case. Some twinge must be telling us that success is just around the corner in this case too. The code is taught as well as learnt. It is thickly distributed through the poetry itself and through the whole cognitive environment of the late 20th century. The curious reader will succeed by scanning the whole landscape and the effective poet will show not only the message but also the means which carry the message.

The orthodox rule remains that art should be clear and complete. Surely there are unconscious and common rules of language which say:

follow the state of the listener's knowledge
remember what is disclosed
explain what is obscure
add information which is itself clear
be coherent
answer the questions which the listener is going to ask
use shared rules for constructing utterances
deploy redundancy to help with difficult parts
reduce ambiguity by confirming one or other possibility
strengthen the difficult parts
avoid contradiction and repetition

and as poetry is a form of language it is also governed by these unconscious and perpetually applied rules, and if it breaks them the effect is that the reader cannot find out what the poem might mean, and the pattern behind the negligent application is a heresy.

We would expect poets to be expert at language and so better at applying these rules more continuously and effectively. Reflexive monitoring of communication is such a basic human behaviour program that to be without it would be bizarre, to be ill even if not heretical. Insight into other people's states of mind is a climax state. Everything else rests on it but it is fragile and depends on intricate and easily perturbed faculties. Clarity does not mean simplicity or vacuity. Obscurity is failure.

Where a reading of a poem fails, there are (at least) two humans involved. We are forced to start from the position that we do not know which of the two is at fault for the failing. We could even blame third parties. Even the search for an individual to blame may derive from the urgent search for clarity which animates the court system, so that clarity in blame is only a function of a need for clarity. Perhaps there is no need to find fault and to find that someone has to pay. An alternative would be to look at the entire process and possibly find amendments which would improve the process. My assumption is that there are texts which are badly written and so abidingly obscure. I first read *Odes* more than 25 years ago and I am very familiar with the rest of MacSweeney's poetry. The social process by which one acquires insight into people's attitudes and into cultural expressions is continuous and partly unconscious. We need careful observation in order to capture it, as a preliminary to understanding where it goes wrong. A reader who knows nothing about the poetry of the last 50 years is in a weak situation to read a specific volume tomorrow. Poets might be poorly advised to write poetry which is so bare that it can be understood by someone with no background.

The poet and the reader both have their hi tech but home-made equipment but between the two is a third sector which simultaneously resists analysis and prevents communication. This is a sector of infra-structure, a network which distributes the code the poems use and which ideally is common to poet and reader. That is, the poet uses a code but a million other people circulate the code to society in general. That is, a poet may not be obscure all on his own but writes something which is lucid to one group and obscure to others—because the infrastructure has failed. When I "get" a work of art it is simplistic to look at the work of art alone and ignore the 40 years of my cultural life during which I acquired scraps of cultural vocabulary. Where poets and readers are beyond criticism in different ways we can still find fault with the institutions of poetry. We have also to define how they should work.

Moving away from a common language seems to be a move away from a common culture. However, the most original poetry is a product of the same geological forces that produced the whole of the landscape—I am suggesting that everywhere there are imperatives, and the extremes are reached by over-fulfilment of them. Any vector will take us to an extreme unless it is stopped in its tracks. The first question we have to answer, then, is why don't you want to write exactly like everyone else?

The increase of information and distinctions has given rise to the balkanization of the scene, bemoaned by Eric Homberger in 1977 in *Art of the Real*[3]. 22 years later, John Matthias, in a significant review article (for the *Electronic Book Review*)[4], was saying something very similar, and asking for the different sectors of the poetry scene to read each other. He asked why no anthology could unite the many vertexes of the stylistic space. It is balkanisation which leads us towards the overall shape of the period—an uncontrolled growth in the range and amount of poetry being written, which forces individual poets to mutate and differentiate in order to avoid vanishing in a mass of indistinct ideas. This is effortful for the poet—but it's good for the reader.

I suspect that the rule governing acquisition in a society dominated by leisure is that pleasurable activities should last as long as possible. That is, poetry will continue indefinitely to become more complex, and poets will tend, indefinitely, to differentiate from each other. So far as I can see, the clientele enjoy the act of shopping—and want a field which is not visible at a glance. Surely running out of new possibilities is the prospect which fills everyone with dread. The project of prolonging pleasure necessarily implies differentiation. Over decades, this differentiation necessarily implies incomprehensibility to the naive reader.

Journalists like to claim that poets waste time by differing from each other. A typical description of the poetry world by people who don't read poetry is 'endless energy wasted on squabbling'. Unless you see the breakout into self-definition, stylistic freedom, and unknown territory as pride and joy, I think it must make no sense at all. It must seem perverse. People want to stop it happening. I think it has a lot to do with narcissism and exhibition. I can see that it doesn't fit in with an Anglican approach to art—where pride is something you try to purge away.

I know that arts administrators would like poetry to be cut down to one simple, instrumental, utterance like a business plan. I know they would like the variety of magazines, so inefficient, to be cut down to a single one, which they could fund—or cut funding from—with a minimum of paperwork. I realise that they hate something which they can't understand without actually reading it. But to me the differences between poets actually mean something. More—the offsets are actually the essential fabric of the landscape, a honeycomb of tiny complete domains like a bubble raft. The 'squabbling' might just be the sound of poets realising how different they are from each other, and the energy it produces is actually what hurls someone out into boundless unexplored areas. Finicky attention to very slight differences is actually the most productive thing which poets do. The differences between a good poet and a bad poet are hard to detect— since both use largely the same techniques, words, rhythms—and lie in tiny verbal discriminants which journalists consider useless. Bad poems are essentially good copies of good poems. The millimetre scale is where everything happens.

Because poets don't work in teams—like actors—they don't need to collaborate. On the contrary, conformism is death for them—it prevents them from generating the new forms which are their memorable achievement. If they clung to the centre, they would simply hammer away producing cover versions of what already existed, and which no-one would want. They must take decisions which will allow them to go out into the unknown. We have suggested that differentiation is the key function of modern poetry—the focus on superfine detail is because the differences between poets are also on the millimetre scale. This is a disturbing suggestion; surely we need to consider the possibility that self-seeking is a minor activity of poets, associated with phases of insecurity and immaturity—and that the renewal of perception allows the 'small-scale' poetry to deal with all the subjects of great poetry—birth, death, the nature of the stars, the origins of society, the sources of the personality, the appearance of water, love, animals, architecture, the weather.

It is stressful to deliver poetry, live, to an audience two-thirds of whom will hate it. The differentiation of poetry gets in the way of the *communitas*, the psychological unity of a temporary group, which is so central to art. However, reconvergence is the least likely of all outcomes. Before this could happen, British society would have to abandon its nature as consumerist, individualist, and valuing differentiation. I suspect that the people most inconvenienced by the balkanization are the reviewers, who would prefer the field to be completely transparent, so that they could make authoritative judgments (without having to do much work).

There are few sources of relevant knowledge except protracted reading of the poetry itself, and few reviewers bother to do this. One of the typical experiences of naive readers of this poetry is to find themselves in the middle of the sound but unable to hear the music. We have to learn the semantic context of this poetry just as we have to learn the names of flowers in order to study botany.

Because there are hundreds of other poets, you have to differentiate yourself somehow. We can suggest that this can be achieved by another over-fulfilment—pursuing yourself along your own axis. The means for differentiating are learnt in childhood, as part of the war for adult attention which never stops; mixed too with dawning awareness of how makers sell their goods—a lesson drilled into you by the frustration of how much you need something special that you want to buy, and what the features are which make it a must-have rather than just one of those hundreds of things you can do without.

The increase of affluence and the spread of education have been producing far more people who want to write or read poetry. This means that the number of poets you have to compete with is far higher. If we imagine the poet's work in terms of a shared space, it means that the space available for each poet is smaller, or that there are more people competing for the same niche. This makes it desirable to specialise—to dissimilate. The new landscape—the one which became visible to everyone in the first half of the Sixties—both created this pressure to dissimilate and supplied the economic resources which made it possible to sell such a large number of niche products. Perhaps people reached reflexivity through the experience of endless rejections. The new stylisation generated far more information—this is how diversity was made possible. When fully flowering—and after say ten years of accumulating—this produced a data-rich and niche-riddled landscape which, from the viewpoint of a single bewildered critic, could appear as balkanised. From the point of view of the consumer, this divergence was nothing but good—it prolonged the possibilities of consumption.

Some poets innovated in the way they wrote, in order to stand out and so fix themselves in your memory; and others relied on their social identities to provide brand recognition, without changing anything in the standard model of the mid-century poem. They relied more on the prose biography on the book jacket, or in the back of the magazine, than on their poems. They expected readers to vote for themselves by admiring someone sociologically similar to themselves. Among the former, meanwhile, stylistic differentiation was achieved by fine distinctions. A shift into subjectivity created free variation which could be used to develop personalised stylistic niches. It occurred, necessarily, by weakening the functional characteristics of language. The speech channel was carrying a double load of information.

You realise your poetry is unoriginal and drop out of the mainstream. After years of fruitless effort, you succeed in writing poetry which is utterly distinctive and yet complete in itself. At this point cultural analysts come along and tell you you're guilty of balkanisation.

Everything happens as if modern poets are expressing, in their metrical, lexical, grammatical, and thematic choices, a protest against the assumptions of predictability made by sociologists and government policy-makers. An early statement of this position was made by D.S. Savage in *The Personal Principle* (1944)[5]. The difficulty with regular verse is that it is predictable, and exceptionalist poets want to use this moment of decision to indicate that the human being is in conscious control of their behaviour patterns, and can elude predictive formulae. Thus any violation of expectations in a poem may be a protest against the norms of society in the broad sense. Savage's concern was pacifism, a dissent from the machine for making war which the State had largely become in the 1940s. But later poets found other reasons for an equivalent level of dissent from the government and from the whole, far more extensive, project of rules and predictive knowledge which underpinned it. Unpredictability was often the key.

A great deal of poetry in our period was exceptionalist (as we may call it)—and few poets wished to be unoriginal.

Even poets who want there to be a big all-inclusive symbolic order, if only so that they can dominate the market by occupying it, end up with bitter complaints that it simply doesn't hold up. Can we pause to contemplate a despairing view of British history where the lifting of censorship circa 1644 unleashes a latent wish for religious self-determination which leads to the collapse of orthodoxy and a growth of a landscape of cults which has prolonged itself into secular culture and has grown ever more dissected from that time to this? There are two views of the proliferation of sects. One is that the history of reading in this country is so much tied up with Protestantism and the instruction to understand the great truths by the light of your own reason that the themes of breaking away from authority and founding your own sect are things you breathe in every day. The other is that England was an individualist society in basic institutions such as landholding and family customs, long before the Reformation. Each view has an interpretation of the large-scale transition of the mid-17th century, with the collapse of censorship in the 1640s followed by a permissive post-revolutionary settlement after 1660. The second view would see the law which (grudgingly) tolerated Nonconformists as bending to survive the pressure of the real society even though the powerful in the land were violently against tolerance. Both views concede that suspicion of authority and theological creativity by learned and unlearned alike have shaped the landscape. Most of the poets discussed here have an imaginative place they go to and much of the discussion is about the structural rules prevailing in these places. The significance of these places—other than England— is probably that they fit into the empty space left by the evacuation of sacred histories—either Biblical or classical-polytheistic—important to an earlier, orthodox literature. I emphasize the personal quality because this is how we read poetry today: Anthony Thwaite is not a heretic but all the same his poems are quite different from the Anglican hymnal—and fill a different role in the life of Anglican readers. I have written at length about the sources of imaginative journeys but the point is not to reduce them to factual experiences. Rather, the way Raine uses Neoplatonism or O'Sullivan uses shamanism is part of their creative patterns. There is an artistic question here. Many voices have been raised saying that modern poetry is obscure, there must be a problem with 'unshared backgrounds', but these imaginative realms also allow these works to expand to their full extent. It is interesting that Mottram's imaginary place is the USA, that Thwaite's is Libya, that Logue's is Troy, but their work is not necessarily obscure because it contains fog-free climates. We would surely not accuse them of an artistic crime because not all their poems are set in a suburb in England.

I must pause to ask after the balkanised reader. Surely you don't identify with this tribalised environment? No, you want to find good poetry wherever it is, even if the whole landscape conspires to hide it. You don't feel hostility to people you have never met. You don't see the merit of purposes in poetry other than experiencing beautiful poetry or producing it, and are equally happy whether they are achieved or not. This is my attitude. It would be pointless writing a book of explanations if everyone was loyally tribal. Taking up the cause of an individual who has been badly treated is a temporary deviation from detachment, which limits perception and should be followed by a recovery. It is possible that the hard core of balkanised agents are the professionals, who are so snarled up in loyalties, resentments, and feuds that this distracts them from poetry as art.

We are bound to ask after the conventional poets of the era. They stay close to the rules of everyday speech (especially between people who do not know each other well) and do not reach a personal style or a personal interpretation of human events. Their language is plain and the events they describe are predictable. All the same, there are a large number of them. Thus, balkanisation can be made to disappear if we ignore all the nonconformists. This is not very appealing. The orthodoxy of inhibited poets is an artistic disaster which is theoretically so wrong that we can attach to it the label of heresy. Meanwhile, thousands of tedious mainstream poets form the 'shadow knowledge' which hides a few dozen excellent ones from sight. The life of the group can throw up unexpected sequences of events without a revolution taking place. I am enthusiastic about the work of, say, Peter Levi and Anthony Thwaite.

Another line is opened if we posit the opposite of individualism[6] as being communalism. Certainly there is an amount of communist polemic against personalised art, for precisely this reason. A whole realm of protest poetry uses straightforward language because it wants to deal with public issues, not ones which apply only to a minority of one. This would apply to the feminist poetry of the anthology *Purple and Green*[7], for example. The Left is completely split between exceptionalist poetry and plain, documentary poetry, thoroughly continuous with the fabric of daily life. If we accept as a fact that the avant-garde does not exist in Wales (and surely the counter-proofs are only stragglers, and hard to interpret), this would point us towards communal values which are expressed in poetry and which are fulfilling for those who share those values. Anglo-Welsh poetry is expressing an ideal, even if that ideal is close to social reality. The flip side of individualism may be alienation—a whole society of possessive individuals, alienated from each other, not forming a neighbourhood.

The open style offers the poet the possibility of creating a world of their own, where everything belongs to them. The problem is the allure of megalomania, the Alexander complex which incites creators to advance too deep into empty space and to annihilate themselves. The question of why a second person would want to enter this private, and privately owned, universe, is not easy to answer. The set conditions of this period reward someone with huge narcissistic drive, creating a place so warm that the reader wants to be there and identifies with the creator. This personality type offends widely held British values and is not encouraged by teachers, mentors, and peers. The mention of values reminds us that we cannot understand the impulse to revolt and self-determination without understanding the battery of socially approved acts, feelings, and relationships which inspire the revolt. This would call for more descriptive detail than we have room for.

Notes

1. Raymond Garlick, *The Delphic Voyage and Other Poems* (Llanrwst: Carreg Gwalch Cyf., 2003). p.64.
2. Barry MacSweeney, *Odes 1971–78* (London: Trigram Press, 1978).
3. Eric Homberger, *The Art of the Real: Poetry in England and America since 1939* (London: Dent, 1977).
4. John Mattthias 'British Poetry at Y2K' (*Electronic Book Review*, at: http://www.electronicbookreview.com/thread/electropoetics/exhaustive
5. D.S. Savage, *The Personal Principle. Studies in Modern Poetry* (London: Routledge, 1944).
6. Emmanuel Todd, *L'invention de l'Europe* (Paris: Seuil, 1990); Alan Macfarlane, *The Origins of English individualism: the family, property, and social transition* (Oxford: Blackwell, 1978); *The Culture of Capitalism* (Oxford: Blackwell, 1987).
7. *Purple and Green: Poems by 33 Women Poets* (Sheffield: Rivelin Grapheme Press, 1985).

TOWARDS A PRIMER OF THE AVANT-GARDE[1]

(The mimetic; The Full Emptiness; Sensory deprivation; Procedures; A soft containing skin: Narcissism and collusion; Games of the gifted; cryptic canons; Memory jars; Disinvestment)

There is a problem, and the identification of it may start with the lack of any overlap, of poets, between the anthologies *Conductors of Chaos* (ed. Iain Sinclair, 1995) and *The Democratic Voice* (ed. Crawford and Armitage, 1998)[2]. Only one living poet is to be found in both anthologies. The twenty-six poets in *Conductors* are representatives of a group which, however disparate its internal range of styles and assumptions, is rejected by the official taste of the day. The poets we are going to discuss are probably absent from the anthologies in your borough library or school library. It may be that conservative editors dislike this poetry or do not understand it. It may also be that most, or all, of the artistically serious poetry is being written by this group. Much of their poetry is quite easy to follow. We are going to deal with a fraction of it: the avant-garde.

It would seem a little difficult for anyone to be involved in teaching or writing about poetry at all without a basic expertise in the avant-garde. Everyone engaged in the field stands to benefit from a primer of the avant-garde. I am proposing some components of such a primer. Scattered through this book and others.

Everyone on the scene recognises a scale of good and bad. This is something which emerges after expertise. One thing is more pleasurable than another. Of course good avant-garde poetry is surrounded by a morass of bad avant-garde poetry. I am not promoting the latter. It would be quite legitimate to write off the avant-garde, and the British Poetry Revival, the generation of 68, and so on, after gaining a proper understanding of the material. What is not legitimate is to write it all off without knowing what it is. The whole operation of location, understanding, and primary experiencing has to take place before any discrimination and evaluation can occur. My proposal is simply that you would want to be able to compare Sinclair and Crawford/Armitage, to understand both positions, and possibly to describe where they diverge—not simply to find the whole pattern tiringly chequered and incomprehensible.

The starting-point was the idea that people familiar with the avant-garde find it easy to follow and relate to. This suggests that there is a body of implicit knowledge. I also feel that a lot of people find the surface of the avant-garde alienating and outside their comfort zone, and so don't get beneath the surface. The project was to force this implicit knowledge into words, so that people who hadn't been following new publications over the last 40 years (if that is the right count) could be given a bit of context.

It would be a simple matter to produce hundreds of pages of analysis of a major avant-garde work. My friend Franz Josef Czernin chose to write an entire book about one poem by Reinhard Priessnitz, 'heldin' ('die matrix lau auf einmal. vögel lähmen' etc.). 'heldin' is only 14 lines long. Priessnitz (who died young) holds an exemplary position in the modern Austrian avant-garde. But I am proposing to record the information which a competent reader has before reading a, or any, poem. This is a primer and it is trying to teach procedures.

It may be advantageous to clarify what the avant-garde is. I see a large mass of wholly unoriginal poetry, which we will skip; an area of poetry which is innovatory (without being experimental or detached from natural language); and a field of avant-garde writing (including graphics and sound poetry) which has a specialised audience and clearly is detached from natural language. It should be clear that I don't write avant-garde poetry and have never felt myself drawn to that area. The discussion will be more likely to succeed if we identify who is avant-garde. I nominate: Peter Finch; *However Introduced to The Soles* (by Nic Laight, Nick Macias, and Niall Quinn); J.H. Prynne after *Brass*; Tom Raworth; Maggie O'Sullivan; Edwin Morgan (mostly); Allen Fisher; Eric Mottram; Adrian Clarke. No doubt hundreds of others could be found, but I need a limited field for my mind to bite on. This is a public word and not able to be defined in an arbitrary way by me. So there may be quite a lot of give and take around the margins of the word. This primer assumes that there was no avant-garde in Britain between 1940 and 1960 (and that the avant-garde of an older era is covered by existing textbooks). Sound poetry has quite a long history but I am still determined to call it avant-garde.

The intellectual background, where modern ideas live and evolve, involves hundreds of vital works and is not susceptible to easy summary. Each of the key ideas can be found in thousands of books, most probably; they are the kind of thing which authors, rightly, rush to put in their books.

So I have not tried to describe this background. Without it, of course, you cannot acquire expertise in modern poetry. What I am saying is, you will have to get it from somewhere else.

The mimetic

I would like to start with an idea presented by Oliver Sacks in *An Anthropologist from Mars*[3], about a million years of the mimetic. He is discussing people with quite major impairments of brain function who have exceptional artistic gifts. In discussing the nature of the gifts, he draws on ideas by Merlin Donald, who suggested that Homo erectus, our immediate ancestor, had the mimetic as their primary mode of cognition for a million years, before the arrival of a symbolic and abstract capacity (which may be associated with H sapiens). Mimetic means imitative (from the Greek). By mimetic he means directly imitative of physical objects and processes, without any verbal or conceptual input at all. Someone who gets into a car and when the motor starts yells "broom broom!" and then imitates the engine sound, with the right timbre, tempo of changes, right changes of timbre as it slows to corner and so on, sounds like an idiot. It's something we all did as children. And—a sneaky admission here—that ability to mimic and be carried by dumb processes is closely related to artistic ability, or at least to one of the abilities on which art is founded. Mimetics reproduce what they see but do not personalise it: what they do does not amount to a statement of how they feel, or their personality. It does not have a symbolic tier. The more complex faculties of the brain, which deal with classification, analysis, integration, or planning, are not present at this level of functioning. People who are undistracted by analytical overlay may be superior at mimesis to people who do have such distractions (and "live in their heads"). Its role in art is controversial—a role fundamental and yet also primitive, resistant to conscious direction.

In Werner Herzog's film of *Kaspar Hauser* the hero is shown playing with a toy horse. ROSS he says. Horse. It is the only word he knows (at that stage). He is enthusiastic, identifies himself with the horse. This is the mimetic stage of awareness. At the basis of a poem is a series of primary identifications of objects or scenes, underlying everything else but very simple in nature. The verbal structure of a poem includes a base level where someone walking down a street is identifying "wall. Car. Kerb. Moving car. Pedestrian. Crisp packet. Tree. Car" and so on—a level which we can hardly live without but which may not normally be conscious. More complex mental processes reveal themselves linguistically by structures linking words. Conversely, the mimetic level is displayed by noun strings. These are a favoured device of the London School.[4]

My proposal is simply that the mimetic is something very important to the avant-garde, which may seem like the most sophisticated group of writers. Disintegrating various artistic conventions allows earlier and more robust functions to flourish—of which mimesis is one of the most visible.

As the mention of the horse suggests, rapid imitation of the actions of animals, and of other human beings, is also a part of mimesis. Dances which imitate the movements of animals are a primordial form of art. We find poems about animals problematic—as well as Elvis singing 'Do the Clam'.

Sacks came on the radio while I was writing this and revealed that he pronounces the word *my*metic, to show the root 'mime'. Perhaps this is how he thinks of the concept. A performer who can say a lot in mime, who can continue a play all evening in mime (the 'pantomime', i.e. without words'), but is not good with words, is a good example of a highly mimetic personality. The artificial banishing of language from mime shows reminds us that one faculty flourishes at the expense of others—and that suppressing a modern faculty may allow something else, archaic, undignified, but expressive, to reach an unfamiliar fulfilment.

By abolishing artistic convention, the avant-garde started from zero—to release something suppressed (and undignified). No doubt the poetry from the more unconscious, excitable, and spontaneous years of the Underground[5] shows its basic structures in a more naked and awkward form than the more sophisticated productions of the 1990s. The former are more revealing. They are also rather hard to locate now. A sample quote, from a recent poem by Doug Jones:

I met her on the Barking Road—
this silly woman
very still
like something waiting to be silenced but not quietened   yet
but just alive who would stop and give her attention
a beat that your glance passes   on her face
until your eye wanders
                            off to fill weavers   folded
                            patterned   fields

her her and the table she   later elided, empty thing   that boomed
            with gales

molecules like wood   pebbles make flesh for meals   the Thames
                        for sweets that ground down   who was
                        and honeycombed   used to
                                hospital bricks, who   making these
inhaled very empty souls of birds   things first before
                                            her made blood/
        (from 'Bloods')[6]

This is not necessarily an important poem. It is three A4 pages long and is poorly represented by short quotes because of its multiple overlapping tracks and the coordinated but oblique nature of its theme, about poverty and food (the making of blood). It has a direct assault on the brain, offering a mass of urgent but unresolved information, withholding the conventional pathways of verbal association which would make it palatable (and forgettable). The bit about weaving may relate to consciousness, or awareness, as a fabric, something woven. It is interesting that Jones, born circa 1980, has absorbed all the implicit knowledge of an avant-garde whose existence has been persistently denied by conservative critics. The poem is not aestheticised or encoded, but full of unfiltered information— physical details and scraps of speech. The poem does not tell a smooth and pointed story because it is mimetic. The material of the poem is not tapered and stitched to exhibit the poet's reactions. I may say that in 1973 I might have thought that a poem was a chance for the poet to display sensitivity (and for the reader to collect the result). By the time I left school, though, I probably wanted something else—and was tired of dutifully collecting the results (and storing them). It is quite apparent that most situations do not give the poet a chance to display sensitivity—and therefore are simply eliminated from conventional poetry. Jones is much more interested in what is happening than in reproducing his own voice on the page. Saying no to the mimetic avant-garde means saying no to large stretches of the real world. That is—the no stance involves a decision that the (object) world is only acceptable if filtered through the sensibility of a talented poet. It would seem on the contrary that many things in the world are interesting in themselves.

The relationship between the personal Voice, the Who, of conventional poetry and the What of the mimetic is one of the most difficult issues. The Mimetic is not the sole principle of the poems under discussion, but a component in a whole.

Look at this passage from the 'growth-rings' section of Robert Hampson's poem *Seaport*:

> layer by layer
> tools weapons shards of pots
> bones
> stone bronze iron
>
> history seen as technological change
> antler-hoes ards
> beam-engine steam-train
> transistor
>
> born
> when the records changed speed
> pre-history now
>
> economic organisation / social change
>
> uses botany / archaeology / atomic physics
>
> *whatever comes to hand* [7]

(An ard is a light wooden plough.) Hampson's poems tend to eliminate from their documentary sources the logical structure with its interpretative persuasion and direction. This leaves a conduct of noun phrases only; the typographical layout is deployed to remove any suggestion that there is a syntactic connection between successive lines. *Seaport* is a major work, where the recovery of pure facts without explanatory annotation allows the build-up of a new understanding on the large scale. This was a painful process; the poem was written "during the late 1970s and 80s", but the 1995 edition excludes, as a prefatory note says, Part III, which has not been finished. The poem consists mainly of mimetic detail; as we said, to exclude avant-garde poetry is to exclude many parts of reality. Here is another passage.

Item three: Brunswick Dock:

> vast quantities of produce
> imported from starving Ireland
> decks turned into pens
> for oxen and sheep;
> deck-passengers
> penned in like cattle—
> Irish labourers
> to bring in
> the English harvest.

Item Four: Merchants' Exchange:

> flagged quadrangle; colonnades;
> brass statuary;

> Nelson dying; a wreath hovers
> over his sword-point; death
> reaches for his heart.

> round the base:
> captives in chains,
> emblems of Nelson's victories:
> the limbs & manacles
> of slaves
> in the marketplace.

The parallels—between Irish harvest workers and African slaves, between commercial freight and naval warfare, between sculpted display and bare want—are not verbally made: we have to draw them for ourselves.

Something prominent in this awkward poetry is the list structure. Any stretch of language from which you remove the pointers and element of argument converges on a list—a string of nouns with simple qualifiers. A comparison would be in conceptual art, where the function of imitation of Nature was moved to the margins, but where simple accumulations of objects were also quite prominent. An example is the person (Susan Hiller) who collected and showed photographic postcards of waves at British seaside resorts. Whatever the theoretical overlay, the basis was a rather simple act of collection and accumulation. Exhibitions of such art offered "the disappearance of the art work" but also showed large amounts of unmodified visual data, like a few dozen postcards of storm waves breaking on promenades, giving a rather direct and uncomplicated optical satisfaction. The conceptual movement would not have worked without these drafts of raw data. It is arguable that the demand which was being made on the intellect to imagine the world afresh would not have worked without the masses of unprocessed data to build the new images with. Conceptual poetry—if we can use that phrase—also relies on unshaped collections of data. The reflexive function relies on the unreflected and sensory in order to have some way of achieving itself. Those postcards showed the force of convention: it was exactly the same shot, in however many seaside towns. But simultaneously it showed something protean: the sea and waves, something the eye can never get tired of.

If we look at the elemental actions for compiling lists, which are so simple that they can be applied by anybody and yet have unpredictable results, we may find that they are half way towards the fixed and arbitrary procedures carried out by the conceptual art movement—and also by underground poets. A useful metaphor may be of headless demonic servants. The servant carries out procedures reliably and without overlay, without using rational procedures to interfere with the results. (The headless demon is one who appears in the Greek magical papyri and also in Paul Holman's poem 'Dog Mercury'.[8]) This may be given by the nature of the brain—if it is composed of thousands of efficient and straightforward local programmes of predictable result, in which consciousness has a limited power of intervention. The case for using 'procedures' has to do with the restrictive and normative nature of conscious thought. The term 'decentring' often crops up in discussions about this. The mimetic person may have great abilities of reaction and imitation, which are weakened by the arrival of a central power of reason and purpose, achieving continuity by damping peripheral excitements. The mimetic faculty gives us list structures without further overlay. This list structure by Peter Finch—

> Bighead
> Executive bighead
> Senior bighead
> Southern development bighead
> Bigheads, publish with us
> Bigheads needed, send sample
> Competition, thousands of bigheads to be won
>   (excerpt from 'Bigheads')[9]

is obviously modified, even if the modification is rigid and impersonal. It is not quite the collection of postcards of storm waves. All the same, it takes place within everyday language. This avant-garde poem sounds like pop poetry. For many of the poets in our view, what happened is exactly this: they were writing pop poetry and got tired of very short forms and the shallow involvement which they entailed. They pushed out the limits of the pop poem and so reached something which was then called avant-garde. (Imagine if you have a tricky advertisement film and extend its world from 90 seconds to half an hour.)

Something like this collecting of objects is direct quoting of other people's words—capture of other flows of speech (again without overlay). The poet here appears as someone passive and infantile—registering without speaking. But soon after follows intervention in the quotes: cutting them up, distorting them, binding different flows together. This passage from Finch is made by cutting and reconnecting phrases from poetry reviews in well-known Welsh magazines:

Richness. His richness changes. He becomes less accomplished. He analyses; he fails to confront the reader's notion. His hands, milling, fray out like overloaded copper wire, blown, blackened, weakened. The strain shows in a kind of willed aggressiveness, a stylistic overkill, a metrical gimmick crackling with unfocused violence. It's a matter of manner. He would argue, between bouts, that his depression is now the focus and that everything else is irrelevant. He has abandoned control.

(from 'On Criticism')[10]

This is perfectly mimetic—that is, imitation without meaning. It's also sophisticated, precise, preplanned, and in general intelligent. Let's just compare it with a passage from Raworth's *Eternal Sections*, which, we suggest, is made entirely out of quoted phrases—

sharply defined periods of individualism
fade with age, as a rule
sensation is registered
expand around me
the substrate of emotions
merely act as gatekeepers
disrupted by stress
unlike scientific instruments
gripped by hands
reversed right to left
an inhibition of the recall mechanism
caused by oxygen shortage
swamps the cortex
before we know about the external world[11]

These may be parallel passages. Finch is recombining 'given' words to react against a world which he (all the same) has to live in; Raworth is recombining words which perhaps he objects to just as much. If we look again at *Eternal Sections*, its samples may now seem very much like a list structure—a part of the outside world captured by the essentially passive poet; a pane of documentary through which we look at the strangeness of the world as a given thing. The editorial actions—of registering, collecting, cutting, stringing together—are those already needed to bring list structures about. Now we have put Finch and Raworth side by side, it is apparent that they are deploying similar processes. If Finch explicitly relates himself to music hall—Raworth may not be a million miles from satire and parody of authority. It is impossible, though, to see him as a mimetic poet.

Eternal sections may simply mean 'forever snips', i.e. scissoring up found texts to compose a poem. A section is also a preparation of something to view on a microscope slide. However barren of titling and labelling Raworth's poem may seem to be, we can perhaps recover something of it more than verbal scraps blowing past like leaves. It would appear that all the phrases in the 14-line poem (or stanza) quoted come from a textbook of psychology. They are impersonal because they represent the common stock of knowledge. The stripping off of syntax does not permit precise and personalised utterance. It takes us right back to generalised knowledge—hegemonic knowledge, in the eyes of a Marxist. Raworth has said that the heart of art is pure politics. The poem quoted starts with a comment about the fading of individualist revolt and ends with 4 lines which if read together say that a blockage of memory drowns the brain before we come to understand the outside world. As a cut-up of instruction in psychology, the poem retells the operative knowledge by which the individual is known, the menial intellectual fuel of corporations, schools, and welfare departments. The passages cited tell of alienation and loss, which, in a framework where dialectic is a central procedure, contain the nucleus of a tale of liberation and fulfilment. If our powers of recall work properly, we could then become conscious. We are hearing an account of ordinary life while hearing a spare melody which tells us about transformation. Another line tells of the reversal of left and right; in a psychological context we might well connect these with the left and right hemispheres of the brain, which are functionally specialised. One deals with logical procedure, one with emotions and intuition. The reversal of the two might therefore point to the dominance of instrumental reason, in late capitalism, and dialectically to a reversal back into the true relationship of human faculties—the restoration of noble human feelings and relationships based on emotions. (The context is somewhat clearer if we take the succeeding poem, which may derive from the same source text, as an extension of it.)

We can ask now whether Raworth is summoning up any autonomy against the world of money and power, or whether his switching off of his own voice is an admission of helpless entrapment, abandonment, plunged yards deep in that world; where he summons up selective listening as the smallest purest share of freedom. We can guess that the use exclusively of found material functions to preserve the implicit cognitive framework of the real situation. This framework contains a huge mass of information, silent though it is. The way in which we know it without conscious understanding suggests how dominant social structures implant themselves—and forcing it to the foreground summons us to make social structure conscious. The poems thus partake of a documentary quality which invented material would lack. Society reproduces itself through the unconscious structures.

Long discussion of these two poems, both on page 51 of the original edition of *Eternal Sections*, could follow. For example, the noun missing before "swamps the cortex" is evidently "inner subjective states" (from the limbic brain), or something equivalent. This missing sentence is talked over by the sentence which we apparently have. If we add the last two lines from the previous poem, we can make a continuous passage with a good fit, thus:

> moments of revulsion were rare
> indulged in with caution
> sharply defined periods of individualism
> fade with age, as a rule

The four lines are a transition area which ambiguously relate to two verbal centres. The whole avoids clean discontinuities but by doing this also avoids clear labelling and framing. Rather than set out all possibilities for a single stanza (as the book defines the separate 14-line 'poems'), let me point out that the whole poem consists of 111 stanzas.

Suppose we describe a procedure as follows. *Take a speech by a famous politician. Wipe out the connected meaning but keep the mannerisms so that it is recognisable. Recite it.* This is something comedians do. You can see it on TV any day of the week. We know how to respond to it—by laughing and not trying to piece the sentences together into a source of information about a subject. We know to focus on the style and on the person being imitated. If we find this procedure throughout *Eternal Sections* (or, throughout late Raworth in general), the text suddenly starts to seem so normal that the label avant-garde hardly applies any more. The problem which disappears is one of unfamiliarity: we could not process the poem because there was no label telling us which procedure to follow. On television, signs such as the name of the show, the name of the comedian, the music, the laughter track, etc., signal the right way to respond.

I must admit that this description is not adequate for *Eternal Sections*. The book is composed of snipped-up quotes and the conscious intent of the source texts is consistently effaced. But the result is radically ambiguous—and not simply satirical and comic.

The use of lists, collections, catalogues and so on has a relationship to metre. Rhythm in poetry is a series of emphases involving the movement of attention of the speaker. It traces the movement of a mind. This is scarcely relevant in a list structure. This kind of verbal passage is bound to be awkward rhythmically. It is not tracing the movement of a sensibility— it is mimetic. Such passages may occur as enclaves within an overall structure which is more than mimetic—and more than merely ugly and psychologically blank. They certainly come off worst in comparison with highly integrated passages of classical poetry. The direct incorporation of quotes from prose yields passages in this category. Identification is mimetic, something human and pre-human. Rhythm is fundamentally linked to mimetic cognition. The 20th-century crisis of identification and rhythm, in poetry, may be illuminated by cognitive psychology. There is a joke underlying all this, which is that I must have a mimetic ability in order to describe the poets properly. It's no good writing long sentences and citing lots of important authorities if you can't loyally absorb and express what the poets are like. Intelligent critics may be less mimetic. They make all the poets talk like academics and philosophers.

Adorno uses the word mimetic in a quite different sense, to refer to the act of emotional identification which underlies art, something irresistible and yet primitive. Communication of mood is not at all the same faculty as perception of things and their conditions. I mention this only to avoid confusion about what I mean by the term mimesis.

The Full Emptiness

There is a term *page rage* which describes what happens when critics decide that they know what the procedure, valid within the poem, is and the poet doesn't. It is my conviction that 90% of the misreading of poetic texts by the critics is due to the latter's imposing on them procedures which are irrelevant to the text as written by the author. Almost all the primer work that has to be done, therefore, is to unlearn the procedures used for reading conventional poetry. Academic critics are not generally interested in discovering the meaning of a text so much as in finding out what mistakes the wretched poet has made, punishing him for them, and demonstrating their own knowledge of the timeless rules of poetry. There are variants for Christian academics (discover that the poet is morally and doctrinally unworthy and punish him for it) and left-wing academics (discover that the poet comes from the wrong social stratum, gender, or ethnic group, and punish him for that). Reading poetry is so simple once you give up the habits which matched the poetry of the 1950s.

Not finding what you expect causes anxiety. There is a class of anxieties about your social set, along similar lines. Part of this is the fear of being rejected– of not having the right assets. Moving into experimental poetry is a social process as well as a conceptual one, and it arouses basic anxieties about being accepted. At the first moment, you actually do lack the usable assets—you don't know anything about experimental art. When going into the unknown you are vulnerable. Art is a highly social thing and involves crucially openness to new people, who will be very important. The invitation is a vital function in art. Come into my world, it says. Moving into a new constellation of friends is an experience so basic that it wouldn't occur to you to say no. The sense of uncertainty is unpleasant, but is only part of a whole range of other sensations reaching you at the same time.

What hurts about modern poetry is the emptiness. I'd better qualify that—it's fairly obvious that we're not all sitting around gazing into space. So: it's about the manipulation and projection of negative space. Take this passage from a Tom Raworth poem:

major acts
reshaping the period
proved a paralysing choice
a crucial feature
quoted but never fully explained
at the very core
experienced as arbitrary government
undermining the independence of towns
to reassert central control
from the mobilisation of resources
despite the risk
of an immeasurably greater alarm
conscious of difference
under the law[12]

After the first line, there are a number of things you would expect, from memories of ordinary language behaviour, to find as continuations. They do not arrive. The naïve reader gets agitated by these gaps, whereas the experienced reader simply relaxes. The poetry becomes enjoyable as soon as you stop thrashing around in the search for structures which aren't there. The word discursive is sometimes used for the aspects of language which avant-garde poetry rejects. It is a capacious word, whose meanings might include continuity, coherence, disambiguation of portions of discourse by other portions, progressing a logical argument. The emptiness, meanwhile, is actually a resonating chamber that lets you hear fine vibrations. This specialisation, removing the functional, is like the sound ornament of melisma; however dissimilar it is in other ways. I find it helpful to recall something that Rudolf Otto said, when discussing the 'numinous' (a term he invented to mean the unearthly, eerie, sublime) in art:

> Besides Silence and Darkness oriental art knows a third direct means for producing a strongly numinous impression, to wit, emptiness and empty distances. Empty distance, remote vacancy, is, as it were, the sublime in the horizontal. The wide-stretching desert, the boundless uniformity of the steppe, have real sublimity (...)

He talks about Chinese architecture, and then says:

> "Still more interesting is the part played by the factor of void or emptiness in Chinese painting. There it has almost become a special art to paint empty space, to make it palpable, and to develop variations upon this singular theme . . . For 'Void' is, like Darkness and Silence, a negation, but a negation that does away with every 'this' and 'here', in order that the 'wholly other' may become actual."[13]

This (as translated by John W. Harvey) seems like an excellent description of the mature Raworth. What Otto, writing in 1917, does not expound is the terrible plenitude and over-activity of Western art—caused, no doubt, by the didactic and browbeating imperatives of the Christian Church. No more did he detect that emptiness was going to enter the repertoire of Western art—in abstract painting, for example. Today, poetry stands against the gush of audio-visual representation as the empty against the full—at every step. It may be that abstract thought is only possible in the absence of relevant sensory stimuli—only emptiness can induce us to withdraw into the realm of thought; which is a full emptiness.

Otto, a pioneer of comparative religion, left a tradition of such studies at his university, Marburg; and founded the Eranos gathering, to discuss such things. Another quote:

> dark streets of Europe
>
> litter the quest with
>
> leaden nouns from extra
>
> territorial an imperative follows
>
> WHERE THE STORY LEADS
>
> MYTH IS THE SWIM
>
> versed in measured despatialise
>
> frames 'definition" reduced her
>
> fluid demonic the simile
>
> flowers rigid in the
>
> dream decisive surfacing LIFE

SENTENCE *italic Seed* inked

the fetish performance lacked

a character voiced recorded

figurative for barbaric in

the transcript account what

tautology suppressed doctored obliterate

with the medium term

(Adrian Clarke, from *spectral investments*) [14]

I don't think the point with Clarke is to explain what philosophers he reads or to identify references to rational discourses. The problem is in a different category—more pervasive but harder to name. The realisation you have to make is how fast the whole thing moves. Once you stop looking for the missing elements of structure, the space becomes limitlessly rapid—it's like travelling at 100 mph. All the problems come from projecting patterns that you expect but which aren't there. It's like being exhausted by the shadow of your own body image. It's really difficult to remember this problem once you have made the adjustment. It's this threshold situation which a primer would carry us through. We can call this kind of poetry dromoscopy—a view while running. This is a reference to Paul Virilio, a writer dear to Clarke, who simply wrote about the effects of speed on perception. Clarke's poetry is artistically brilliant. It is exciting and its subject is excitement. It shows associational processes with the speed and verve at which association works, not with the pedestrian, due process, manner of essays or legal proceedings. Clarke's poetry has been stripped down to go faster—it is not empty.

Emptiness can cause the reader problems. I must admit my suspicion, though, that realisations are very often not made by the methods of discursive prose; and that such prose can easily confuse people—law and philosophy are not known as the most transparent of reading material. Intuition may both belong to the Stone Age and be more rapid. If you asked a lot of people why they are concerned with poetry, and what the difference between poetry and prose is, many of them would probably reply that it's the way poetry puts over information which matters. It's quite likely that the whole nature of poetry is to rely on inexplicit and intuitive links, emotional identification, figurative language, feelings rather than facts. Quite possibly, people who are satisfied with clearly labelled and logical procedures don't read any poetry at all. So when Raworth abandons the discursive method, we have to be careful about attacking this—in case we prove that poetry is unnecessary. It is possible, in fact, that Raworth is an example of overfulfilment—that if you take the rules which separate poetry from prose and apply them many times over, you end up with something like the mature Raworth. That is, Raworth is further out on the axis than everyone else—but the axis itself is common, and can be identified quite readily from any point within the literary culture.

It is difficult to define the common ground between Raworth and the uncoded sound of the magical strings we are going to see later on. But, at some level, both are works of emptiness—rejections of the discursive mode.

A key concept for understanding the emptiness is the threshold level of resistance to ideas. Resistance to distraction allows focus and makes business life possible. Lowered resistance—a low threshold—makes one suggestible and is suitable for dealing with art. If you flood the poem with rational, literal details, it will not be suggestive. In order to make the poem suggestive, you have to throw yourself into it—miming a state of lightness and freedom by avoiding any definite and realist details. This produces the empty text.

In the 1940s, there were problems with radar observers on long shifts when nothing was happening. After watching a screen intently for hours on end, they began seeing things which weren't there. This led to what are now known as sensory deprivation studies. Really a lot of research money went into this area—the radar stations were the front line of defence against attack by nuclear bomber. The hallucinations came as less of a surprise to Gestalt psychologists than they may have done to the military authorities. The flying saucers mythology was a by-product of the same problem area. What Gestalt taught was that the brain was constantly active, spontaneously generating search patterns, and that impinging information actually damped down these patterns. Blank screens, or indeterminate but suggestive patterns, could permit the formation of spontaneous imagery —self-amplifying patterns. And it is these which we must now turn our attention to.

The use of solitude

In *New Scientist* for 30/5/93, p.30 John McCrone reports:

> "subjects were shut in a ganzfeld, a simple sensory deprivation chamber where bright, red lights are shone onto ping pong balls taped over the eyes and white noise is played into the ears. For subjects the effect is much like staring into a formless fog. After a quarter of an hour or so of such blankness, most people begin to experience brilliant dream-like images, much like the so-called 'hypnagogic' images that are often seen on the point of falling asleep."

There is a second world of vivid hallucination waiting outside the real one; itself the product of a complex mix of perception, error, unmodified fantasy, and arbitrary interpretations. To reach this second world we need intense concentration, going under in the words. We spoke of emptiness. Something we may feel in an avant-garde poem is a vacuum. A grey feeling of the air being sucked out of our lungs as the text offers us no goal, no explanations, no comforting texture of lived experience, no-one to identify with. Clammy as this may feel, it is intentional. People do not necessarily regard a puzzling and uninterpreted environment as a challenge. They may well have ample access to films, DVDs, television, radio, video games, etc., which offer no such problems. They may experience no sense of triumph on cracking the problem.

The key question is why the reader would not simply break off contact here and find some more fruitful way of spending their time. None of the supporting literature around the avant-garde ever addresses this question. Nonetheless, it is reasonable to think that the great majority of readers stop reading when they find the vacuity. If leisure activities are guided by pleasure, it is not easy to see why someone would pursue an activity which is unpleasant and even seems to have stopped being an experience, to become a distant environment of vague stimuli. A certain percentage of people will interpret the vagueness as "this radio is broken"—something has utterly gone wrong with the text.

The motive to persist past the vacuum may be the memory of past pleasure—curiosity as a legacy. You would continue because of expected pleasure, from the memory of previous pleasure, from previous encounters with similar material. There is an amount of argument in the promotional literature about what the recent avant-garde is similar to. Claims are made that it is similar to the avant-garde of 1900 to 1930, to the European literature of the present day, to post-structuralist literary theory, etc. This is part of a claim for space, for public funding, for airtime, etc., which I find excessively businesslike. I got into avant-garde poetry as a legacy from watching non-narrative cinema. At that time the London School quite often did gigs (poetry performances) in the same building, in Gloucester Avenue, as the one used by the Film Makers' Co-Op, where I was going to watch all these non-narrative films. I could reason that if I got past the problems with these irritating texts they would offer pleasure as films by Brakhage or Jonas Mekas had done. So eventually I got into this area of poetry, after a decade or so of tentative contacts which didn't do much for me. And my map of the aesthetic universe evolved to show people like Raworth and Fisher as bright stars.

Anyway, it doesn't matter too much why you choose to persist.

A German philosopher—Gadamer?—described how the proper movement of a text was from the unknown to the known. A poem is not a treatise on philosophy, and has means proper to its own nature. But it may thrive, all the same, on an outset which says, "We know nothing. What then do we know?" No poem can present knowledge without first assuming that the reader—the observer invisibly present within the poem—lacks the knowledge in question. A poem can allude to a great deal of knowledge and still be a meaningless poem. Conversely, the value of a poem may lie in the extent of the absence of knowledge which it delves at the outset. The virtuous movement of starting with doubt, acquiring and testing information, and reaching new knowledge, is made possible by an emptying at the outset. This may be called kenosis. The word literally means emptying, and refers to a theological concept about the ignorance of Christ as the most important part of his incarnation. Because he truly became a man, he did not know that he would live again after death. As a god he knew this, but he had forgotten it on being born. There are a couple of references in the *New Testament* to Jesus' loss of divine knowledge.

The critic Peter Fuller, familiar with the theology of the incarnation which preoccupied the Church of England, and English Nonconformity, from around 1890 to 1910, applied kenosis to modern art.[15] To the modern art, that is, which has shed the acquired knowledge of how the world of objects and anatomies is constructed. Forgetting geometry. For a school in Paris and some other places, a necessary step was the disappearance of illusionism, of the picture—replaced by something more primeval and uncoded. Fuller was looking, in the 1970s, at abstract monochromes by many different artists. Emptying was, clearly, the process which had led up to them. Theology was already in the realm of discourse about them, brought there by Mark Rothko and Barnett Newman amongst others.

The leading kenotic theologian in Britain was Charles Spencer Gore, who is also credited with bringing the Church of England from Toryism to Labour. The kenotic movement played a noble and central role in British culture which really had nothing to do with abstract paintings, or the New York school. Its applicability raises problems, since there are thousands of modern artists and it would be impossible to collect the views of all of them, let alone sift them to find evidence of how they saw modernity. Fuller was such a genius as a cultural critic that he overrode the evidence in pursuit of his own dazzling and all-embracing conceptual schemas. His theory works better for one strand of Abstract Expressionism than for the rest of modern art. Unless the artist is also Christ, kenosis is a misleading term in art, because it has too much of a load from the theology of the incarnation.

Two topics of which modern poetry has made much are the relation of the perceiving ego to the world, and place—the way things fit together to make a place. It is reasonable to say that these are matters we know a great deal about already (and that what we do not know is of limited relevance to the lives we lead). Poets can only make something of them by assuming an ideal listener who knows nothing (and who is eager to know everything). Within the field of a poem, the kenosis takes the form of abolishing conventional elements of poetic organisation and of semantic reference. If you are faced with the resulting emptiness, the wished-for response is to imagine a new structure which would fill it. Whether you choose to explore this behavioural playground is up to you. I am here only to suggest what the appropriate response is for the text to work best.

The razing of a cognitive structure does not deny what that structure asserts. It simply puts the matter within the scope of discourse. Suspending old knowledge makes it possible to re-imagine the universe. You can choose to follow that route. The erasing of cognitive structures is sympathetic to alternative structures rather than to a void which supports only the absence of cognition. This is why the avant-garde is adjacent to radically anthropological poetry—for example by Tom Lowenstein, David Wevill, and Martin Thom.

Procedures

A key text for me is the catalogue by Richard Cork of an exhibition of *English Art Today 1960–76* in Milan in 1976.[16] The exhibition seemed to include exclusively conceptual artists. This era has so much to do with the poetry we are talking about now. It is certain that the poets are using made-up procedures at many levels. One of the illustrations in the catalogue is of a series of photographs made in 1971 by John Hilliard called 'Camera recording its own condition'. The photographs are taken in a mirror which reflects the camera (and very little else). They are arranged in a grid, of 7 by 10. The separate exposures show all the settings (aperture size and shutter speed) possible for the camera. Within each image is the image, on a different scale, of the controls of the camera: the image shows the inner state of the device which created the image. The whole work makes some kind of comment on self-consciousness. It shows a completely explicit and exhaustive set procedure. It offers considerable richness of possibilities for reflection. Do we have as many as 70 different subjective states? In the corners of the grid there is no picture—the surface is whited or blacked out in apparent ecstasy. Is this an analogue for our emotional states, subjectivity invading perception? misery and delight?

Or take this account from an interview[17] with Allen Fisher of how one of his books was composed:

> It's quite a fun book. Produced as a consequence. Rather a mechanical poem. Lots of the devices used in *creek in the ceiling beam* crop up, are Ur-examples of later works. *creek in the ceiling beam* is first of all a recording in time in one place in the room I was sleeping in and whenever the beam creaked I would record its time. And then I'd map this out on a graph. And the shape that the graph made I used as a device for selecting from the books that were lying by the bed at the time of the creaking. Mainly a series of poets, in the books. And so that was how the creaking seemed. And I conjected different reasons for the creak, to do with plumbing, and pigeons in the loft, and to do with ley-lines, and the idea that maybe there was a ley-line coming through the bedroom. Which obviously was more than tongue-in-cheek. And then I realised that the beam running through the bedroom was potentially on a ley-line which connected all the cemeteries in South London. So that's what the book's about. So we went round all the cemeteries photographing all the sites.

This was circa 1973, I suppose. The procedure sounds like a lot more fun than the actual book was. Because I'm writing a book, it's easier for me to focus on the didactic aspect of strict procedures—that they make you think about what the unconscious procedures are which (unconscious) poets follow. The making conscious of the unconscious is what any writer does, the core of most verbal acts. However, from the description it seems more like the procedure was a game and a laugh, an excuse for wandering around town taking photographs. I think the atmosphere of 1973 was more benign to this kind of thing than the atmosphere now. The learning was linked to playing, something as relaxed as musicians jamming together—a social thing which they are going to spend so many hours a week doing anyway, whether there's an excuse or not.

The contrast of such explicit procedures with traditional poems is meant to make the unconscious procedures break the surface. Trying to explain the difference with traditional (or intuitive) procedures is bound to make us notice the latter. If we put these tasks together:

occupy a symbol
write a story about it transforming
expressing an unresolved feeling
based on natural analogy
create an ordered arrangement of charged objects
achieve release of pent-up feelings

—we may start to find the inherited procedures strange. There is perhaps a character-revealing divide between those who instantly abandon these procedures when they are exposed, and those who simply admire them.

A picture is something outside you, whereas your voice is part of you. Visual art is more externalised and detached—literally, physically. It may be that poets have clung on to intuition rather more than visual artists, and that they are less popular than contemporary visual artists because they do not radiate that heroic autonomy from inherited codes and modes. The public still assumes automatically that the poem they see is the result of conventional romantic self-dramatisation and appropriation. Visual artists were incredibly strong at documenting their procedures. But there are very few examples of conceptual poets doing documentation. I think this is regrettable. I think a lot of readers have had bad experiences trying to find psychological, or political, motives in poems (or "projects") which really only make sense if you know the procedure which generated them.

In order to grasp how these procedures are original, we would have to describe the conventional procedures of reading. This could be quite a voluminous project, but we can claim that the basic procedure is identification, and that consequently another procedure has to be searching for someone to identify with, beforehand. The reader may experience frustration because this is not possible. The frustration often brings up the issue of what the laws of art are, so that the reader starts arguing with the poet, and drawing down general laws of art as proof of the implicit contract which the poet is in breach of. Art may have no laws, but it certainly has rules. The artist has greater liberty if they invent their own rules, which also allow greater liberty to the artistic work. Presumably every rule (that exists) was brought into existence by being invented. Therefore there is no essential difference between a rule invented in 1600 and one invented in 1970, or 2005. To be sure, if this argument is born out of frustration it is unlikely to reach agreement. Arguments run more serenely if based on comfort and concord.

So, the avant-garde poet thinks you should stop trying to identify. Once this big central thing has vanished, you can look at the varied peripheral things.

A basic law of art is that the work of art should share a set of rules with the audience. It is hard to talk about what happens when this sharing is not so. Either the artist has to change, or the audience do. A catastrophic phase will follow, and then it will be one or the other.

In a poetic project where emotional identification is being prevented, and there are no characters to project onto, we may well experience an intense series of involuntary visions of what is being withheld, and this may be appropriate experience in that space.

What is omitted, is being foregrounded. This is implicit in the whole process of kenosis. My most intense responses inside conceptual art involved thinking about intuitive and subjective art, and why I preferred it to conceptual art, and why all my poems were intuitive. Thwarting is quite close to the concept of making rules naked—lay bare the device, as a Russian Formalist said.[18] Because the acquired procedures are so strong, they keep churning away although they are frustrated. This gives you the chance to look at them. I could think about the kind of poetry I liked because it wasn't there to distract me. This takes us into the area of reflexivity, role detachment, critical awareness, and so on. This important area is reached through negation.

We heard Robert Hampson say that history could be seen as the story of technological change. The prefixed 'seen as' points to an observer, other than Hampson, who holds this opinion; typically, we are not told who this observer is. Perhaps it is Hampson. The belief in technical knowledge rather than psychological dramas, or the spread of morality, as the central process in history, reduces most works of literature, and most works of history written before 1900, to the sidelines. It is tempting to draw a link between this and the expulsion of personality from the modern poem: technique, something the avant-garde are obsessed by, would then come to the foreground in poetry, parallelling the realisation that the state of society depended on the technical skills of the workforce. I say this is 'tempting' because I don't think this represents how avant-garde poets think. It is a position which may have influenced some of them.

There is something comforting about these strict procedures. They show people taking up something unique, following it with persistence and fortitude, and triumphantly bringing it to a conclusion.

The procedure *identification* is part of a common stock. It does not belong to any individual. It raises the question of what the generative procedures of writing are. Do we think of multiple parallel processing as a model for the brain which composes? The routines would be decentralised and below consciousness; partly derived from spoken language, partly acquired by imitating other writers? Writing may be the action of Symbolic Machines, thousands of coherent pieces of logic rolling on the brain's hardware.[19]

Things were changing every few months, it seems, in the 1970s. The thing about that John Hilliard photograph about self-observation is that it's clearly impossible to look at it now in the way that a qualified observer would have seen it in 1971. It really was a revolutionary time—things rolled on, and the earlier states have become irrecoverable. I'm afraid that lucidity is a product of calm—when culture is conserved and congealed.

A soft containing skin: Narcissism and collusion

As Sacks pointed out to us[20], the mimetic mode has no symbolic tier. It is good at telling *What* but does not have the means of signalling a *Who*. We can now wonder whether personalising experience means added value or reduced value. We have to ask what is happening as someone is remembering a scene of some kind. Perhaps they reproduce it literally. Perhaps the act of memory involves a transformation of some kind—an infusion of their sensibility. We would have doubts about the literary ability of someone in whom the first faculty was depleted—they could not recall the order in which things happened, the objects present on a tray, the words which other people had used. But this faculty might exist in isolation from the ability to express feelings and psychological states.

The world is so constructed that it can survive without my personality. Or without reflecting my personality. Something we should wonder about is the transformation of the world into strips of owned sensibility. This is central, but we are allowed to think about it. I take it, of course, that this is what those poets are doing who are anti-mimetic, who spurn list structures and cut-ups of alien texts and metrically blank passages. We should consider the possibility that there may be a bad poem which is thoroughly personalised and where the mimetic level is weak and decayed. Key terms to be applied here include teleology, self-projection, mediation, affirmation, selectivity, hegemony, and consensus. An avant-garde writer would argue that a poet's personality is a convergent function. Its product, that is, is less diverse than the intake—the world itself. It produces self-similar, repetitive blocks of language, which are recognisable (and marketable) for that very reason. There is a virtue in reproducing raw, unfiltered data. It is more diverse than fully finished poetry. There is also the issue of ideology and filtering. Perhaps we do not want to encounter the world as filtered through a smooth and reassuring voice. The voice is homogeneous, and we may wonder what happened to everything that was in any way different. The convergent function is the telltale of narcissism, which on a large scale shows the imaginative limits of a class and a literary stratum. A shared sensibility produces a reduced verbal world, where variation is lost simply by exclusion, where preferences are applied recklessly and repetitively. Convergence shows us where the borders are, unconsciously creating an image of the ego by making its prejudices, limits, and investments plain. Here wish-fulfilment betrays group interests.

We can call what is negated before this poetry starts the concentric-egocentric zone, meaning by this a centre in the poet's ego, with the reader's ego wrapped round it, in a process we call projective identification. They share a centre. The assembly is concentric. Egocentric processes are organic, archaic, circular, repetitive. A world without that centre has a greater range of different processes taking place inside it and allows sense to move at much greater speed.

Also in thinking about poetry, the benefit of abstract and objective schemas is that you can see the whole range of poetry and not just the bit you are in love with. This may also feel like disenchantment and alienation.

Moves which loses you points in the avant-garde game include identification, expressivity, realism, imagination, appropriation, aestheticisation, generalisation, pastoral. I am uneasy about the point-scoring aspect because evidently most of the players would fervently deny that it is taking place. (The claim would be, conversely, that anyone who is not doing these things is stupid and unreconstructed.)

What the neutralisation reveals is that art as we know it relies on big central human identification objects, and takes place as if it were the fantasies of the figures about themselves, which the spectator drowns in, as if exchanging their identity with the central figures. We may well reflect that the society we have is organised around possessive individualism, and that our legal system has an overdeveloped theory of individual rights, with a weak development of traditional restraints or collective interests.

One mainstream belief is that the more a poem personalises experience the more poetic it is. One strand of the unconscious beliefs is that the difference between novels and poems is that the latter have far fewer characters than the former, and are much more the expression of one individual self. The central convention of advertising, too, is to make a personal link between a human and the consumption object, so that the act of consumption is naturalised by being linked to an identification object, and the potency of the human object is presented through their powers of consumption. The conventional poem thus bears a strange resemblance to the scenario of an advertisement. The noise given off by the big central figure wraps us up, comfortably perhaps, and drowns out any signal coming from other sources—from other people, from people acting as a group, from strands of experience which do not lend themselves to self-indulgence and expressions of power and autonomy.

It is open to doubt whether this personalisation was so dominant before Romanticism. The exploitation of narcissism has been one of the great technological breakthroughs of Western art in the last two centuries. Weighty arguments have also found this development starting with the Mannerist era, from around 1520. The geography and history of this change are of great interest.

Remarkable effects can be attained by non-teleological art through exposing the conventions of art and the social imagination. We may think of John Hilliard's photograph here. At some level, turning a bright light on your own vanity is one of the favourite effects of art; as soon as the artist exposes an imaginative scene which I have invested in, the flash of self-knowledge is painful and memorable. This is not exactly hedonistic but it does turn your brain on. There is a loss of pressure on realising that everything is possible. The going is firmer if things are certain in terms set by a social group. The new style does not offer an environment but something receding and intangible. The destruction of the centre reveals, not a preset syllabus of new ideas about collusion, but a stabilised space in which an unlimited population of new ideas can emerge from thin air into substance.

The two big processes we have to notice are the removal of rhetoric and the removal of the central reference back to an ego. Most critics would agree that the dismantling of rhetoric and of Romantic self-protection is a process widespread in all 20th-century poetry. The avant-garde takes these processes much further but they are deeply scored into the culture. One of the dogmas of mainstream academic poetic activity from the early 50s on was to dredge out 'rhetoric' from the poem. This was an austere development programme which defined adulthood in a poet as a stage reached through learning progressively to purge one's poems of emotions and expressivity. Practical Criticism called for precision in poems and in reading poems. It tended to isolate the bits of poems you enjoy and remove them. 'Rhetoric' seems to mean words which transmit emotion; words which dramatise a situation; words which involve us in the immediate moment, losing detachment; words which cause us to identify; words which express deep, inarticulate states of feeling rather than rational, cut and dried, notions; identifications and appropriations and projections; ornament, especially as this transmits mood, with light parts of language expressing light and transient mental states; and many other things. You lost points for liking these things.

If we look at this process in the round, it may seem that the academic poet of the 50s purges rhetoric partially and the avant-garde poet purges it thoroughly. That is, there is a procedure of identifying and removing certain elements of ordinary language, which can be applied recursively. The avant-garde poet is someone who over-fulfils this procedure. Perhaps this is widely so, that recursive application of rules separates the extremes from the centre.

One of the semiotic strands cut out by kenosis is collusion. We have spoken of narcissism, as a quality in the self-process of individuals. However, art is a social thing, and we have also to consider very similar acts of selecting and heightening as parts of the group process. These can be summed up as collusion. It may well be that the defects brought to an individual's behaviour by narcissism are brought to the behaviour of a group by collusion. Status can be seen as the voice of a group's subjectivity, and this includes low status. Laying bare structures of self-esteem may answer the question "Why is my status low?"

Liquefying and estranging status raises two questions, at least. One has to do with Marxism. Within the general context of the conceptual movement, individuals were saying "this collusion is with members of the bourgeoisie, income groups A and B, and so is unacceptable to me". It is possible that all the avant-garde writers withdrew from the visible literary world because they were Marxists and rejected bourgeois culture. I don't know if this is true. It would be so neat if we could say, a multitude of young people were alienated; they rejected the self-praise of a society which they found basically immoral; they were especially keen on Adorno (and his negative dialectic) and Herbert Marcuse (with his attack on affirmative culture); their new critical art exposed the ideological hegemony underlying bourgeois art. The trouble is, this doesn't ring true. No-one ever talked to me like that. Certainly it would be wise to read Sartre, Adorno, and Marcuse in your background studies. But it may have been accidental that the collusion exposed was (male, white, middle-class, ethnically British, educated, literary, pro-Christian)—since the artistic interest of the group of creators we are looking at was against collusion everywhere, and they rejected easily available modules of Marxist propaganda art, based on working class solidarity, just as much as they rejected Hollywood assumptions about character and narrative coherence.

Considerable numbers of people were also saying "this collusion is with members of the male sex and so is unacceptable to me". Literati from Wales, Scotland, Ireland, and even the North of England, have frequently or even generally felt English literature as a hegemony of the South, a club to which they could not gain admission. Was the attempt to remove the personality as the core of poetry an attempt to satisfy and alleviate these complaints? Hardly so. There were too many other reasons for deleting this core and moving to the periphery of the perceptual field. But it is easy to misread implicit intents. These critics from the out-groups generally wanted egocentric, personal poetry with their own favoured figures at the centre.

People seem to be more agitated about group narcissism than about individual narcissism. The idea that 'all male poets collaborate to project and suppress' agitates people more than the idea that 'one male poet, the one we are reading, projects and suppresses'. I don't really understand why this is. The vanity of an individual seems to be a major problem when you're reading their poetry.

The other question has to do with collusion as social reinforcement as a force which does away with anxiety. The withdrawal of collusion can mean the collapse of illusions which leave clear an essentially fertile void. It can also mean a collapse of emotional temperature which rapidly draws on depression, wretchedness, melancholia, loss of ideation, the need for reassurance. Depression can be seen as the internal version of low status. The object world is simple and unkind compared to the rich world of other people's psyches. The experience of avant-garde art can be like the experience of depression. In general, it seems to me that narcissism is quite fundamental to art. This is an area which would repay research. I suspect that art can be successful even though it reflects the vanity of a social group. But a draft of new information and new patterns is always welcome. The problem with self-regard is artistic, not political: that the poem becomes utterly predictable, reinforcing group identity by saying what thousands of other poems say. Educated poets do tend to demonstrate their command of classical models by reproducing the models.

The avant-garde poem thus removes the vividly coloured centre and the darkening effect which it has on every other sector, and presents a picture in which everything is periphery and a uniform, quiet grey. The value of this transformation rather depends on just what was being obscured before—the riches of this periphery. What do we find emerging from under the dazzle? This whole area is immense, obscure, perhaps sublime. It partakes of the random, the intact and primitive, the forbidden, and the unrecognisable. It dissolves orientation points and exposes us to bodily experiences of nausea and magical flight. It brings on the nameless, the unbounded, the dimensionless. It opens up a world of orderless, dispersed, perhaps anatomically incomplete, entities. It corresponds to a stage of the material world called chaos. It is without words but contains what perhaps precedes language. It may be that it represents fantasy after wishes have been removed as a limiting factor.

Games of the Gifted: Cryptic Canons

When I was in Ofsted's research division, I spent an afternoon idly reading a research publication about Gifted and Talented children (known as G&T in the trade). It arrested my attention, because the description it gave of games which these children play to stave off boredom made Tom Raworth's poetry flash before my eyes. I think it probably applies to Allen Fisher's poetry as well. The writer thought that gifted children were hopelessly bored by what the teacher had to say, picked it all up in five minutes, and spent the lessons in deep inattention, playing games of arbitrary variation on the flow of words or text in the textbook. The games were deliberately complex and cryptic, because their purpose was to fill up time—but they also involved lots of short cuts and omissions. They involved re-ordering things, building variations, spotting unusual and unintentional patterns in the words (defamiliarising?), collecting 'matches'. Cutting out and recontextualising were fundamental. It was misreading; focussing on the ambiguity and never on the conscious message.

So maybe . . . modernity in art isn't based on Parisian philosophy or on elite and unshared codes, but on a childhood play strategy: G&T children invent these patterns spontaneously, and do so in large numbers. Quite probably they have always done so. This is not to do with the collapse of shared social values within the last century; except in the cheating sense that a profoundly bored child is withdrawing from shared values simply because they are couched in an unstimulating flow of discourse. If you are talking about alienation, you have to look for its source in the right place. The problem for me as a critic is whether these 'cryptic' 'puzzle' practices will be attractive to a broad audience—since after all the G&T are maybe 2 percentiles of the general population.

There is another question about this kind of 'arbitrary complexity' 'overdevelopment' 'puzzle quality' being present throughout the history of culture, rather than just since 1850 or so. Personally, I think it's there if you look for it. And these devices have become mainstream many, many times. But that's another story.

I couldn't find that publication again, but there is one on the Ofsted website called 'Educating the Very Able'.[21]

It's arguable that the withdrawal from the High Street poetry scene is a re-enactment of the withdrawal of a seven-year-old child from the classroom into a private world full of games and protected by dissociation.

This is just a hypothesis. I am not sure what to think about it. I think being intelligent and being bored are related conditions. It does explain why avant-gardistes can be poorly socialised and yet all seem to share the same values. The values were not socially acquired. It's remarkable that they, as a group, are facing away from the social aspect of language as well as from the aspect of meaning and showing. This quality of being more excited by a 'hidden' or deliberately mis-read meaning than by a simple meaning is a giveaway—a sign that you belong to a certain group (even if you don't know it yet).

There is a specific condition of fear of boredom. It's underrated. Probably, it's a central factor in the disposition of the poetic field. It's something acquired early in childhood, and, because it comes from that age, it's an overwhelming feeling, led by cunning rather than reason. I think people are making a big mistake by taking a sociological approach to taste; if intelligent people have a paranoid fear of reading Tony Harrison, it's not to do with social conflict, it's just because they're frightened of being bored. Explanations using 'politics' or 'the wish to be associated with admired international elites' may be *post hoc* rationalisations. The G&T are bored by political discourse because the rate at which it presents information is too slow for them, and the language it uses is not tricky and puzzling in the way they like. This resistance is really nothing to do with politics or government or administration. This group would find good government equally boring and frustrating. Switching off is their specialism. Avant-garde government is a null concept. There may be an alliance between currents which are angry because the TV is boring, and groups who want political change, but really they don't want the same things and their ways must part. The notion of mainstream poetry was not the product of organised research but of an intuitive and 'allover' reaction at the base emotional level; fear of boredom. Like other intuitions, it was essentially right. Divisions between artistic groups are not based on orderly and articulate debates, which draw on secure and thorough collections of facts. They are much more internal, intuitive, and involuntary than that.

The research didn't actually look at similar behaviour among less intelligent, normal children. Do ordinary children find school boring? yes indeed, this is not an experience securely confined to an elite of the super-bright. It's something everyone shares. I just mention this as one of the problems with using research in studying aesthetics. Many people have had the experience of being bored by avant-garde poetry, too.

A classroom is a great example of a central institution. Problems with the sociological approach to poetry may be summed up by looking at this central place—children aren't all getting the same socialisation because a lot of them aren't even paying attention. If they go off into some self-made world, it's that world which is teaching them response patterns. This may demonstrate why in looking at poetry we have to forget central institutions and think more about software. Styles of information processing are much more of a vital function for children, because learning is the central thing in their lives—as not for adults. The little strategies they develop for self-stimulation during the boredom imposed by dull adults may be the very basis of poetic activity.

Mainstream poetry quite literally is boredom imposed by dull adults.

Memory Jars

One part of Allen Fisher's poem 'Enclosed Delight' is titled '15 Objects in two sets', of which this is part:

> Etching of Count Alexander Cagliostro with brief biography.
> Photograph of Michael Bakunin and a letter from Bakunin to
> Ogarev November 2, 1872.
> Drawing of injection moulding construction.
> Map of the Americas showing distribution of Indian tribes.
> Drawing of boot types 'through the ages'.
> Photographs of busts depicting Homer, Hesiod, Solon, Sophocles,
> Euripides, Socrates, Plato and Aristotle.
> Painting by John Constable, 'Study of Clouds'.
> Painting by Edward Hicks, 'The Peaceable Kingdom'.[22]

The vitrine is something associated with Francis Picabia and the years around 1918; he put objects into a case of glass (and wood) and exhibited them. As this implies, the juxtapositions involved in the collections may be surreal. Although unrelated, they seemed to form new wholes—encapsulating a time and a place. The objects may be naturally associated—as in emblem painting, a European genre which died out with Romanticism; or be arbitrarily associated, to create a new unique whole. The boxes were inspired by junk-shops—or museums. The vitrine may be evocative in itself, or a comment on the act of memory. I think everyone reacts to those Picabia works with delight, and most people respond similarly to the verbal heaps of objects. Although, the original vitrines have a simultaneity and primary quality which verbal forms do not.

A partial description of 'Museum Pieces', another work by Fisher, follows:

1. using Frances A. Yates' *The Art of Memory*, where a system of places and objects is collected to give a set of triggers for memories. In less useful terms this could mean an ashtray from Southend reminding the owner of a holiday there together with a set of notions connected with the place.
2. bringing together objects that would otherwise be disposed of such as empty pill cartons, broken pencils or out of date coins.
[...]
4. Some pieces have been extended to act as "Reversal" objects. They include sardine cans in oil, a broken purse surrounded by out of date coins and so forth.[23]

The word assemblage is also used sometimes for a non-random collection of objects. This is in common use in archaeology to describe artefacts frequently found together—and which as a grouping may have a semantic load, signifying social status or ethnic allegiance.

It is interesting how technically unskilled art, art on the margins, can abandon most features of pictorial realism but still cling on to emblematic objects. A Bronze Age statue-menhir can show that the subject is a male by depicting a sword—while showing facial features is too demanding. Grave goods (the word assemblage is often used for these) can say a great deal about the status of the person buried, in a language without words. The ornament on a metal cloak-clasp may be part of a system—it is differentiated from the clasps of neighbouring ethnic groups, so that the enamel griffins etc. say who the owner is. This coding, while apparently very efficient, has of course the limit that it can only reproduce meanings which already exist—it is tied to a real social structure. The system works because the cloak-clasps are very similar—slight differences have a precise value.

The virtual objects which are drawn on in metaphors are stores of knowledge. States of mind are loose, flighty, mutating things. They are hard to share, but that is the task of poems. Metaphor seems to rely on objects of unusual familiarity and firmness. There is as if a virtual store where these objects are kept. The memory jars may be an attempt to supply a new set of objects to act as vehicles of meaning. Conceptual art was so named because it was art which left no objects behind and could not be taken over by the gallery system. But my memories of conceptual exhibitions, checked by surviving photographs etc., show (also) the opposite—piles of objects with no ascribed meaning. In fact, the apparatus of conceptual art shows large resources of concepts without objects, objects without meanings, and object/symbol codings which are detached from objects and symbols. This apparatus permits freedom. It was a response to the ideological over-coding of the Cold War.

Fisher was referring to the Renaissance theatres of memory described by Frances Yates. These were technical aids used by people making speeches—and so resembled the conventions by which poets cue memories in the listener. The use of poetic tags is a basic feature of poetry. It has undergone damage in modern poetry. The classical poet Claudian wrote: "Then arrived the legion set over the furthest Britons, which governs the bloodthirsty Scots and gazes, on the dying Pict, at his bloodless pictures impressed by fire; even the battalions set against the blond Sigambrians, and those which tame the Chatti and the turbulent Cherusci."

These are tags. The Roman listener could, obviously, summon up conventional images of these barbarians, once stimulated by these epithets.

It would be possible to represent well-known poems by a series of photographs of objects. Some poems might be recognizable from these series. In any case, poems depend on series of objects, around which their action takes place. Much English poetry describes the routine of agricultural work in a village. Literary people spent much of the 20th century recreating this village so that literature would not collapse without it—the Imagined Village project. The custom of decorating pubs with disused agricultural implements (horse gear, brass pans, etc.) is part of this project, and connected with Georgian poetry, which often described these implements as stores of integrity. It is obvious that the weight of symbolic ethical values loaded onto the image of the ploughman at sunset, and so on, vanishes when we are reading urban poems. It is the sensuous support of poetry which has vanished. Perhaps a new set of object codings would be useful.

The industrial activity of visual art had developed an efficient keying of scenes to objects or physical features. By the time a poet had mentioned "crib" "stable" "ox", the reader knew the poem was set in Bethlehem.

Classical mythology had a hardly less effective system of keying. The collapse of inherited narrative complexes or myths, as a basic aspect of the modern condition, left poets with an "empty world", a state of disenchantment. This world was however full of all kinds of objects. The vitrines bring to light something long obscured—that poems are based on collections of objects. Realising this made it clear that the cognitive frameworks bound to the objects were limited and inherited—and that building new ones might involve building new assemblages of objects. The action of storing memory in the blank, freed, objects could fill the world again. The activity of uncoding and recoding could now come under conscious control—freed from inherited, rigid, structures. This is perhaps what we are seeing with memory jars. The vitrines seem to be collections of objects to stand for scenes yet unwritten—objects in a state of freedom.

It would be a mistake to look at these assemblages as references to a story which you are supposed to know. In reality, they are props for a story which does not exist yet.

The memory jars are the opposite of kenosis. They represent irrational plenitude.

It may be that, in order to bring new poems about, one has to collect new assemblages of objects first.

Because ideas cling together by habit, it may be easier to rearrange groups of things than groups of ideas. Fisher arranges these groups of things and we go along with it—whereas we call arbitrary groups of words "meaningless". Suppose an art project in which a thousand people were given access to an endless store of objects and asked to construct new assemblages. They would make the assemblage, photograph it, break it up. Make another.

One can reduce poems to series of objects—they would then be noun strings. This suggests list structures underlying discursive speech, as a kind of archaic layer.

Breton proposed the assembly of dream objects of unknown purpose. This is a breaking of borders. Maggie O'Sullivan produced, in around 1995, a poem listing a set of lead animals. I was present when David Sellars suggested to her that she actually produce the objects—perhaps as castings or textiles. The poem later came out in *Palace of Reptiles*.

Disinvestment and entitlement

Part of the components of consciousness is the product of social agreement—this is collusion. They are also likely to be optimistic—*narcissism*. They are also adapted to create the impression of continuity and predictability—the element of *control*. Someone who feels trapped by all this will turn the volume controls up on dissent, emptiness, strangeness. Doing this produces a strange kind of art. People may find this incredibly unpleasant. It probably does give a lot of insight into how the mind works. But also, pure coldness is something you can never achieve. You simply can't have awareness with the functions of teleology, collusion, coherence, switched off.

What is appropriate behaviour in this emotional realm? Some kind of personality crisis is appropriate. The loss of collusion means the destruction of the assets which those other people valued. They don't have value unless someone attributes it. To put into question the relationship between an ego and the assets which it is invested in is an urgent process—one which flashes up an x-ray image of a whole psychic anatomy. The ego engulfs objects like a phallus, technological power, military power, education, Western pre-eminence, and when they are pulled out the ego slumps and falls down. Within the realm, emptying, rebuilding, refilling, re-emptying, the ego at incredible speed is highly appropriate behaviour.

Whereas we have said that it is the central role of the poet's ego which is under attack from the avant-garde, the central thing which people attack is more probably the identification with a nation, a gender, a social class, etc. Groups are just as capable of self regard (and selective blindness) as egos.

Arguably, most art rotates around the withdrawal or acquisition of symbolic assets. The shared game, or collusion, involves assets as the tokens on which the play depends. Withdrawing from the praise industry (propaganda, advertising, etc.) must promote the exploration of uncertainty and disenchantment. The avant-garde intensifies the game by dramatising the moment of loss and gain. At a technical level, the panoply of 19th-century poetry has stopped working; forfeiture of assets is a daily fact for a poet even if they have no wish to think about it.

In the 1950s, writing poetry was the activity of a small group of people who had a great deal in common. At that stage, the working class were a huge Other for the literary world—about 80% of the population, they were simultaneously absent from the scene and referred to all the time. Anyone hearing the cultural discourse over the last 40 years will have noticed discussion around disinvestment of the dominant cultural group. This has rarely been posed in terms of the working class, but frequently in terms of myths embodying the values of patriarchy, colonialism, militarism, possessive individualism, etc. This proposed disinvestment is related to the extraction of the ego from the centre of the poem. The attempt to make procedures conscious contributes to a critique of how judgements of people, and attachments to them, are formed.

However, a scan of the Left critique of artistic taste shows that the modernist myth and the related myth of personal creation of forms from nothing have been the subjects of cogent criticism. That is, from the standpoint of a committed feminist, a committed Third World nationalist, etc., the figure of an autonomous and reflexive creator is just another part of a male-Western myth, and this includes the avant-garde in all its forms. The heroic claims of modernist poets to autonomy, self-definition, a leadership role into a new future, and also to innocence from the crimes of 'bourgeois civility', are just the kind of triumphalism which the Left critique is directed at.

If a person A has a status which they dislike, they can rightly see this as an act of collusion between other people which excludes their opinion. The assignment of status is one of the fundamental classificatory acts of a society and can be seen as arbitrary. Feminism shed a spectacular light on this process, but it is even wider than the ascription of roles to women. Fantasy rather generally involves an exchange of roles. For the individual A, the idea of occupying any other status than the one they have is part of a fascinating and repressed world. This vision of status as arbitrary and subject to rapid change is crucial to enjoying avant-garde art. It draws on evidence which is hidden beneath the ordinary structures of perception. Negation of what is will always show up the world of what is negated but which might be. It can be argued that the repressed, in a society based on possessive individualism, is always socialism—the loss of individual ego boundaries to feel and work as a group.

The processes of disinvestment, depolarising, depressurising, reconfiguration are quite extreme experiences for the individual. Because every bond is changing, the exposed and sensitised surface of the ego is at maximum. In a certain sense, this must maximise consciousness and acuity of awareness. This is a real experience, even if the posited universal transformation of relationships in the march into a revolutionised society is not.

Disinvestment fits in generally with a landscape where there are numerous different social groups, each with their own internal sets of values, and where the individual may need to float from one to another. We could rephrase the shift as being from longstanding and heavy, involuntary projections onto light, rapid and voluntary ones. We saw that a key quality of avant-garde poetry was velocity. Emptying out the centre of the poem allows speed and disengagement. This has certain advantages.

The avant-garde is perpetually pointing towards the uncoded part of the world visible beyond the boundary of the artist's personality, and unpicking all the points where the text has been adapted to give the illusion of continuity, and to display the poet's virtues to best effect. We may pause to think how little this approach would appeal to mainstream poets. If the mainstream totally relies on an attachment to the personality of the poet, and the avant-garde is persistently pointing out the artificial nature of a text set up in this way, the mainstream poet will see this as treachery, the equivalent of someone turning up the house lights at the high point of their performance. It may be arousing in their brains a nightmare in which modernity rolls on by one step and their poetry abruptly loses all its credibility. If we look at the functions which the avant-garde is trying to isolate and switch off, it may seem that in general they are the functions which artistic talent permits, and which separate good art from bad.

People have very diverse views on how interesting the dissolution of the real role structure would be. We may suppose that the audience for the avant-garde is made up of the dissatisfied.

Conclusion

Another disclosure which sheds light on how the scene works is the existence of pacemakers. These are the people, probably not creative but on the scene, who besottedly test poems for their true avant-garde status, jeer at people for failing their home-made tests, loudly announce the results, and ignore any artistic values. The avant-garde may depend on a social scene of insecurity, competition, stress, and lack of legitimate assets, to support it. It is only because the pacemakers have total belief in the rules of the game that they are clear enough to apply as a principle in revising texts. The role of the pacemakers is to increase insecurity and screen out any alternative rule-sets, all the other games.

The converse of the fear of humiliation by the pacemakers is a faith in modernity, and in the power of the classical avant-garde of 1910–25—and in the possibility of owning these as assets today.

Of course I can't paraphrase everything. That doesn't mean it doesn't affect my brain. I would argue that there is a large gap between what I can apprehend unconsciously and what I can paraphrase, and that this gap has to do with intellectual performance. I regret the gap, but I don't think that I can put everything I know into words. This floating and inexplicit knowledge is precious, and quite distinct from poems which I do not understand and which leave me cold.

I talked, a while ago, about a body of implicit knowledge. The problem with verbalising this is not only how much of it there is, but also, and perhaps even more, that different people own different copies of it—the process of putting it on paper makes obvious disagreements which had been blissfully latent up till that time.

Image before leaving

A Canadian psychologist in the 1940s showed chimpanzees a clay head and elicited responses of horror and alarm. Further experimentation showed that in fact they were very disturbed by any element isolated from its normal whole. In fact, the presentation of any figure with an element missing was extremely disturbing.

This is clearly related to the device of omission in modern poetry: the missing element is foregrounded, and is the source of disturbance.

The psychologist was Donald Hebb (1904–85)—the same one who pioneered sensory deprivation studies. He was not a follower of the gestalt school, although the interest in wholes and parts of figures (*Gestalten*) seems akin to the interests of the gestalt school. Actually he seems close to his teachers, who worked on brain physiology and on modelling neural networks.

The mainstream critics respond to poems of unusual design with the same horror and alarm as the chimpanzees in Hebb's laboratory.

The image of a figure in a controlled, laboratory set-up being put through artificial experiences which project them into strange and unknown states of mind was of vital concern in the 1950s. The transfer from this image into the radical art of the 1960s is rather important. The interest in total environments seems to stem directly from it.

The idea of cellular assemblies, cognitive psychology, etc., is fascinating for the kind of people who read modern-style poetry. However, we have to ask about the horror and alarm. How is this compatible with aesthetic experience? Or, does it simply disappear with familiarisation (and would this prove that familiarity is after all basic to pleasure)?

Notes

[1] The case against the avant-garde is usually resolved in complete silence, but the case against is made in Peter Abbs (ed.), *The Symbolic Order* (Brighton: The Falmer Press, 1989), pp.89–142. In his contribution Fuller developed the most illuminating critique of the avant-garde and the conceptual scene in the visual arts, the scene from which he had emerged as a critic and fan. Fuller spent much of his time with artists and was unwilling simply to repeat the glittering propaganda lines wheeled out so often by dealers and catalogue writers. The matter is one of unusual complexity and Fuller did much to clarify it. Consult *Beyond the Crisis in Art, Marches Past*, etc.

[2] While I am using these particular anthologies as my main examples, little has changed in the ten years since they were published.

[3] Oliver Sacks, *An Anthropologist on Mars* (London: Picador, 1995).

[4] School of London: for a practical definition of this term, see the Balkan Gazetteer at page 302–310 of this volume, or, see pages 262–7 of my book FCon.

[5] The Underground: For a practical definition of this term, see Balkan gazetteer at page 302–310 of this volume, or, see pages 138–208 of FCon.

[6] Published in *Cul de Qui* (periodical, London) issue no. 1, 2002.

[7] Robert Hampson, *Seaport* (London: Pushtika Press, 1995). A revised and expanded edition is due from Shearsman Books in late 2008.

[8] in *Angel Exhaust* (periodical, London) issue 19, 2007.

[9] from Peter Finch, *Selected Poems* (Bridgend: Poetry Wales Press, 1987), p.144.

[10] 'On criticism': ibid., p.116

[11] Tom Raworth, *Eternal Sections* (Los Angeles: Sun & Moon Press, 1993), p.51.

[12] ibid., p.40.

[13] Rudolf Otto, *The Idea of the Holy* (trans. John W. Harvey; London: Humphrey Milford, 1923; orig. 1917), pp.71–2.

[14] Adrian Clarke, *Spectral Investments* (London: Writers Forum, 1991).

[15] See note 1 above.

[16] Richard Cork, *English Art Today 1960–76*, Exhibition Catalogue (Milan: Electa Editrice, 1976).

[17] in Andrew Duncan (ed.), *Marvels of Lambeth: Interviews with Allen Fisher*, Cambridge, Salt Publishing, forthcoming); henceforward referred to as *Marvels*.

[18] see Viktor Erlich, *Russian Formalism. History—Doctrine* (New Haven: Yale University Press, 1981), p.77.

[19] This was a phrase of Structuralist criticism at a certain point—*machines symboliques*, or virtual machines which act on symbols.

[20] Oliver Sacks, *op. cit.*

[21] 'Educating the Very Able'. http://www.archiveofficial-documents.co.uk/document/ofsted/veryable/able-04.htm#gen29

[22] in Allen Fisher, et al., *Future Exiles* (London: Paladin, 1992).

[23] in Allen Fisher, 'Blood Bone Brain', *Spanner*, 1981–1982.

Leaders of Heresies:
Eric Mottram and Kathleen Raine

To start with, let's take two schemes as first person fantasies of poets.

I am a mirror for the beautiful invisible things of the universe. I write beautiful poetry full of beautiful things and in tune with the eternal. I practise deep involvement, people are forbidden to disagree with it and cynical people are removed far away. The patterns catch up the reader and go very deep and lock them into a state where they perceive only the beautiful and other sensations do not penetrate. All great art throughout the ages is similar to my art and poets who aren't like me are lost in a corrupt materialist and plebeian error. We are sensitive people surrounded by other sensitive people and go into a state of worship where we are super-sensitised to the wonderful things of the universe. We need barriers around this sensitivity to exclude the complexity of the material world, and the fixed forms of art produce a powerful focus which locks us in the pure and desired state. There are wonderful people, noble spirits, who know each other and who cluster around my poetry. People who dislike my poetry lack purity and faith. Of course the people have a natural sense of beauty and respect and modernity is just an unpleasant fantasy by a few unhappy intellectuals. Of course all the human race except for a few beret-wearing intellectuals in Parisian cafes is in tune with my poetry and rejects this modern nerve jangle.

Or else:

I write new poetry and am in alliance with all the truly innovative artists in the world. A whole new world is opening up and of course it will belong to the people who detach themselves from the old world. People are desensitised to the artistic forms of the past and no longer truly respond to them. Being thrown into completely unfamiliar environments turns on the whole brain whereas repetition of form only turns on tiny parts of the brain and then only to the extent that it has an element of the new, the element we own and control. The shock of neurological dislocation and behavioural uncertainty breaks people loose from basic assumptions about how life is led and so liberates them. Political progress is impossible without detachment from old habits. The state of deep uncertainty is where people improvise most, achieving true freedom, and learn most, using their brains most intensely. Subversion of form provides the most radical insight into form and is also political liberation. Artistic convention serves to exclude the complexity of the material and human world, building a thousand dikes and hedges to defend against it, and exposure of naked intelligence to this complexity is a transcendent experience. Knocking out the dominant faculty may be sufficient to release the minor and normally suppressed ones and set off radical exploration. People have been taught to go to set places and collect set artistic gratifications, this is circular and truly mobile behaviour follows from dislocating it. Exact recording of the past simply reproduces alienated behaviour patterns. Emergence from the set patterns allows much larger patterns to emerge into the light of day, allowing conscious choice at many levels. This is the triumph of the mobile. I can join elite groups of exciting people if I get rid of my attachment to the past.

My suggestion is that this is the sort of fantasy which animates poets, who are motivated by a strong sense that there are winners and losers and are always on the look-out for a personal win. As is the nature of fantasies, these are visibly incomplete, and we have to think of real poets as chasing several of them more or less at once. Another take on this is that readers are animated by these fantasies and expect poets to fulfill them. Being inside the fantasies is of course wonderfully warm, profound, intoxicating. The trouble is staying deep enough inside them to maintain the pleasure and to get poems written. At this point a role emerges for cliques, narrow and unified enough to give the fantasy social acceptability and substance, to echo back an inner state. Being outside the fantasy is an un-poetic feeling strikingly akin to depression.

The two first person fantasies are based on the positions of two theorists of poetry, Kathleen Raine and Eric Mottram. While they were influential on other people at least some of the time, the positions existed before they came along and exist also in other countries. Both of them had an imaginary landscape which they devoted appalling labour to reaching, as if they had the idea that it would blow right out of their hands. Sometimes they flung open the gates to welcome people in, sometimes they moved to seize and expel others, but they were afraid of being expelled by it. The more compelling it was, the more they were concerned that other people would take control of it. They set tests of fitness which they laboured to pass. At this point we can reflect that the urge to overmatch brilliant rivals could be so demanding that it would distract someone from the need for clarity, and that they would forfeit this basic virtue of language in order to win. That is, when style signals control of scarce assets it can evolve towards exclusiveness and become the most desired virtue of language—displacing clarity, lucidity, explicitness, and so on.

I was lamenting earlier how few shared events there are in the life of poetry. The exception was the disagreements of 1976–7 at the Poetry Society—which were not 'shared' events, in the sense that different participants agree about anything that happened. Of course we can go down to a richer level where we register every book publication as an event. We then lose the illusory promise of events as turning-points—they are numerous but lead in all directions. Instead, we have a flow of time without loss in which immense sensations of power and beauty wax and wane and wax again. It is difficult to speak of 'shifts of sensibility' unless we mean these cyclical ones which come and go like the weather. It is exciting to find moments at which things change. However, with both the sensibilities discussed, what I see is a temporal plateau—after a stage of rapid development, they do not change very much and arguments and attitudes cannot be dated to within a few decades.

The Enemy of Modernity: Kathleen Raine

In the Middle Ages, there was a current of idealised literature in which the protagonists were saints or heroes; the Grail cycle went further by having knights who were also holy. They carried out wonderful feats and had simple perfect characters, and the story depended on these features. The stories were very predictable and lived in a sealed realm which they never chanced to break. There was an odd symmetry between this branch of literature and the social order in western Europe, in which either nobles, defined as knights and warriors, or senior clergy, owned most of the land and most of the power. The saints, like the prelates, were typically members of the aristocracy. This social order still persisted into the 18th century, and the slow rise of democracy correlated with the spread of the

Enlightenment, associated also with a new kind of history which dealt with the other ninety-nine percent of the social order and was based on facts rather than on idealised biographies. It had a critical attitude towards the hereditary powerful families and towards the subservient narratives which glorified them. By the late 18th century there was an opposition in Europe between the Enlightenment and the defenders of the old order, a sort of Counter-Enlightenment. The latter received mighty intellectual stimulation from the resentment and enforced idleness among French monarchist exiles in the 1790s (and subsequent years), and this phase of creativity produced a tangle of ideas (I would prefer not to say, a system) which was able to be drawn on by conservative exiles from power over the next two centuries. This Counter-Enlightenment is the larger landscape in which Raine wandered as an individual.

She says in a review of a reprint of Thomas Taylor (his version of Iamblichus): "It was Taylor, first translator of Plato into English, who supplied the texts from which the English Romantic poets learned the Neoplatonic metaphysics, with its accompanying symbolic discourse, which wrought so revolutionary a transformation in the theory and practice of poetry at the end of the 18th century. Blake, Coleridge, Shelley and Keats all are, in various modes and degrees, polytheists (.) [...] It is possible that the impulse of quantitative science has almost spent itself, and that a return to the traditional concept of mind as the only substantial reality may have already been reached through the following of scientific investigation to its conclusion."[1]

So, the application of psychology, politics, and sociology to art has to stop. Knowledge derived from precise measures, e.g. documentary, photography, psychology, must be excluded from art. Raine (1908–2003) studied natural sciences at Cambridge and associated with a brilliant group of students remembered for the magazine *experiment*, who were interested in linking science and art; Raine wanted just the opposite. Criticism, realism even, seemed to interrupt and frustrate beautiful states of mind which led to happiness. The lifelong search for a solution to this problem guided her development. Generally people justify the piercing of objectivity into art by saying that modernity is a good thing; Raine was happy to reject modernity in its entirety, and this was clearly a heresy. I will quote more passages from her prose work:[2]

> Perhaps it is impossible finally to create even a fairy-world when the idea of the sacred is entirely absent. [...] Perhaps this is the first society to build no environment of the arts for imagination to inhabit; and our cities have become all but imaginatively uninhabitable in the absence of those numinous presences. For if I were asked what contemporary English poetry [circa 1966] most conspicuously lacks, I would say, the imaginative, and especially the mythological sense[.]

> Art becomes formless when it becomes soulless. The Platonists spoke of the 'souls' of stones, plants, and animals; the 'soul' of a crystal is the form—the mathematical formula—of the crystal [.]

> We find only what we are qualified to see; the neglect of the importance, to the Romantic poets, of the perennial wisdom in its European guise of neo-Platonism is a reflection of the metaphysical ignorance of the post-Protestant West. [W]e are beginning to realize how little we have understood in works long familiar. Indeed, the entire European tradition of imaginative poetry . . . proves to be strung upon a single thread.

> Indeed, nothing seems more unnatural, in the art of poetry, than 'natural' diction, common speech, the conversational tone. It is a mark of imaginative inspiration and content to write in a high and mannered style, removed from common speech[.]

> But there is another influential minority who are no friends to the beautiful—those academic critics whose conceptual apparatus criticus the beautiful transcends and eludes. [...] The climate of critical opinion is indeed at this time increasingly plebeian and quantitative [.] They even appear to regard direct access to works of poetry as an infringement of their own territories (which some might say they have in any case usurped, as the rabble after the French revolution parcelled out more concrete estates).

> Indeed a revival of the learning of the imagination, and especially of the works of Plato and the neo-Platonists, has been the

inspiration, not only of the Florentine renaissance and all that followed (in England as elsewhere) but of every subsequent renaissance. Spenser laid the aesthetic foundations of all English poetry since, in his four hymns, of which one is to the earthly, another to the heavenly beauty. [...] Yet as our culture as a whole has drifted farther and farther away from its old roots [...] it has come to seem almost as though the poets speak a secret language.

This is based on a theology which almost nobody else shares. However, there is also the saying of Henry James, "what do such large loose baggy monsters, with their queer elements of the accidental and arbitrary, actually mean?" James is attacking the whole line of 19th century English novels here. The demand for more intense and precise patterning, and the elimination of the shapeless bulk of mere prose reality is the essential thing for Raine, and was, as Chris Baldick has reminded us[3], a concern of several critics around 1900. They were too eminent (and Baldick points to Pater, Symons and Wilde as well as James) to be viewed as heretics, so Raine is not so isolated here. Much modern poetry is a banal paraphrase of the newspapers or tiresome details of daily life.

Two tags say something about Victorian poetry: 'the utterance of noble philosophical truths wrapped in melodious sounds' and 'The spirit of man is each a string vibrating to the sweeping arm of an unseen eternity'. There is a kind of poetry which had a shipwreck in the 20th century, and which Raine was still trying to write. My guess would be that her verse before the start of publication in 1943 was too Victorian, and became successful when it became more condensed and modern. Such poetry did not suddenly halt "on time" when Victoria died and was obviously still being written in the 1930s and 1940s. It was pushed off camera by an alliance of interests which occupied modernity.

It is difficult to accept that neo-Platonism[4] was the *only* factor which inspired the Renaissance. It was though an asset which Raine controlled. We all love the belief that you can pick up a piece of driftwood on the shore and find a worked pattern on its underside, beneath the mussel footings and the seaweed, and find in it knowledge so stunning that it will change your life, and displace the poets who are your rivals. This is what Raine found in the Late Empire Greek texts such as Iamblichus (as well as Porphyry, Proclus, and Plotinus).

> The dust sweeps through the figures of a dance,
> Moves in its ritual transit like a bride
> Imprinting shells and flowers with primal forms that pass
> To fossil wastes and whirling nebulae,
> Weaving the rose, the lamb, and the world's darling child,
> And then unmakes again the world the dance has made.
> (from 'Dust')[5]

Some people have protested that Plato was rational and so magic couldn't possibly be neo-Platonic. However, the theory of Ideas is profoundly compatible with magic, and the idea of influences beaming around shaping the universe is fundamental to magic in the Near East and Europe. Here we see these waves giving dust its shape. Magic is simply the search for a shape lens with which to control these beams, and that is what Iamblichus and the author of *Picatrix* are describing. The engagement of major Platonists with magic and theurgy in the third century AD was thorough. Raine is not promoting witchcraft but believes that art works because certain shapes have an effect on our minds in the same way that talismans capture planetary influences.

In 1919, Edwin Muir was psychoanalysed by a Jungian, allowing the first entry of Jung's ideas into the bloodstream of British poetry. In the 1920s, after the collapse of the European monarchies, opposition to the Weimar republic and to the new regime in Russia produced radical innovations in the Counter-Enlightenment camp. Raine was married, in the 1930s, to two of the brilliant undergraduates of her generation, both poets: Hugh Sykes Davies and Charles Madge, closely associated with documentary, science, rational thought. Yeats' *Oxford Book of Modern Verse*, which we have already discussed, is the forgotten storehouse to which we should go to find the direct ancestry of the work she wrote a few years later. In the same year, 1936, came Muir's extraordinary *Variations on a Time Theme*, in which we can again recognise the tone of her poems. He was articulating a strange intuition about the inevitable and grandly repeating nature of spiritual situations, denying personal identity. Raine's poetry is much closer to Empson than it is to Blake or Shelley. Another look at Madge's works shows a strong attraction to surrealism, dream, and even religion. His work *Poem by Stages* is full of religious imagery rather than photographic recording.

Raine's first book of poetry did not come until 1943. She was up till then part of a network of speakers, but did not see herself as the primary speaker. It may be that her husbands and their friends simply talked so much that there was never time for her to interject. We can see this simply as being dominated by men. Or, we could suggest that she had a great admiration for left-wing intellectuals, including marrying two of them, while her spiritual urges led in a completely opposite direction. This led to silence—and a vast sequel in which she expounded a theory designed for completely silencing Marxists, intellectuals, and the whole Enlightenment thing. Her reaction led her eventually to spiritualism and the editorship of *Light, a review of psychic and spiritual research*. Her poem 'The Invocation' (in *Stone and Flower*, 1943) 'a spirit/ that I would make incarnate'—is about a medium, cast in terms which suggest a link between possession and poetic inspiration. The *possession* by which a few intellectuals felt that science belonged to them with its enormous power, by which consequently a few occultists came to feel that the huge power of spirituality belonged to them, made the conflict between them peculiarly long-lived. Raine reached poetic fruition in the 1940s, an era dominated by the New Romantics, and like them took a stand against documentary and machines. For me, she was a New Romantic but an atypical one. Her poems are lucid and theirs are obscure—she was not influenced by Dylan Thomas. The callsign apocalypse relates to the prophet John (on the isle of Patmos); Raine's book and poem *The Pythoness* relate to the prophetess who officiated at the oracle of Apollo at Dodona. However, both are prophets.

Raine's voice is that of a devout worshipper reciting the liturgy of some unknown religion. The naïve stylisation of vocabulary and rhythm has the intactness of childhood faith. Almost by mistake, we catch a glimpse of an unsuspected, integral universe where everything is connected to everything else—where starlight is a messenger beam floating down ideas which govern the conduct of plants and humans. *Stone and Flower* is not yet perfect, but the subsequent volumes, *Living in Time, The Pythoness,* and *The Year One* are splendid achievements. Her flourishing as a poet barely overlapped with that of her two husbands, who in fact fell silent at much the time that her first book of poems emerged, and remained silent, poetically, over the subsequent half century, in which she went on publishing. I have caught myself saying that Raine is both "lyric" and "didactic". This contradiction may not just be my brain shorting out: in her poems, she is an acolyte rapturously chanting a hymn. The text explains a doctrine and thus is didactic, but her attitude is one of exalted belief raised in a dangerous excitement above a normal sense of reality. Meanwhile, she does not write about love affairs or marriages, so that the conventional lyric situation of an I in love and interacting with other people is not part of her work. As we expect of lyric poets, her late work is of little interest. (It does include a long poem about a frustrated love affair, an innovation which did not lead to artistic success.) The *Collected Poems 1935–80* is too selective of the essential 1940s poems and generally has the wrong inclusions list. *Collected Poems 1956* is a more satisfactory book. *The Year One* contains many poems influenced by the Hebridean hymns or spells of Carmichael's *Carmina Gadelica*. They focus on a wish and are written in short lines in a repetitive convergent design. The interest in oral and simple forms brings us close to George Mackay Brown, Muir's other pupil.

European literature since the late 18th century has been less and less heroic, with an unending series of exposures of the contradictions of heroes and the verbal or visual apparatus of praise. It has been possible to construct a theory in which the nobility of the older era had access to sources of spiritual power which the modern world has lost through cynicism, so that the knights of the *Morte d'Arthur* and so on are literally described and not merely in an unrealistic and exaggerated (and monotonous) way. This may seem like a belief that heroic statues are depictions of a race of people with splendid physiques rather than flattering depictions designed to please the patron. However, once you accept this theory, it follows that there were arts of power and transcendence which an elite had in, say, the 15th century, and that the structure of societies dominated by narrow elites was a corollary of these awesome powers which the elite possessed and which the serfs readily recognised.

We have heard Raine describe the translations of Thomas Taylor as being the thing which made English Romanticism happen. This notion of ideas blowing in like seeds and expanding like flowers in a field may indicate what she thought her ideas would do for modern poetry if they were listened to. They had to do with intensified pattern, as well as eliminating facts. We may think of lilies slowly expanding over a pond, tranquilly, over 30 years. She also thought of the life of the artist as a slow expansion of ideas and vision. The Neo-Platonist view is of the universe as composed of ideas moving as fast as light to animate the shapes of the physical world, which has no impulses on its own. Pattern is not simply out there in the natural world with its visible structure, or in the functions of the brain, but is a third thing leading both of them. Raine thought also of a mood as the expansion of a pattern gradually acquiring integrity as it grew, so that human consciousness depended on the radiation of ideas and the role of art was clearly to mediate these stretches of pure time. Few poets wanted the critical attitude towards politicians, the actions of government, and the owners of large corporations to be switched off in the search for 'harmony'. Most poets though would be happy for the poem not to be criticised and subverted, so that the experience of the poem would develop autonomously to the extent that the poem had enough structural integrity to sustain that. The monumental sense of authorisation of graduate intellectuals to rubbish everyone else was persistently vindicated by graduate intellectuals but was not always revered by poets.

Her impact on the scene much later, in the 70s and 80s, was due to the integrity of her love for chosen master creators: Blake, Coleridge, Shelley, Yeats, David Jones. This example was inspiring but also raised questions: if you, as a secular, materialist, modernist poet, could write poetry which was sheerly beautiful and inspired such rapt devotion as Raine gave to her favourites, then obviously you would. So, if you didn't, this was clearly a problem. If being critical, intellectual, and so on produced a generally diminished body of poetic work, something needed fixing. Few poets would reject Yeats, Jones etc. for their ventures outside rationalism. Maybe the love of poetry was something sublime and noble in itself and withered without those qualities. Academic works on recent literary history all stress the collapse of authority of the writer and the proliferation of dissident groups who allegedly like nothing better than invading and subverting texts. Even if the hordes of indignant readers actually do not exist (except on the same plane as UFOs and their crews), critics are still eager to use texts as anatomical subjects in bloody and garishly lit didactic displays. So poets are attracted to a proposed island where analysis, puncturing, disruption in general, are utterly forbidden. Raine offers this.

Raine has described how she set out to read everything which Blake had read. Although it is unclear when she started (although already in 1951, she wrote the British Council pamphlet on Blake) this project must have occupied much of the 1950s, and culminated in her book *Blake and Tradition* (1968). A long gap in her production of poems filled this decade. At latest by 1960 (the date of a published lecture on Blake) she was steeped in the knowledge which was neither Christian nor rational—a landscape of ruins left derelict by the Enlightenment, having failed all the tests which the age of reason applied. The word "tradition" is used in a special sense. If you look at the Wikipedia entry for Raine there are references to the magazine *Studies in Comparative Religion* (founded 1963, and originally called *Tomorrow*, then *Traditional Studies*) and to the group of writers involved with it. For them, "tradition" had a very charged sense, given it by René Guenon, a prominent figure of the Counter-Enlightenment of the 20th century.[7] The total number of her different books about Blake is hard to count.

The 1940s were the moment when it seemed possible to tack Blake round from a wonderful primitive into a contemporary whose stylemes could be directly incorporated into new poetry. During the 1950s, that current was stood on by everyone with literary authority. In the USA, the Beat poets were "turning on" to Blake, although with them the abandonment of reason was a sign of intellectual laziness and spiritual self-indulgence. The mass reception of Blake must have been a thing of horror for Raine, and it was obvious that the end of persecution for her favourite poets could also be a moment of defeat for her. A new era of spiritual hunger was dawning, and in the 1960s Blake became a cult figure for youth. One strand of the new culture was the New Age spiritual movement ("Rouze up! ye sons of the New Age", Blake had written), from about 1968 on, and one tiny group in this was the Research Into Lost Knowledge movement, or RILKO, which included the architect Keith Critchlow. Their revival of 'sacred geometry' seemed to be showing how Neoplatonism was visible in the design of buildings, designs decorating ceilings or manuscript pages, and in whole landscapes.

In the 1960s, the most famous English poet was Ted Hughes. He was just as much devoted to the Muir and Jung heritage as Raine. In fact, what seemed to be happening was a dynastic struggle over that heritage, which Raine, read by perhaps a twentieth or a thirtieth as many people as the fascinating and dominating Hughes, was in no position to win. Raine wrote a wonderful book, *The Hollow Hill* (1965), and in 1967 *Defending Ancient Springs* collected her essays on poetry, setting out her position. In 1971, she published *The Lost Country*, which showed a serious decline although it had some of the old virtues. In 1973, there followed *On a Deserted Shore*, which seems to be the end of her creative success. It is an account of a love affair but set too far in the past to have the sense of immediacy and of possibilities which love poetry needs. Its egoistic theme is not redeemed by exhilaration or intensity. It is depressing. Hughes shows a universe of autonomous entities, driven by uncompromising ideas and almost ignoring the outside world and other entities. By focussing on the conflict process he shows how you get from complete entities to incomplete entities, of which the real world is full. The pattern (molecular or neurological) completes itself by acquisition but destroys other patterns in doing so. The cosmos is full of carcasses and ruins. The Jungian system is strong on individuation but does not really leave room for second or third parties. Hughes was the most mythologically creative English poet since Blake.

In 1981, she launched a magazine called *Temenos*[6], subtitled *a review devoted to the arts of the imagination*. "*Temenos* . . . rejects the premises of secular materialism." It was co-edited with Critchlow, Brian Keeble and Philip Sherrard, a Greek scholar attacking reason and science from an Orthodox standpoint. Part of its initial capital was to present the anti-Hughes position. She picked up a stratum of poetic survivors from the 1940s, but the magazine carried little poetry and especially little by poets born after 1920. Its ponderous attacks on modernity seemed to be expected to fail, as there was no anticipation that creativity could be reborn after the murderous purging of elements that did not accord with Tradition. Raine was not the kind of editor who takes interest in the work of other poets and develops an art politics which could affect the progress of poetry. *Temenos* was more oriented towards the agenda of Tradition, occult and only partly public, than towards living poetry.

The belief that Europeans prior to the Enlightenment had had supernatural powers, controlling miracles, heroic feats, divine knowledge, etc., could easily be adapted into the world view of Nazism, with its besetting drama of heroic and noble Ancestors and modern decadence which has lost touch with archaic principles. In the constant evolution of the forces of the Counter Enlightenment during an uninterrupted series of defeats, a merger with modern Nazism was inevitable and seems now to have been effected. Julius Evola was the central figure here. Tracing internet links shows that Aleksandr Dugin, leader of a movement which is both pro-Nazi and pro-Stalin in Russia, is a traditionalist and follower of Evola. A similar group exists in the Ukraine.

Hughes' vivid depiction of organisms in conflict graphically updates Raine's sweet picture of abidingly autonomous and timeless beings. Her landscape supplies boundless space to each entity, so that limits and conflicts never arrive. This is something which poets deeply desire, and it is inspiring. Evidently it means that few poets ever get considered, and it is not surprising that *Temenos* ends up with nil poets, so that infinite benevolence is offered to a total of nobody.

An essay I posted on my website in about 2003 classifies Raine as a Christian.[8] This follows Kathleen Morgan's 1965 book on *Christian themes in contemporary poetry*, which I admired. But with more familiarity with

Raine's work I am inclined to doubt this assignment. I don't think you can be a Christian unless you are a monotheist.

The Acolyte of Modernity: Eric Mottram

Pattern, symbols, and consciousness are closely linked, but despite Raine's constant interest in the links it is hard to agree with her version of them. The narrow intense focus on pattern which allows someone to write poetry about an idea seems to belong to intellectuals, and Raine's relationship with this group is elusive. Ideas are abstract patterns shared and contributed to by many people, and Raine's ideal of art would seem to be fulfilled by art which is animated by ideas and constructed according to formal ideals.

Mottram (1924–95) belonged to a generation of intellectuals which matured during the Second World War and the ground-breaking Labour Government of the 1940s, and was marked forever by Socialism, egalitarianism, belief in progress, a world perspective, and the excitement of the newly visible might of America. He was young in a time when the power order was crumbling and soon to be outworn. Practical anti-Fascist activity on a battle-cruiser included chasing the battleship *Tirpitz* up a Norwegian fjord, and sailing to Murmansk as escort to one of the White Sea convoys.

Academically, Mottram, who graduated from Cambridge in 1950, was one of the pioneers of American Studies as an independent area of study; he co-wrote one of the reference books (a volume of the *Penguin Companion to Literature*, replete with information about modern American poets and movements), and was, from 1960, the first full-time teacher of American Studies at the University of London. Culturally, he lingered in the atmosphere of 1963, when he was pushing Ornette Coleman, Charles Olson, and William Burroughs, was in a fervent minority, and knew that his opponents would be proved wrong. He never could be involved in English poetry full-time: his immeasurable influence on it is because the new language, almost as much as the language of pop music, had come in from the USA. Evangelizing for Black Mountain poetry also meant promoting the best tendencies in British poetry. He bet on a rapid rise in the market and won.

"A culture exists in limited mobilities of complex fictions, which function as both permissive and restrictive patterns, stories and repeatable points of reference These perform as a system only in so far as they constitute a mythology of behaviour and justification, a history of assumed origins and ends which can be used to permit both control and liberty—in government, economics, sexuality and law." I think this suggests his brass-necked assertiveness, but also his concern with the original simultaneity of experience, which came I think from regarding the jazz gig as the privileged moment. Eric's best work came from his ability to perceive many scattered individuals as a shared space full of a shared excitement: to restore to self-isolating, fragmented, freaky modern art the sense of conviviality. His ability to isolate common underlying forms made good new poetry possible, because it pointed out to various original or rejected figures that, if they were all writing the same Poem, some of them were doing it badly. His kind of cultural morphology dispelled any unimpaired personal essence.

This jazz belief in spontaneity and conviviality provided a theoretical counter to the determinism implicit in the approach to art which relates it to rather stable sociopolitical structures, and indeed to the immobility implicit in academic accumulations of knowledge of the past. Eric held these three systems in balance, as indeed any cultural actor must do.

The apex of his involvement with the British end of a shared excitement was from 1971 to 1977, when he was editor for twenty-two issues of *Poetry Review*. Some public interviews, put on as Poetry Centre events, were printed in *Poetry Information*: with Ken Smith, Tom Pickard, Barry MacSweeney. These are first-rate sources for the study of these poets. In this period he also wrote his two Catalogues for Poetry Conferences at the Polytechnic of Central London, 1974 and 1977, defining the British Poetry Revival, a phrase he coined: "Since the 1930s officially sanctioned British poetry has favoured minimal invention and information, and maximum ironic finesse with personal anecdote covered with a social veneer or location of elements in the country. It favoured the urbanely witty or baroquely emotional rather than the thoroughly informed intelligence and the risk of imaginative form. This preference could not tolerate an art which went beyond a leisure-hours consumer's inclination to rapid reading to work which might necessitate concentration, trained ability to read, and a willingness to entertain the prospect of new forms and materials." These are still the best explanations of modern British poetry; one is now available in book form, but then almost none of the poetry they describe is in print. The Catalogues remind me of nothing so much as a tank, firing to left and right without slowing down; stringing hundreds of names of publications together, they tell off a polemic with irresistible cumulative force. They illustrate his ability to recognize simple patterns in complex events; to link thousands of disparate phenomena; to isolate historical consequences in the flux of cultural production; and, not least, to inspire followers.

The image he builds up has these features. The 'Poetry Revival' is (a) a unitary phenomenon; (b) a progressive phenomenon following immanent laws; (c) it is bound to triumph; (d) English poets cease to be provincial through intervention from abroad as a module or transit route of "world culture". The fifth feature is its status as an American Exarchate, a reflex of events over the ocean, with a temporal delay which allows foresight. (The Exarchate was a part of Italy run from Byzantium, with its Governor appointed from there.) Anyone who invokes a historicist time pattern is bound to be disgruntled when the listed trains don't arrive on time, or when other trains arrive along the same tracks. I think that this historicism is akin to the jazz sense of occasion: the time-line of poetic vitality which Eric saw was made up of very many points, each of them a gig, a burst of conviviality, which *you had to be there*. It may be that the only way out of individualism, in writing about art, is to think in terms of these "hot social moments", and perhaps the imperious time-line is then inevitable. Mottram's view of art was singularly anti-individualist. Yes, the British poetry revival was less of a cohesive historical object than Eric's "complex fiction" has it: but I am more interested by what three dozen poets share than by their unique differentiae. What of speech is not shared is spilt.

Mottram recalled that, at the outset of his involvement with the Poetry Society, it was still being run by people who rejected all poetry since Tennyson. It is partly because Mottram and his allies succeeded that we can't even imagine the position of their enemies; but any look at documents of the period (Poetry Book Society choices, for example) will show how marginal the new styles were to the poetry business during the Sixties. They are not marginal today. There has been rapid progressive change. He was a great editor; the railroad called in Pat Garrett. The dead crows came home to roost. When Mottram's job at the *Poetry Review* came to an acrimonious end in February of 1977, it was along with thirteen resignations from the Board of the Poetry Society. People have acted as if this deprived everyone else of legitimacy; but there can be no reinstatement. Instead, this self-exile wrote a whole generation out of history, and meant that its influence on the British poetry emerging over the next two decades would be nil.

The personal effect on Mottram of that confrontation with institutions and fund managers was disastrous; while commitment to a world imagined but not lived in proved a weak basis for poetry. *Towards Design in Poetry* was a disappointment in this way, pleading for a marginal kind of art without apparently considering that something energetic and well-formed creates its own centre. "Composition is a series of decisions within choices, but improvisation can be simply repetition, as most poetry and jazz in the established modes always is: that is, it has become commercialised design, or it has become the fearful recapitulations of minor artists. The degree of alert creativity within intelligence and sensitivity reaches vanishing point and is supported by patronage." Mottram was a grand marshaller of detail and a knockout polemicist, not a theorist. From 1977 until 1980 he ran a series of readings at King's College in the Strand; these were continued by Gilbert Adair, and continued for twenty years as SubVoicive. As a venue for new writers, as a focus for the elusive avant-garde audience, and as a forum for discussions, this series has kept poetry alive in London. Eric taped all the readings he put on, and this fabulous spoken archive may be made available to the public. The belief in the unique complex of simultaneities, the kairos, caught by taping, dislikes the fixed quality of the Book: but the tape also emanates a simulacrum of the event when the kairos has gone. Immersing in the great critical art of the past, we reduce it to property, ourselves to administrators, and rob that art of its critical potentials. Concentration is loss of peripheral awareness.

I was surprised to learn from the obituaries that Mottram had published almost two dozen books of poetry, starting with the cultural percée of the late Sixties. His work is not celebrated, partly because of his inability to write a good line, the strained quality of his most startling juxtapositions, and even because of his underlying positivism, the cohesion and administrative efficiency with facts which make a good scholar. His moral principles got, in a typically Cambridge way, in the way of mere sensibility and freedom. He is the most literal of the avant-garde Socialist poets of the period. Nonetheless, the sheer accumulation of data, so reminiscent of his prose, builds up to quite a tonnage; one would call him an Alexandrine who hankered to write an epic, or even found a mystic rite. The long poem *Tunis*, where the wealth of detail is evocative without dispelling the mystery, is perhaps his best. *A Book of Herne* (1981) is interesting for its reception of Ferenc Juhász and the Hungarian myth of pagan and Uralic origins. *Interrogation Rooms* (1982) is a Leon Golub-like detailing and putting to scorn of the hidden chambers of States where violation and collecting statistics are the same project.

The Exarchate charter perhaps explains why England produced so little theory, and so little prose criticism, to support its great poetry. The theory already existed. The BPR has been great poetry flourishing in the absence of great criticism. The traditional inarticulateness of the Small Press world points us back to Mottram's major writings, chiefly the PCL Catalogues, as the only proven style for writing about this novel poetry.

We are *post* a classical era in which Mottram was one of the guides and great editors. The polemic points made by Mottram to support the 'British Poetry Revival' in the 1970s and 1980s were so telling that they have now been appropriated by the Mainstream, for example in the 'New Generation' sales literature and the Bloodaxe *New Poetry*: the view of England as a province, the vividness of unofficial and peripheral cultures, the heraldic claim filed to the Modernist estates, the Abroad franchise, the opening to an information overload. Such is the fate of ideas. The questions of the invisible radical 1970s, and the Lying History promulgated by 'market makers', are the principal ones hanging over contemporary British poetry. 1977 was the end of the 'British Poetry Revival', a horizon of invisibility bounding a new generation: conviviality was lost. Does the "lost poetry" offer a solution to contemporary formal problems? That would imply that the arrow of time stood still; those poets themselves were inspired by American poets, French philosophy, and by pop, jazz, cinema, new textiles, politics, social experiments, etc.

Mottram published "almost 200" essays, most of which, I presume, are about American studies. His section of the Paladin *the new british poetry* ("A treacherous assault on British Poetry") is offered as a summation of the era of *Poetry Review* under his editorship. His essay in *New British Poetries: the Scope of the Possible*[10] is a rehash of his 1974 Catalogue, indicating how much he'd drifted away from the scene after the campaign of 1977. I sometimes wonder how much of modern British poetry he liked, apart from seeing it as a reflex of his beloved Americans. One certainly wonders if he admired any of his followers.

Mottram was an impresario figure, imperious, decisive, and animating. The avant-garde is short of these. Yet radical poetry is born from bursts of febrile enthusiasm, not from earnest, dull, protracted labour. You can't be an actor without a theatre and a production; the illusion that a society of the poem exists allows the verbal space of the poem to exist without blowing apart. Eric was the leader of the bank raid, a theatrical deviser of the social space inside which strange language could emerge.

The Mottram family have given Mottram's archive to King's College, for a centre which makes both papers and tapes available to students.

Update 2008

Comments in this essay relate to a 'time now' of 1996. The SubVoicive series closed in about 2003. The poetry which was 'not in print' in 1995 now mostly is *in* print, due to heroic republication programmes by Salt Publishing and Shearsman Books. The comment about Tennyson fans comes straight from Mottram but is not in fact true. He may have encountered people who in the mid-70s still wanted poetry to be like Tennyson, but in the 1960s *Poetry Review* was not run by these people and did not publish their work.

Heresy as Autonomy

In 45 years, Raine and Mottram can barely have overlapped. The opposition between them is an example of why 'poetry wars' is a misleading term. No war took place, no border province was identified where campaigns and seizures could take place, no record of dialogue between the two camps exists. Their followers can barely have paid attention to each other. There is a tantalising moment in Professor Barry's book[11] which shows Kathleen Raine visiting the Poetry Centre in 1976:

> I went to read poetry in the company of Robert Gittings. I was frankly disgusted at the dirty state of the premises (a beautiful house and formerly well cared-for), and by the nameless boors who hung around the bar until they deigned to come upstairs (late) bringing their beer with them. One vomited over the floor during Mr Gittings' reading. I left as soon as possible, courteously escorted to a cab by Mr. Cottrell (p.164).

Would that she had continued "I made it my business to interrogate several of these bar fixtures about their views on poetry and soon realised that many of them were destined to be the most important English poets of the next thirty years. Suddenly I realised that poets did not have to dress as aged members of the Spiritualist Association. I also talked to the personable and erudite Professor MOTTRAM who explained some aspects of Blake which I had previously misunderstood and suggested I read one Henry Corbin." Alas! reader! I must tell you she did not.

Why put Raine and Mottram together? My suggestion is not that they represent the whole landscape of poetry, even for a while during the 1970s, but simply that they belonged to real factions and were prolific writers whose views we can reconstruct effectively. Both offered salvation knowledge and formed cults. Placing them in a set of common terms is almost impossible, so a discussion of points of opposition would be strained. I would have to make up the words of both sides in order to stage an artificial debate. Yet both are leaders of heresies. The details of their positions are unfamiliar to the general reader and are a constant source of surprises. It may be that a detailed understanding of these two strangely original figures would lead us into the centre of poetry, in a period which has now closed, and into the middle of the poets' private worlds.

Poems based on ideas we cannot accept as true are also heretical. The poet would then attack the usage of the word "we" but this does not affect the substantive point. Both Raine and Mottram were heretics of this kind, in the system of ideas which they wrote about and gave access to. It may be that Mottram used ideas we just haven't evaluated whereas Raine used ideas, either about cosmology, supernatural religion, or aesthetics, which we reject because we have better information. Mottram relied on an apparatus of value judgements and artistic experiences and insights which few people were able to share when he was an editor of national importance, during the 1970s. At present this apparatus may seem slightly dated, and the American avant-garde of 1963 rapidly evolved into something else. The Eisenhower era, with its Cold War intellectuals and effective stands against civil rights by people like Senator Richard Russell, has vanished and the revolt against it is hardly a heresy. This justifies Mottram's broad position, and meanwhile the artistic techniques he defended have become familiar to far more people. Mottram was a heretic in the sense that he published in *Poetry Review* a mass of poetry which a large number of subscribers found irritating and tendentious in its entirety. Also, in the sense that some of his critical work shows dislike and indifference for central areas of poetry, investing in the marginal in a risky and disoriented way. This is my broad conclusion. The details of the case for the defence have involved constant discussion over the last 30 years and cannot really be said to be exhausted. Mottram's poetry is also obscure, but this is not vitally related to, or implied by, his ideas about political and cultural change. The fragmentary quality of (much of) his poetry is founded on a belief in plunging people into unfamiliar environments so that they can react totally, with all their might. However, this brevity generally means frustration and incomprehension rather than intensity. He wanted immersive experiences but the flashes of his poems made of chains of flashes are shallow. If we consider the notions of momentary intensity and disruption, we find that they are in no way heretical, and that they are principles found at the core of popular culture. His specific beliefs about the dulling effect of habit and self-repetition led him into conflict with institutions based on conservation, but they are easy to identify with. We could indeed equate them with existentialism, the philosophical attitude fashionable when Mottram was a student. Looking at this belief in the immediate moment as the location of virtue, we can readily believe that he did not also have a system of knowledge, i.e. abiding knowledge and reaction patterns, and therefore that he did not subscribe to a heresy, as opposed to guesses and hopes.

Raine's dislike of quantity means that poets' share of the qualities she idolises is either all or nothing. This, when applied to a whole range of poets, is grandiosely unjust. Her method is not suited to distributive justice and, once again, is suited to an empty landscape. It is wonderfully warm for the favoured, for example Gascoyne or Muir. Do poets want a set-up where they are utterly vulnerable and sensitive people rush in to protect them? This role is only available to a few people and the demand for attention may seem infantile to others. Virtually everyone agrees that poets are emotionally vulnerable and that there are remarkably aggressive people roaming the poetry world. We have to wonder if the difficulty of accommodating the whole cultural field leads naturally to a sectarian landscape where a cultic order creates receptive warmth for specific poets and where the core values of those cults evolve *naturally* into heresies separated by linguistic fractures.

At some level, the complexity of a text must depend on the extent of information which it contains and which we do not possess at the beginning. Raine proudly tells us how Yeats spent four years studying one of Blake's works and seems happy to share with us that "Yeats, a poet of this century, can no more be understood by those who do not possess the knowledge of the 'learned school' in which he himself studied, than can poets of other periods[.]"[12] The knowledge in question is heretical and we are being told that we are cut off from Yeats and presumably from other occultist poets. At this point Raine *is in favour of obscurity and is justifying it*. The complexity of the work of Raine and Mottram is partly the extent of wrong information included in it and which makes the gap between inside and out more violent at the same time that it makes the insides huge and vague. It seems possible that the complexity of their work is consequent on the extent to which they adopted ideas which are radically unfamiliar and so contain dazzlingly large extents of new information. The unfamiliarity is intimately related to error—the more error built into the semantic structure which the work lives inside, the more unfamiliar the whole is. The theses are not part of our previous experience because the other people we have listened to avoided saying or singing them, this because they found them to be wrong. It may be that a linguistic structure which is both complex and unfamiliar is likely also to be wrong.

We spoke earlier of an Alexander complex, where people rush into an empty space because of an urge for territorial aggrandisement, possibly at the expense of truth, sense and proportion. The product of such a rush, pursued over decades, is a specific kind of heresy.

To me this recognition points to two possible new speculations. First, that some modern poets seek out autonomy in a counter-creative way by plunging into universes of falsehood and feeble hypotheses. Secondly, that the creation of a counter-universe may create a complexity which is also wealth. A sector of the audience is willing to acquire this groundless complexity because it offers a more autonomous and sustained imaginative experience. A speculative conclusion would be that people who have spare imaginative or intellectual time in big quantities want more labyrinthine and less reality-true art. Someone else might feel distinctly irritated and delayed by fighting their way through structures of information which in the end mean little, because they do not correspond to the structure of the universe and will never be confirmed by the evidence of our senses. In a sense, you acquire this knowledge only to forget it again.

Clearly this sort of heresy can lead to obscurity in poetry, but supports also sustained work in which every section yields new information. Both Raine and Mottram are to a large extent didactic poets, writing large amounts of prose in order to exploit their didactic urges, and they wanted clarity.

Raine was a heretic in the sense that her prose work relies on assumptions about the universe which most people do not share, and which are also perplexing and irritating. I should say at once that this stricture does not apply to her poetry. Her views on poetry are also heretical in the sense that they firmly invalidate the judgements of taste made by most modern readers, and the way 20th century poets write. The cult structure and the self-referential structure damage a shared understanding. However we need to take her criticism more broadly and consider the solid descriptive content of *Defending Ancient Springs*. What she says there about the poetry of the 1930s and 1940s is sensible even when she is facing ideological opponents. It seems that she became less open to new ideas and more fanatical about the ideas she believed in as she grew older. Her prose came significantly later in life than her best poetry, and the poetry comes out of a less bigoted and authoritarian and cranky pattern of thought.

She was impressed by her student associates, like Madge, Empson, Sykes Davies, Humphrey Jennings, to the point that she never got over them. The story tells us something about the clique as the unit structure of the poetic world. Inside it, you drop your defences but demand loyalty in return. It was a close knit group, but the others disagreed with her about certain issues. She found this unpleasant. It is true also that she attacked them in print and over a period of several decades. This may not simply have been benign and friendly reminiscence. I suppose it is unbelievably lucky and rare to have people around you and also find them in sympathy with you. It is nice to think of cliques being all warmth but we might also have to register competitive and denying forces of unbelievable strength blazing away within cliques. The shape of small groups may be effectively the structure shaping language. Something crucial may happen to poetry when a writer drops the barriers between them and the few people close to them. We mostly agree that poets are fearfully vulnerable and that richness of language grows from intimacy. Beyond these simple truths the patterns are very complex. Of course obscurity and heresy are also products of these patterns.

NOTES

1 *Studies in Comparative Religion*, 1968. See:
   http://www.studiesincomparativereligion.com/Public/journalinfo/default.aspx

2 Kathleen Raine *Defending Ancient Springs* (Oxford: Oxford University Press, 1967); the quotes come from pp.132, 172, 94, 120 & 169, respectively.

3 Chris Baldick, *Criticism and Literary Theory 1890 to the Present* (London: Longman, 1996) has the quote from Henry James. Both tags on Victorian poetry come from Baldick's excellent book.

4 For sources on Neo-Platonism, see notes to chapter on Mediterranean Cults below, p.218.

5 Kathleen Raine *Collected Poems* (London: Heinemann, 1956)

6 See:
   http://www.studiesincomparativereligioncom/Public/journalinfo/default.aspx
   Tradition: see the website Traditionalists.org, hosted at http://www1.aucegypt.edu/faculty/sedgwick/trad) Ukrainian group: see http://hnn.us/articles/23821.html). For my earlier essay on Raine, see www.pinko.org.

7 I have written about this in *Origins of the Underground*.

8 See www.pinko.org.

9 *Live all you can* (Twickenham: Solaris, 1992) is a book-length interview with Mottram. There is a list of his works at
   http://www.kcl.ac.uk/depsta/iss/archives/collect/1mo70-03.html .

10 Peter Barry and Robert Hampson (eds.) *New British Poetries: The Scope of the Possible* (London: Routledge & Kegan Paul, 1993).

11 Peter Barry *Poetry Wars* (Cambridge: Salt, 2006). The book is discussed at length in another chapter of this book, pp.276–289.

12 *Defending Ancient Springs, op.cit.*, p.173.

THE DECLINE OF POLITICAL POETRY, OR,
THE RISE OF CHRISTOPHER LOGUE

I find it embarrassing that the best British poetry of the period 1995–2005 has been written by two poets, Christopher Logue and Geoffrey Hill, who made their debuts in the early 1950s. It almost seems as if the waves of freedom and subjectivity which opened poetry up so much from the 1960s had made it harder for poets to describe social action—where freedom is constrained by rules. The unifying frameworks—Christian for Hill, Marxist for Logue—limited as they seemed in the heady days of the counter-culture, at least make it possible to discuss public events. In the new society, writing about other selves arouses conflict. The movement of poetry over the last four centuries has been away from the authority guaranteed by closeness to the hierarchies of Court and Church, and towards individualism[2]. Writing about politics was easy for a Court poet: their status as servant also granted them access to the conversation of the great. There was something wonderfully and depressingly visible about the location within a few yards of the king: all you had to do was look, and the story displayed itself to you. Historians have moved towards the story of the million households, and away from the story of the hundred dominant families.

The proposition, that the central role once played in poetry by saints and heroes is now stoutly occupied by the poet, is alarming. However rich the detail of verbal projection and virtuosity, the scale of poetry must have been reduced. There is a problem with this in modern times, and to discuss this we have to go back to the point where personal art breaks away from civic or patronage art.

The Hungarian Marxist Arnold Hauser described a subjective style of art as arising in the early 19th century, and linked to the rise of the bourgeoisie[1]. This is a more specific concept than Romanticism. Later, in his book on mannerism and the origin of modern art[3], he drew a chain of connections, almost conventional within the terms of German art history, leading from the start of Mannerism in the 1520s, and running right through the Baroque, Romanticism, the rise of formalist art, etc., in constant growth. Attention was shifting, already with mannerism, away from the life of the saint who was being painted, and towards affective distortions of style, which express the personality of the artist. This is the genetic burden of modern Western art, strikingly different both from mediaeval Western art, from eastern European art, and from folk art. It is unstable but constantly productive.

It is dominated by style, *maniera*. Style shows the slighter movements of the poet in a rich detail which argues closeness to the poet. The fact that the poet preserves so much fine and subjective detail in the finished work implies that they concur with this vital closeness as the correct standpoint for the reader. This is the literary admission of privatisation. We might almost say that it recognises domesticity as having replaced public affairs. Attraction and identification dominate the stage. We may suppose that in this poetry signature is prevalent over other considerations (although intellectual exploration is obviously important). Forces like individuation, personality, competition, and differentiation seem to be at work here. There may in fact be a sociological explanation for this.

From the 16th century onwards, the nobility changed the arrangement of their domestic space, to emphasise comfort and intimacy. The military and display functions of the nobility shrink away in favour of a newly attractive domestic space. This privatisation has implications for the fate of a heroic and oratorical style of poetry. There was a halt called to the privatisation of art during the era of ideological confrontation, say 1933–56; over a further short period of time the economy was redirected away from heavy engineering (military, nuclear, etc.) and towards producing white goods and homes for a consumer market and the baby boom. Art since that time has been an exploration of the privatised realm. Art has lost interest in the governance of the State.

We actually ask artists to be more narcissistic than other people, and we enjoy a momentary rush of narcissism in art. The work of art and its subject dissolve away in favour of the luxurious distractions of the artist's personality. If art comes along which is really all signature, with no content of narrative and action, you will not have a right to complain. Domestic space has engulfed us like the Incredible Shrinking Man in the 50s horror flick: he couldn't leave the house, but its space became boundless. An old Situationist tag says "department stores are our new cathedrals", but really monumental central symbolic spaces have been replaced by an infinite flat set of suburban homes, full of subjective spaces, and these are the niches that art must fill. Much literary energy was spent in the first half of the 20th century on what Georgiana Boyes has called "the imagined village", an English shared fantasy. It could be argued that the old "imagined village" was really the parish, and that the cultural war was the Anglican Church resisting displacement. In the new society, teachers replaced farmers as the source of the conventional scenes. The conflicts staged in poetry show where diverse family idioms meet the pedagogic arsenal of the State, rather than world trade patterns, or relations between ideological blocs.

Of course it's possible for poetry to address politics and the collective well-being. Christopher Logue has in recent years published two new volumes (*All Day Permanent Red* and *Cold Calls*) of *War Music*, his translation of the *Iliad*, purely political poetry and a modern classic[4]. It is the work of an "action specialist" in Hollywood terms, a study on civic virtue and the errors of the States in artistic terms. It is also great poetry, heroic in scale as well as in manner. It is never discussed in the cafés where poets meet— he doesn't feature in the debate. *Songs*[5] included a substantial extract from Book XXI of the *Iliad* (the combat of Achilles and the Scamander), so that this translation has now been under way for almost 50 years. During which time—it has had no influence whatsoever on other poets. Fortunately we are allowed to read it all the same. Subsequent volumes were collected as *War Music*. *All Day Permanent Red* is a continuous present, one day of combat between the aristocrats, with their overdeveloped display weapons:

> On either forearm as on either shin
> Lightweight self-sprung wraparound guards
> Decked with a slash of yellow chrome without
> Dotted with silver knots and stars within.
>   And now —
> As he moves through the light
> Downwards along the counterslope, his shield,
> Whose rim's ceramic fold will shatter bronze
> Whose 16 alternating gold and silver radiants
> Burst from an adamant medusa-Aphrodité boss
> (Its hair bouffant with venomous eels

> The pupils of its bullet-starred-glass eyes
> Catching the sun) catching the sun
> Chylábborak, Aeneas and Anáxapart,
> Quibuph, Kykéon, Akáfact and Palt
> Cantering their chariots to the right of his [. . .]

The duels which Logue describes do convince as reproductions of the duels favoured by Iron Age aristocrats, that they wished to be recorded in the poetry which they paid for. But his stories also bear a tantalising resemblance to the scripts of advertising films. The protagonists are carrying out elevated acts which they have dreamed about, lent significance by the objects with which they carry out the glamorous acts: the objects are fabulously expensive, status-bestowing, specialised, permitting soaring aggression. They give a sense of invulnerability. They reinforce the physique of their owners. The stories have a dreamlike smoothness. They vividly resemble the short films which advertise cars. As each hero goes down in the dirt, we reflect that these vain and callous people are in control of their societies, spending the surplus wealth which the agricultural base affords.

The poem dwells on fine perfections of aristocratic kit and small blemishes—the 'lipstick-sized' arrow hole in a neck—through which life departs. The extravagance of resources is almost as wasteful as the wilful waste of lives. Everything here is concentrated with tremendous force into the visual—and the events are packed into the human body. We are all happy to laugh at the tableaux of history paintings. History has become much less frontal, less pictorial, since its theme expanded to include the affairs of the non-noble families in the land. Shakespeare can have a messenger dash on, to avoid showing a battle on stage, but you can't really have a sociologist dash on: "My liege, the affluent society is hard upon us / Privatisation is a-voiding the public realm / And suburbs doth vaunt status competition through objects / Like unto a ravening hamster gloating on its wares." Poets are well advised to stand off, going to extreme range, and use the archaic mode of allegory. This is what Logue has done; there is no doubt that his sports journalism on Bronze Age bloodshed is aimed at contemporary Western governments. You can't see ships sail to somewhere in the Near East, and spill thousands of soldiers onto the strand, without somehow thinking of American, British or French foreign policy. When *Songs* came out, the reference would have been to the botched Anglo-French-Israeli expedition to Suez, in 1956. Who could really have expected that wars would still be fought to secure the flow of Middle Eastern oil in 2006? But, there we are, and Logue now seems way ahead of the policy professionals.

When he published his ground-breaking volume of political argument and direct address, *Songs*, in 1959, it must have looked as if an era of political poetry was on its way, displacing the glowing or guilty self-regard of bourgeois subjectivity. Logue's ironic staging of the slip between purpose and outcome is dialectic in intent. He is showing the destruction of the land-owning class because that is the event he dreams of. Analogy is unmodified by all the measurement which the rise of science and technology brought along; but it can be persuasive. Logue's poetry cannot be accused of subjectivity. Its scale is undiminished—little less than warfare, the modern state, the conduct of international affairs. A large part of his success is that he has gone back to the company of kings. In his *Iliad*, politics rotate around the few royal families, and come to regular climaxes in single combats.

> My liege, the geometry in which you were before all eyes
> Has been redrafted. Thousands of civil servants
> Have gently taken o'er your high office.
> The Chief Druid hath retired behind his waterfall.
> The serfs are coming onto the stage.
>   ('Two Sociologists of Verona', Act II)

Modern government is too complicated to fit naturally into poetry. It is hard to dramatise committees, although there was a noble effort in a film called *The Small Back Room*, dir. Michael Powell, 1949, which we will pass over. Further, the location of ideological commitment and structural resistance in Western society is not in the government all, but in millions of households dedicated to consumerism and to the system which assures their prosperity. In Iraq, western armies and air forces knocked over the government and expected that to be the end of the war; the idea that the rest of society is passive and not attached to the central ideology is a fantasy. A change of dynasty can be shown on stage, but hardly a change of way of life. However, the poet can create something integral and artistic, which hangs a mirror in which part of the Western way of life can be seen. The resultant book naturally has the shape of the mirror as well as the information floating onto it from the society in view. Who, though, could look into this mirror and not recognise what gleams in it: arrogance, materialism, narcissism, militarism, the lack of all restraint. What society is shining in this mirror? Contemporary Britain?

NOTES

[1] For the theory of individualism see books by Todd & Macfarlane, *The Origins of English individualism*, cited above at p.22.

[2] Arnold Hauser, *The Social History of Art* (London: Routledge and Kegan Paul, 2 vols., 1951).

[3] Arnold Hauser, *Der Ursprung der modernen Kunst und Literatur* (Munich: Deutscher Taschenbuch Verlag, 1979).

[4] Christopher Logue, *War Music* (London: Jonathan Cape, 1981); *Kings* (London: Faber, 1991); *The Husbands* (London: Faber, 1994); *All Day Permanent Red* (London: Faber, 2003); *Cold Calls* (London: Faber, 2005).

[5] Christopher Logue, *Songs* (London: Hutchinson, 1959).

See also my essay on Logue in *Angel Exhaust* issue 13 (periodical, London, 1994), & a long interview given by Logue to *Thumbscrew* (periodical: Oxford, issue 1, 1995).

Tango of Gematria: Asa Benveniste

In Benveniste (1925–90), the containing conceptual structure is of absolute determinism, but on a scale so complex that the world of the senses is durably mysterious:

> surmounted by butterflies sleeping asses
> and thick rainwear assigning tickets
> to aragonese boxes where visitors
> familiar in deep religious fat tango
> to the music of gematria
>   this is where it all fails.

The point of gematria (number divination) is that everything yields meaning (and, to a certain extent, everything is prefigured in the Bible); and Benveniste's poetry has this thorough structure. But he is using a heterodox Jewish divinatory system . . . within which the "scatter" of individual sensory data is a way of glorifying the complexity of the universe impinging on the senses. *Gematria* derives from the Latin *geometria*, but is in fact an arithmetical system, whereby the numerical equivalents of letters in words from sacred texts are held to contain secret correlations: thus the text holds a second meaning. Benveniste is interested in this second meaning, and his poetry is about a second meaning in the parts of the world itself. He remarks in the foreword to *Throw out the Life Line*[1]: "I have included the long poem 'The Alchemical Cupboard' which, as I recall, concluded the study I was engaged in for ten years into the sources of Kabbalistic congruities. It was something of a black period in my life, and when I stepped out of that space I moved on to the ground of light which language anyway has always been for me. (. . .) Most of the poems here have a basis in domestic experience, though it may be hard to believe . . ." Clearly Jewishness was important for Benveniste, although I am unable to say anything very much about this; the Kabbalah is another Jewish system of divination, about which a great deal can be discovered from Gershom Scholem's *Kabbalah*[2]; this devotes a chapter to the *Zohar*, or Book of Splendour, evoked in the first poem in *Life Line*:

> I address you with the fact
> that lethal gas rises from the five books
> of splendour in the morning

post everywhere announcing
herons have begun to leave
the province of Choan
you come early and I wish to say
you are a part of the conflict
in my mind

Someone who could spend ten years studying the *Kabbalah* is a long way away from the English poets around him. He is fond of imagery involving the physical reality of written language:

O fibrous Egypt you will conclude
this codicil by walking over posthumous ice
pursued by naiads hoping to drag you
into the serifs of blind paper
            ('Coloured Mansion 1474')

paraphic Canaanite signatures
            ('Doctrines')

Yellow paper conceals akkadian scribe
(. . .)
navigation by blind goddess
he ruins his sleep
testing purities of water
cylinder seal 3.8 centimetres
high again at side of page
and assumes a seasonal mask
of bristles and cheekbone
            ('Who Left the Door Open').

            the possession
of edict, the semiotic
placing of uncial
to its rightful line;
of letters and their shadows
and all the beauty
            of passage
('She Passes Through the Poem')

and this comes from the sacredness of the written object in Judaism, as well as from his profession as a typographer. (The Egyptian fibre is the papyrus reed; Akkadian was a Semitic language written in Mesopotamia, from the 3rd millennium B.C., standing for the early history of the culture to which the Hebrews belonged.) The rapidity of flow of Benveniste's ideas is the idiom of someone quick-witted and easily bored, and this is why his poetry appeals. Every detail of its fabrication is expressive; the details bear out the intellectual message. Unintelligent people grasp ideas as if they were objects: if you are laborious, ideas lose their life and become part of an authority situation. Ideas in poetry can only be intelligent if they are fluent and transient, mere analogues. His technique reflects a way of talking, it is the expression of a personality, an idiom; the "break of sequence" is actorly, almost an impersonation. This is why his poetry is confined inside it. Even though the "non sequitur" is typical of an era (cf. Tom Raworth, Spike Hawkins, Harry Graham, etc.), we have to analyse its specific function afresh in every poet.

Benveniste, American-born, was the publisher from 1965 to 1981 of Trigram Books, one of the vital small publishers of advanced poetry which were so essential in the later sixties and the seventies. Others were Fulcrum, Rapp & Whiting, and Goliard—later, Cape Goliard. Unlike most editors, he printed and physically made his own books; another reason why the book as object preoccupied him. Dealing with books is a religious activity for a Jew. He called one of his books *Grip Edge Lay Edge*, terms relevant to fastening a book for binding or glueing. *Throw out the Life Line / Lay Out the Corse* was Collected Poems 1965–85; this was followed by *Pommes Poems*[3]. I never met him, but reports show him as someone generous, positive, and quite indifferent to obstacles and group inhibitions—just what you would expect from an American. I'm not floating the idea, quite widespread in the 1960s, that 'English poets should all be replaced by American ones', but just that 'if you fellows had a can-do attitude, the landscape would be changed within weeks.'

He entitles a long sequence 'Tabelli Linnaei' and sub-titles it '15 poems of Linnaeus by way of self-portrait'. His attention to the activity of the biological systematist and originator of the binomial system of naming species, suggests an interest in epistemology. The classification of knowledge is fundamental to any intellectual system. If knowledge depends on a grid like the one in which type is inserted to make up a page (itself resembling the orthogonal lines on tablets used by Akkadian scribes), then redesigning the grid alters knowledge. Perhaps quite other paths of naming, investigation, and establishing affinity are possible. The juxtapositions of which his poems are made up could form a new system of connections. If you classify a species with its ancestors, you obscure its relations to its prey species and competitors, dynamic influences on its anatomy. Above all he is trying to assert the complexity and surprise of life, in opposition to any monopolistic system of determination. Linnaeus successfully classified *H. sapiens*, alongside a hairy mountain species no longer known to science: did he successfully classify and predict human behaviour?

Apart from the pre-Hellenistic world of the Near East, and the medieval Jewish world of mature Kabbalism, somewhere else he has an affinity for is the pre-scientific world of European magic, the writers of the sixteenth and seventeenth centuries involved in occult knowledge which had not yet given way to science. Benveniste was more involved in the occult than any poet of the period except Peter Redgrove. There is a passage in 'Alchemical Cupboard' which goes in part:

& Fludd awakens Paracelsus the skin Pythagoras to Kelly your
Dee names Lully who turns Bruno Dellaporta the axis Ashmole

—a sequence of names covering the whole history of occultism, several of whom we have encountered while considering the sources of Kathleen Raine. (*Recte* Giambattista della Porta, author of *Magiae naturalis* (1558)). Benveniste is reasonably similar to Raworth in the way he edits his material and in the reliance on editing to produce a personal voice. But there is this palpable link to Raine—they were reading the same texts from the 'hidden tradition' of Southern Europe and south-west Asia. Does this allow us to draw a line connecting Raworth, Benveniste, and Raine? To develop a class of which they are the members? Hardly so. The connection is real but it would not suggest that the people who read Raine overlap, by more than say 1%, with those who read Raworth. I raise it just to shed light on the Tabelli Linnaei and to imply that the classifications we generally use may be surrounded by the ghosts of other ones. I have to admit, also, that the research on occultism which I undertook for some other parts of this book has proved of no use for this poet.

Notes

[1] Asa Benveniste. *Throw Out the Life Line / Lay Out the Corse: Poems, 1965–85.* (London, Anvil Press Poetry, 1983).
[2] Gershom Scholem: *Kabbalah* (New York: Penguin Putnam Inc., 1997).
[3] *Pommes Poems* (Todmorden: Arc Publications, 1988).

FROM CLUSTER I: ANTHONY THWAITE

Anthony Thwaite's *New Confessions* (1974) is a series of fifty poems, partly in prose, spoken in the voice of St Augustine, a 4th Century convert born in what is now Algeria, with a very inflated style; he wrote an autobiography, the *Confessions*. Part of poem XXVIII goes:

> The reticulations of the centipede
> The ripe haze of the clogged orchard
> The brief gamut of rain sounding in gutters
> The moss still warm in the quail's empty lair
> The thin crushed touch of gravel to the nostrils
> The spectrum smeared on the narrow paths of snails
> The wind heaving the canvas and bracing it taut
> The pierced arrow from which stormclouds bleed light
> The nipple rising in its stippled disc—
>
> > Ask
>
> What binds them in perfection, each perfect,
> Distinct in harmony, joined in separation,
> Poised to admit, administer, reject,
> Supple in passiveness, precise in action . . .[1]

This passage, notably close to an Anglican hymn, names the beauties of the world and in doing so chooses transient, slight, and unusual sensations, with the implication that this is where we reach higher alertness—an idea which he shares with the underground poets. The passage is beautiful but tightly integrated into a rational structure of argument, in the part of the poem which I have not quoted, so that the aesthetic and the intellectual do not slip away from each other. Thwaite (born 1930) is close to Browning—and is keen on collecting large series of data, rather as the Victorians did, to serve as the weight-bearing structure of a poem. He has the retentive and discerning powers of an archaeologist or a scientist. The exultation in fine distinctions is the argument of his book.

A note explains the relationship between 'Letters of Synesius' (in a 1967 book) and *New Confessions*; both are more or less biographical monologues, by ancient theologians, in verse, set in North Africa. Biographical scraps show that Thwaite was a professor in Libya sometime during the 1960s, but also did National Service there around 1950. The poems are based on strong memories of places, objects, even of dust and wind. Do they connect with the poet's own life? 'These quiddities [. . .] are foreign to me; I must transpose them. But in the transposition lies all the knowledge I have, and all the knowledge I have of what I do not know.'

The force of this poetry lies less in narrative or argument than in what has been called the figural complex which it abidingly draws on. When we read

> . . . But a tumulus looms across meadows, low burden of old sacrificial compulsions, plundered relic of vanquished theologies. Stone knife, bronze dagger. As the builders' men move in, under the earth or by the lintel they uncover a stone salt-glazed jar, whose grimacing mask warns of a lock of hair, a handful of nails, a stain of urine, a pierced heart cut from musty cloth. The heat of the winter sun chills to an icy meteorite, as men believe in witches and old women die in fire.
>
> (XLII) [2]

—it is not obvious that this account of a witch jar relates to Augustinian themes. Yet, this horror made of organic smears is a parody of incarnation. The curse connects to original sin, often described as a curse. The central concept is substitution—as Christ suffered becoming a substitute for sinful humanity. The jar turns someone into a victim—a sacrifice. These links may not even be conscious, but the complex of images underlying these poems is so strong that it shapes everything into its deep patterns. It is helpful to read other volumes by Thwaite to see how the figural complexes lock into place. The first twelve or so poems in the 1973 volume *Inscriptions* are also about North Africa: along with the Synesius and Augustine poems, they form one vast complex, inexplicit and reverberating. The pot is a recurring theme, and this is how this witch-jar—an English jar, lost in Africa—steals into the poem. We have to ask how much the book is really about Augustine. This is difficult, but I suppose that (a) some passages do not refer to Augustine at all (b) the whole text can be read in two ways, as relating to 4th Century Latin Africa and to a 20th Century English poet.

Augustine was a Manichaean who converted to Christianity; Manichaeans held that the trapping of souls in carnal bodies was bad. The sensations in the passage I quoted to begin with are possible because we are minds locked into physical bodies, by incarnation. This in distinction to being mere souls, moved by rays of influence—like the influence which the curse jar exerts on its victim. The theology of incarnation is here sustaining Thwaite's mastery of facts, the unrelenting energy with which he commands series of data.

I read an interview with Thwaite by Peter Ryan, in which he revealed how strongly he was influenced early on—during the 1940s—by George Barker. In his interview, he says roughly that abandoning self-idealisation, and abandoning Barker as an ideal, brought him to the point of writing memorable poetry. We have to decide what the relation is, in this book, between the declared source, Augustine, and the undeclared one, *The True Confession of George Barker*, whose presence we can hardly doubt in the genealogy of the work. Barker was preoccupied with grace and original sin: a mixture of the two writers is not unreasonable.

Thwaite overlaps, stylistically and thematically, with Geoffrey Hill, who started at Oxford just after him and has also claimed to be of the school of Barker. The work under discussion is unthinkable without *Mercian Hymns*, which has a 'dual time line' moving between the poet's childhood and the work of Boethius, and is also a mixture of prose and verse:

> Old lizard-face, gloating over the loathsomeness of sin, sanctimonious adversary, apostle of the Manichees, slobbering on the confessional. Spiritual teaser, allumeuse of the inflamed conscience. Thus I recall you.
>
> (XL) [3]

Surely the pressure of this writing is wholly admirable—and incompatible with imitative status. (The person invoked is Faustus the Manichee, not Geoffrey Hill.) As a youth, I was reluctant to consume Christian art because I doubted that something anti-hedonist was going to offer serious pleasure, and because the insistence on preset knowledge suggested the repression of individualism whether artistic or behavioural. Other people went with this reasoning, and this is probably why Thwaite is little discussed. The commercial pressure of a blurb is especially unsuited to pious poetry: the blurb of *New Confessions* ('Sometimes oblique, sometimes direct, but always written with cunningly modulated eloquence') is partly circular or meaningless. The economy of reputation starts with blurbs: so also there is room for researching and recovering good mainstream poets from beneath the politics. I admit to missing lots of important poetry.

A stanza of 'The Pine Processionary' runs:

> But some must fall by the way, for we have enemies:
> The hot acids of the ant, sharper than his sharp beak,
> Spill into me and madden me. From my clefts and segments
> I volley out my lances, my brittle hairs,
> In a fine poisonous dust. Some must fall, ants and caterpillars.
> My tough survivors start again, and then
> Huddle together, ready for another kind of burial.[4]

In a barrage of painful experiences and repulsive textures, the keyword here is tough—a rallying-call for the existentialist intellectual. The first line of the poem is 'This is a garden for the cultivation of death.' Literally, this is about a study area for finding ways of doing away with the pest; but the line is also a variant of Genesis: 'This is a garden for [. . .] death', you eat the apple and the Fall ensues. We have to ask how the structure of an array of dingy and unprepossessing objects can embody huge energies which are, this time, exalting and exciting.

We have to ask, too, how *New Confessions* relates to *Mercian Hymns* and its figure of Boethius. A key point is that *Letters of Synesius* came out four years before *Mercian Hymns*. Surely the basis here is Anglicanism, which creates a shared symbolic order—Hill and Thwaite are recognisably voices in the same liturgy because they are part of the same community.

We have to recover the local conditions of the generation of literati who came to maturity in the 1950s. The typical thing was to be watchful Cold War intellectuals suspicious of any trace of Fascism or Communism, and to have hopes of Christianity reviving as a political and cultural force. The decay of Christianity was a source of unease, summed up in the failure of Christians to resist Hitler and Mussolini. Anglicans were aware (because of the new demon of sociology) that the young in urban communities were not Anglicans, and that they were the future. A common reaction to this was to reject the intoxicating eloquence of Anglican oratory, admitted to be the most beautiful thing in the English language. A bareness of style was felt to prove that the young Anglicans were real as individuals, without the support of institutions and the past; the word existential carried this meaning. The Anglicans were, in the 1950s, becoming class-conscious and voting Labour; the association of their church with feudalism, with younger sons of the landowning families, was abhorrent to them. Instead, they were thinking like social workers. To sum up, Hill and Thwaite are extremely different from the Anglican literature of the 19th Century, but they were writing with and for Anglican intellectuals of their time.

The decade had equally a current of suavity—light and twinkling verse which accepted the loss of shared values by emptying out the poem. We have to hear the sound of Christopher Fry, Betjeman, late Auden—the un-tough Anglicans. But our theme is the 'tough' qualities of 1950s academics and the shamefast qualities of Christian writers. Taken together, these sound very drab. It doesn't sound as if the resultant poetry is going to be gratifying in any way. These two poles sum up what later readers found unattractive about the 50s poets. He keeps coming back to dust, stones, graves, pottery. The objects Thwaite studies are humble—dust and clay are Christian symbols for the lowness, the fallenness, of man. A title like Stones of Emptiness sounds amazingly unrewarding—surely we would prefer softness and fullness. *Inscriptions* has a gravestone on the cover. How could we want to read a whole book about graves? The gravestones echo the stones of emptiness and also the pots—turning into quasi-ceramics. But we have to point out that these poems are moving and involving, fascinating works of art. The question is why.

A possible answer is in 'The Pine Processionary', a little masterpiece about a caterpillar of Mediterranean pine woods which moves in long destructive files (the processions). They are furry, wriggly, prolific, have irritating stings—couldn't be nastier.

> I am beginning to be born again,
> My head a steel-hard drill, tunnelling upwards,
> Scattering sand-grains and pebbles, flailing the earth aside,
> Ponderous, blind, earthbound,
> A brown lump of damp tissue,
> Heaving myself over the punishing earth.[5]

(The speaker is the pine processionary.) All the adjectives and even processes stated are unpleasant.

These beasts are squalid but insanely energetic. Thwaite harnesses that energy. His caterpillars are a cumulative series, systematically colonizing and expanding.

First, we identify with the processionary, because of its life force. At the end of the associational series, surely, we identify the processionary with the whole of Mediterranean Man—facing off heat and dust in order to breed, to migrate, to find food, to create cities and civilisations.

I said that Browning is the model—that wonderful fascination with detail. But the caterpillar poem is strangely like Hughes.

One of the most basic forces of our universe is classification. Knowledge is mainly based on this. For me, the classification which allows me to separate 160 contemporary British poets is fierce and full of energy. The frustration with mainstream poets is that they're all the same, you can't memorise their style. For this reason, someone who is fascinated by series of fine distinctions, who never deviates from focus on this, harnesses an energy which goes right to the core of the brain. Thwaite's interview confirms that he was a collector as a child—that he does have that rigorous knowledge of coins, pots, stones. His ability to marshal detail is 19th century—there is this amazing positivist impulse to catalogue and to isolate all the different substances of the world. This is what makes his poems large and involving. His powers are probably related to *In memoriam*—related to the Victorian novel, really.

'Letters of Synesius' is a moment of self-forgiveness—20 years on, the contact with the Christian and Latin-speaking past is being allowed again. At the same time, it dramatises the conflict of Anglicans with a secular and hedonist society in the 1960s: our epigraph shows Synesius watching a barbarian tribe from out of town. A little later, they martyr him.

Thwaite is at the opposite pole from exceptionalism: they want to demolish the orderly structures of knowledge, he wants to make verbal monuments to them, or climb to the top of them, as monuments.

Cluster I is a term from an analysis I once did of the whole field of modern British poetry. The anthologies I was using excluded a group born in the 1930s, whom I nonetheless spotted as a cluster important to the whole picture. As the ninth group, they were coded as *cluster I*. They were hate figures for the 'British Poetry Revival'—as the dominant group over several decades, they were excessively ungenerous towards younger poets, and so were buried by negative reactions, from virtually all factions.

The jacket of the second volume of the Movement anthology *New Lines* (originally 1956) is covered in quotes of reviews of the first which attacked and reviled the book. One of them says that very few books have ever received such a negative press. This signals that the poets included were not at the centre of poetry at that time, and that the sober and academic reviewing staff of the nation's literary magazines were not part of some small literary conspiracy which *New Lines* was the voice of. They actively sought the negative propaganda, and it has never really slowed down.

I have to admit here that I have actively participated in the standard model, whereby the 1950s were a time when squalid poetry was seen as tough and authentic, and dislike of ideas was seen as part of the NATO shield against Marxian idealism. That culturally sterile decade built up frustration released in a wonderful explosion in the 1960s and 1970s, deftly written out of history by neoconservatives. This story started to blur a bit over the last ten years (from 1995, I mean), in which Logue and Geoffrey Hill seemed to dominate the poetry being published—though both had made their debuts in the early 1950s. We sorely need to add empirical detail to some of the grand wings of this model which are still merely schematic.

Some details which could be added to a future modification of the schema are:
  —the Movement were buffoons and obnoxious provocateurs who just obscured the real talents of their generation;
  —the attitude of sniggering put-downs of ideas, Continental ways, and emotion in poetry was not shared by all British academics of the 1950s and was in fact not very compatible with the core values of Christian academics, either Catholic or Protestant;

—it was hard for young poets to break through in the 50s, and the carnival of 60s culture drowned out the rather quiet signals that conservative poets were making; anthologies were not helpful for them;

—people who were not rebels could rebel late and be late developers, so that their early works look average and are bad samples;

—the culture wars of 1968–75 (other dates possible!) involved a crisis for Christianity as the dominant institution of national culture, and this may have stimulated Christian poets to unusual feats;

—a large portion of the poetry readership in the 60s was made up of people who had gone to university in the 50s or otherwise shared 50s values; there was a whole world of poetic activity continuing on that basis.

Thwaite (b.1930) Levi (b.1931) and Hill (b.1932), are examples of excellent poets from the generation described. I was rather startled by how good Levi's poetry was. I am looking for further material in this line. I think one can speak of these three as a 'cluster', what you can call a generation.

I am unsure where to go next with this project. Further recovery operations will need names in order to be properly targeted.

Author's Note:

I include this discussion as an example of a personal mistake—so that this is *my* moment of depolarisation. A burst of memories may help the repentance process. In 1979, Eric Mottram told me a story about Thwaite—of which the upshot was that Thwaite had no sense of rhythm and couldn't be taken seriously. Eric wasn't the only critic whose views on modern poetry became mine. In 1995, I interviewed Martin Seymour-Smith, the other father figure whose views I absorbed wholesale. He had been an undergraduate at the same time as Thwaite, in the early 50s, and absolutely hated him. There was some story about someone becoming Thwaite's girlfriend, to Martin's great indignation. Anyway, Martin had a very firm line on all matters Thwaite. As a direct consequence of this, I never read Thwaite. In 2005, my co-editor on *Angel Exhaust*, Charles Bainbridge, pointed out to me that as a matter of fact Thwaite was incredibly good. Rapidly, I read some of the poetry in question and realised that I really liked it. His poetry is much better than Mottram's.

The point of this story is that you get most of your tastes from your friends—what they know, you end up knowing. This works terribly well but is very unfair.

I offer this as an example of how depolarisation would take place. The process I envisage would involve revaluation of hundreds of poets and would end up with a set of common valuations, ones we could all share. It would be based on wide reading by critics willing to ignore traditional boundaries.

Finally, we should point out that the 'salt-glazed jar' above, with the face, was a Bellarmine jar, so named after a 17th-century Jesuit theologian, St Robert Bellarmine. He was the author of a doctrine of salvation, grace, and good works. Is the jar there to contrast Bellarmine with Augustine? I think not.

NOTES

[1] Collected in Anthony Thwaite *Collected Poems* (London: Enitharmon Press, 2007—henceforward referred to as CP), p.146.

[2] CP, p.156.

[3] CP, p.155

[4] from Anthony Thwaite *Inscriptions* (Oxford: OUP, 1973). This poem was left out of CP.

[5] ibid.

—See also *Anthony Thwaite in Conversation* (London: Between the Lines, 1999), a book-length interview.

Tom Raworth: The Past as Damage

We are going to look at Tom Raworth again, in more detail, because the Primer chapter was animated by a purpose of instruction, and this distracted from a contemplation of the artistic purpose within his writing. We can understand more of Raworth by going inside his work and not looking all the time at objects outside it.

Raworth's creative biography is long and marked with events of a singular intensity. It is not based on narrative and biography and it would be misleading to present a biographical narrative as an explanation of it. The publication of his *Collected Poems*[1], a major achievement for Carcanet, makes the poetic work available; the thorough details published on Raworth's website absolve us from bibliographical tasks. The only issue is to explain why his poetry is so great—the boundless extent of this curious emptiness.

Analysis of poetry of the recent past, for example the sample in the 1940 Day-Lewis/Strong anthology[2], reveals a high proportion of statements referring to timeless truths: immediate experience is only presented as evidence of unchanging truths about life, which dwarf temporal concerns and so provide consolation. Passages such as:

> This clay that binds the roots of man
> And firmly foots his flying span—
> Only this clay can voice, invest,
> Measure and frame our mortal best.
> (C. Day-Lewis)[3]

are taboo now, as generalized, didactic, static, browbeating, moralizing; yet they were then the stock in trade of poets. Out, with these abiding moral truths, go the static frames of classical myth and Biblical story. Genres like the character sketch, or the poem on someone's grave, also disappear, because they are temporally flattened and do not show a unique event. You can't have a high rate of change running through statements which are supposed to remain true for thousands of years. Purging the text of these, either for philosophical reasons or for aesthetic ones, leaves something fragmentary, which asks for a whole which does not yet exist. The goal of unpredictability demands the elimination of statements generalized as to time; the new poem tends to exclude any statement which presents static truths, but presents events which are new and transient. This follows on from Lawrence's call around 1930 for a poetry of the immediate present, its "wind-like transit". It also follows on from a distrust of mediations, an attempt to elude the assumptions about social relations embedded in them by getting at more primary data. The doctrine of a "continuous present" follows from democratic empowerment, the belief that the laws of social structure can be remade by participants and on a continuous basis; the laws bequeathed by the past have no sovereign claims, because they begin with the inherited and unequal distribution of wealth. The past is most demandingly present in the persons of Old Poet Codgers, antiques held to gain value if the arrow of time works in the expected way.

If the past is damage and knowledge is the shape of the past, then one wishes to lose knowledge because its structure is damage. Writing through experimental rules offers severance from experience. This conflicts with the precept of making the personality the centre of poetry: target number one, perhaps, of thirty years of radical poetry. The exemplification of a timeless truth is replaced by the hypothesis: the poet devises a possibility and writes exemplifications of that, perhaps enabling us to think about the nature of language or of social conditioning by doing so. The hypothesis is a form of *ostranenie*. The experiment is like play, which is also a form of free activity governed by rules; we repeat play acts until they lose their fascination, and that is probably also the regime for experiments. They belong to the primary level of art by this playful quality, and, because they produce objects which are strange, perplexing, free, inconstant, they ask for participation. Art which isn't experimenting with the world is a dreary proposition. Admittedly some of the experiments are ruined by a self-important, authoritarian, didactic, humourless, etc. attitude of the artist.

The deletion or slimming-down of the information in a poem has always left more room for procedures to evolve in: Raworth (b.1938) is at one end of the spectrum, in the procedural band. Because reading involves a search pattern as well as passive packages of data, this daring deletion serves an artistic purpose; which does not disguise the intent of criticising inherited wealth, organized knowledge, secret corporate authority, scriptures, and the deeply internalised and partly catastrophic behavioural patterns of English people and groups.

In 1993, Tom Raworth published *Eternal Sections*, which we have already discussed in the *Primer*[4]. The poem, composed 1988–90 according to the first edition, is far too complex to describe section by section, of which there are 111. Every section deals with a different topic. We will analyse one section to make discussion of the poetic grammar possible.

> forced to act
> ostensibly independent thought
> can never admit its disposal
> into a senseless gadget
> paid symbolic tribute
> by an appraising look
> forms of decadence
> exclude schematic parables
> no less seamed
> within tradition
> used to mean
> a product that does not bear
> the compactly economical shape
> of a brutal national economy[5]

The poem is the product of something outside itself: it exploits the possibility of grasping the emotional tendency of a text by seizing on key phrases, but there was a text which preceded the poem, if only in virtual form. We can guess that it concerned the relationship of critical thought (including critical art?) to real politics. Indeed, it may have resembled *Dialectic of Enlightenment*[6] and *One-dimensional Man*[7]. Thus, the act of reading may well include the projection of a phantomatic course of words saying, for example, "Turned to account, academic philosophy can never admit that it functions as an intellectual toy, on which the elite practice their discrimination; the critical process is in decay; commentary on politics is silenced, although the tradition of Western art and thought requires such commentary; thought once meant (simultaneously, is *employed to mean*) something which was not instrumentalised by the process of commodity capitalism, which (compactly) excludes other possibilities." The gap between the poem and the phantomatic prose text is one between non-finitude and finitude, and hence can be compared with liminal utterances versus practical ones. By eliminating the detail which forms the perceptual horizon of those playing the game, attention is drawn away from the winners and towards the rules of the game and its nature as a game. By refusing to make logical statements, Raworth draws attention to the distinctions of category embodied in language, which it cannot make statements about. By failing to define who is speaking, he prevents us from writing off what is being said as particularist and native to a certain point on the social spectrum. *Eternal Sections* is a collection of language with no speaker, with no situation, with no time, where nothing is asserted or controverted. It reveals the structure of social fields rather than showing events.

Early Raworth poems liked to exploit the evocative power of a single line from a period novel, and of old postcards (reproduced in his book *Lion Lion*[8]), or the pictures on cigarette packs. This is recognizable as a device used by the Dada group in around 1920. The device was quite transparent around 1965; expanded to an immense scale in the 1990s, it has ceased to be so transparent. Excerpting a line from a novelette about the Empire reveals the conventions of the genre, which resemble "real" political assumptions; *Eternal Sections* is pursuing this archaeology of conventions. So far as I can tell, eternal sections means 'forever cutting (texts) up'.

Raworth and Allen Fisher share the intention of making an overall structure of ideas, that is, they take the overall design of the Anglican/ imperial/common law system that preceded the current dispensation, and produce something equally comprehensive which differs by replacing every element. To realise what they are doing, we have to grapple with the notion of something that mediates between primary sense data, affects, physiology, etc., and finished symbolic acts, whether communicative or merely cognitive. To point to this grid, we can just compare France and Britain, and ask why identical human physiology, very similar technology, and very similar climates and geographical location produce two things so different at the level of politics, art, and daily life. *Eternal Sections* is not a narrative instantiating a social structure, but a kind of acoustic mirror reflecting what is instantiated. In a sense, it can only be read by someone with a prior knowledge of British social structure, as a set of rules for dealing with situations and for classifying or recognising situations, and as a stock of narratives accounting for the system and its history, and describing the kinds of person in the system. It is, in its way, a complete account of a social system; each section deals with a semantic area, and the set of all of those can stand for the cognitive structures which enable someone to belong to a given society. We can understand both Raworth and Fisher better if we consider the uninhabitable nature of exceptionalist poetry, its painfully visible quality of representing a transient state of mind and therefore not a way of life and a livable social order, or even one that included people who didn't have degrees; a shallowness reflected in collapsing and opportunistic linguistic devices. They chose instead to lengthen and deepen self-consciousness by giving it longer (and better analysed) strips of behaviour to reflect on. Another comparison would be with a compendium of myth like Ovid's *Fasti*, a calendar-poem: both the modern poets offer a mythic cycle without narrative. Something preceded the narrative and structured it; a myth without a preceding something would be just a fantasy.

This is a poetry almost without assertions. To enter its space is almost like becoming able to see an optical illusion: a small transition almost impossible to explain. We have said that much of the effort expended by conservative readers is in fighting with phantoms—useless violence, waste energy. Summing up the experience of it from the inside, once its space has opened up, is difficult.

An analogy which strikes me is that of neutralising oppositions. First, a word about wordfields. Words—permanent words, lexemes—are organised in fields, according to a group of German semasiologists.[9] The meaning of the individual words depends on the way their range is demarcated by the other words linked to them, in a field. The differences between related words are qualities for which no words exist; we learn the demarcations by use which may involve interactions with objects. However, since many words are not to do with objects, learning word fields involves observation of social behaviour. You could say that learning the language is impossible without the social system as an instruction aid. Critical thinking about the wordfield may draw us into critical thinking about the social order. Listing words does not fully describe the field. However, if I display the set:

persistent consistent	innovative
thorough obstinate	avant-garde
dated repetitive	European in scope
out of date true to self	reflexive theoretical
dogged rootsy	advanced modern-style
authentic unmodernised	free rootless detached
regressive unfashionable	unbound developing
steadfast	conjectural formalist

—you already understand how the terms are used, so a full instruction set is nugatory. All the terms in one column could be used for the same artist. Since the wordfields are static—or evolve slowly in relation to the scale of an individual lifetime—it is arguable that poets just recycle the spectrum of possibilities latent in the public system of language. If we set up a wordfield as a matrix, we can apply transforms to produce different matrices with different formal properties—and reflecting conjectural social systems.

Language is structured around oppositions and permits a process whereby one steps outside the oppositions themselves and reaches a point which embraces them. Thus, if I write about syntaxis and hypotaxis as opposed qualities, there is also a term *cohesion* which describes both qualities. It disengages a similarity while receding into vagueness: cohesion is not a quality of any specific stretch of language, or rather almost all language has it by definition, and it is vague because it applies to almost all natural language. In the realm of describing humans, to step outside the lexicon and neutralise the oppositions between individuals is both to bring a glimpse of the whole and to weaken the shapes which we project onto individuals. We are thus deprived of our projective fantasies and obliged to seize the common and collective. Raworth's poetry contains almost no finite statements, tied to time, to a place, to specific individuals and their conflicts. It would follow that the poems emerge, if only tentatively, into the non-finite: a world which is sublime and close to blankness, at one and the same time. By transcending oppositions, language loses the ability to give quantitative information but also becomes close to any possible situation. It represents equidistance and capacity which is never full.

The poems in *Eternal Sections* are generically similar to wordfields, but the continuous units are longer than single words. It is too neat to say that Raworth's procedure is always to neutralise oppositions, but this is one procedure he uses. We could equally well say that what he is doing is serial violence as he fights with texts which he hates, soaked in ideas which he hates. We can also describe his style as simply one of sarcasm—in which he repeats words in order to undermine them. Pursuing the neutralising idea, we can say that deleting the tier of language which makes statements and qualifies them makes wordfields visible. To get away from specifics is then to learn how to think in the abstract—a perilous but fundamental procedure.

There is a certain analogy with abstract painting, which cannot express actual spatial relationships, but which can evoke the sensation of space itself, liberated from objects which define it. It is common and collective—by virtue of negativity. Even a painting stuffed with objects contains a small surviving portion of pure space through which light can impinge and reverberate.

Our minds incline us to seek the pattern constants within the torrent of impinging events, and if Raworth's poetry remorselessly moves into abstraction it is because shedding the merely real reveals much more powerful and permanent structures behind it: the silent rules on which society is constructed. He does not write down these rules because there is no notation in which one could do that. However, the psychological position to which *Eternal Sections*, for example, leads one is one from which it is possible to think about what these rules look like. The idea of a structure diagram of a society is however precious because it takes us to a point where we can think about how to describe a society (as opposed to merely playing out a role within it). Raworth does not need to describe how Britain works, because we already know that. What we actually need is a still place where we can organise what we know into a conceptual form, and this is what his poetry offers.

By discussing emptiness, suggestibility, blankness, the non-finite, analogy, the sublime, at such length, I have tried to create a set of memories which can act as guides for thinking about Raworth and why his poetry works so well.

Raworth's mature work is concerned with language as social memory, and the negations within it suggest what is excluded from memory—an alternative system. The issue of the past is highly involved with the relations of class. Someone preoccupied with the past may not be consciously conservative, but preserving past relations denies the individual the right to define who they are and to make their own way in society. If literature is biased towards stored knowledge, it is also biased towards social hierarchy and immobility; the literature of the past was undoubtedly used by the landowners as a tool for glorifying themselves and for disparaging those of lowly birth. The project of a continuously present poetry is political and aims to abolish all traditional effects and hangovers, to destroy the memory stores where the patterns of inequality are kept.

Elimination of syntactic markers may increase the ambiguity of the text, therefore the number of available information and interpretation paths, and so its adaptability to different conditions, i.e. to different readers. The cult of leaving out organised syntax (both at the level of the sentence and of the higher sense-units binding sentences together) may be entirely rational, the optimum way of achieving polyvalence to face a heterogeneous audience. When Raworth writes

> his extensive library
> the centre of his picture
> merge into the verdict
> one moment threatens
> an explanation of why this language
> representing the glorious past
> belongs, even to those
> following me into this war
> by blending the impersonal ethos
> beyond the reach of satire
> to account for its success
> in demonic or satanic terms
> is irrelevant
> yet the basis of this neutral identification
> (from 'Sentenced He Gives a Shape')[10]

—the lack of semantic labelling is an apparent lack of resolution, even of completeness, which may quite literally leave more information inside the system. The semantic labels can be seen as eliminators of information. Leaving the extra paths in there leaves the poem uncommitted to any social or ideological group; the poet's voice evaporates, in a detachment which alienated much of the reading public, who wanted less ambiguity. Suppressing tribal loyalties makes you invisible in a world of eyes which are sensitized only to tribal stripes and insignia. Again, I have to point out that quoting one stanza understates the polyvalence of the poem. I selected this stanza because it may be about the construction of one-track language: "neutral identification" is the point in the room claimed to be occupied by the objective scholar, accountant, politician, or manager, taking decisions on behalf of other people. In writing this I am directing attention to one aspect of Raworth's work, reducing its ambiguity and probably annoying the poet whose best efforts are thus overruled. Raworth's asyndetic syntax leaves polarities unmarked, which is also what neutrality is, *neuter* meaning neither one thing nor the other.

We could ask whether this language is *before* (a highland region before social language has played its tricks) or *after* (a reprocessing of other language, at the estuary, to win its raw materials). Is truth what we realise after the philosophers have spoken, or what was there before anybody began to fabricate and distort it? The explanation of why *this language representing the glorious past* belongs *even to those following me into this war* carries recognizable traces of an origin, in the mouth of someone, perhaps a wartime politician, justifying the war in terms of a shared community represented by language, by culture, by the past, as the long run of time in which individual differences and interests merge into a collective identity. This explanation is threatened, and one can see why; how could the language belong to everybody when the means of production belonged to a few hundred families? The official record is only one representation of the past, because access to it was selective; it conflicts with folk memory passed on from parents to children. "The centre of his picture" points to selectivity, because space has no centre; wherever we direct our attention is a focus, but different people focus on different things. The idea of a centre is where we pass from the world of light to that of power.

His work is highly distinctive, but has definite analogies with an amount of small-press poetry: characterised by very high indeterminacy. This works aesthetically by allowing free association, a beautiful state; but can also be the expression of political opposition, conflict with a prepotent information authority, rebuilding the rules which say that one thing follows the next. It is hard to imagine the style without a preceding phase of Marxism, challenging the whole social order and seeing it as something artificial and fragile; but poets who use it do not necessarily hold any Marxist beliefs.

One can see the past either as an accumulation of design expertise or as damage. The assertion that history is a convergent process which discards the bad paths and repeats the good ones justifies stored knowledge and so the distribution of wealth as the outcome of past events high up a maximisation curve; the good outcomes are in fact the content of the stored knowledge. Innovation, and the redistribution of wealth, then become dangerous steps back into the unknown. Language doesn't belong to everyone. The area of democratic choice is restricted by rules: a contest of past and living present. Indeterminacy describes series of states: it is difficult to work out the previous states of a gas from its state at any moment; we can say that a gas lacks a past. A liquid, equally, is unsuitable for use as an information store. This erasure of the past implies that the future is not predictable either. All of this implies, when addressed to social systems, that stored knowledge is of little use, because future states of the system are not contained within past states however exhaustively described. So, a belief that society is a highly indeterminate system disagrees with the allocation of power to a few, based on past events; the need for hereditary wealth; the power of the educated; the burying of rules, from the past, which cannot be altered, limiting the area of democratic discussion and decision. The defence that the social system is a success tested by time assumes both that the future is like the past and that there was some optimizing mechanism, whereby the superior system became the real one. The more free the individuals in a system are, the more chaotic it becomes, and the less they can rightfully be bound by rules from a vanished past. That "a library / [is] the centre of his picture" suggests someone who sets great store by stored knowledge; drawing attention to this suggests the alternative, putting faith in living people and so allowing them political and economic power. Because of the privileged access of the upper classes to the written record, intensive study of it may simply make you reproduce their viewpoint, concentrating the toxins of triumphalism and partiality in your tissues. After all, the written records are best at recording property rights, and the genealogies (of rich families only). My knowledge of the fifteenth century is almost entirely of landowning life, as preserved in the texts, whereas my experience of the twentieth century is somewhat lower down the social scale, to say the least.

The lack of causal relations in Raworth's poetry points to a universe, not one where causality does not operate, but where the causes and symptoms of things are not obvious: the past of the system does not forebode its future. He does not eliminate semantic labels altogether: in the quotation, the words *even, to (account for), yet,* and *is irrelevant* define (and so restrict) the relationships between primary semantic blocks. This stanza is atypical of Raworth's style. We can claim that a fully formed clause, such as *one moment threatens an explanation,* implies causal relationships, and that words like *threaten, merge into, beyond the reach of,* also have a pointing and de-ambiguation function. One can claim that the ordering of words implies such syntactic links, in English, because in that language word order is the main marker of syntactic function. Because to know causality implies general understanding, it implies knowledge of the past; and the exclusion of change in the passage from past to present. But certainly this poetry is very ambiguous and non-causal when compared with, say, the prose I am writing. This stanza is soaked in the modern Left critique of the objectivity of managerial discourse, and so resembles the older kinds of poetry, which also contain ideologies; the effect of this leaning depends, however, on the quality of the intellectual system it leans on.

We have to look at one more poem:

contemporary cultures of display
can no longer rely on government funds
to replace the real
creates a sense of sequence

all sorts of insecurities and doubts
living in a museum
draw a screen between
the democratic progress
to offer an improved version of the past
mingle varied and passionate streams
with a garden, a park and a greater estate
nostalgia supplies the deep links
the disease if it is a disease
seems stable and unchanged
           ("Eternal Forgings")

This, of course, is a forgery. I put it together out of samples from a book—as a test of a hypothesis of how *Eternal Sections* may have been produced. I think it sounds like *Eternal Sections*—which, I am saying, is actually a repossession. This forging could be called *the past as property*.

Raworth's work makes one doubt the value of the concept *heresy*. Highly original, massive in extent, almost totally non-discursive and inexplicit, it would be heretical if it were not also a modern classic.

Perhaps we are dealing with the wrong model. We could sketch an alternative one in which there are (say) a dozen centres of poetic art, each one designed like an object complete but surrounded on all sides by error. Near the centres, even in the immediate vicinity, there are tracts of failure. Each poet agrees about the failure and the act of designing the poem is made effortful by the need to avoid the error, by subtle shifts and small distances. The poem is the result of many drafts and we can only grasp that situation by imagining failure scattered all around. Capture spirals lead us also through zones of increasing intensity into foci of unsustainable brightness and totality.

However, comparing any centre with the other eleven centres (which we have just posited) is pointless. Heresy in that sense is meaningless.

It is a question whether these divergent centres have anything to do with each other simply because they all use words. Everyone human uses words. That is no test of similarity.

NOTES

1   Tom Raworth *Collected Poems* (Manchester: Carcanet Press, 2003). Henceforth listed as CP.
2   C. Day Lewis & L.A.G. Strong (eds.) *A New Anthology of Modern Poetry 1920–1940* (London: Methuen, 1941).
3   from C. Day-Lewis, 'Overtures to Death', quoted from the above anthology, p.109.
4   See pages 23–66 of this volume.
5   Tom Raworth *Eternal Sections* (Los Angeles: Sun & Moon Press, 1991), also in CP, p.419.
6   Theodor Adorno & Max Horkheimer *Dialektik der Aufklärung* (Amsterdam: Querido, 1947).
7   Herbert Marcuse *One Dimensional Man: Studies in the Ideology of Advanced Industrial Society* (London: Beacon Press, 1964).
8   Tom Raworth *Lion Lion* (London: Trigram Books, 1970); also in CP.
9   *Wortfeldtheorie* is associated with Jost Trier and Leo Weisgerber. See Jost Trier, *Aufsätze und Vorträge zur Wortfeldtheorie* (ed. O. Eichmann & A. van der Lee; Paris & The Hague: Mouton, 1973).
10   In CP, p.397.

THE MYTHICAL HISTORY OF NORTHUMBRIA
or, feathered slave to unreasonable demands: Barry MacSweeney

In 1971, Penguin did a survey anthology of British poetry[1] since 1945, which included Barry MacSweeney (1948–2000). 27 years later, they did another one, which didn't. There is a story to tell here. This is difficult poetry:

> death beholder
> lynx shoulderblade tundra dart
> in cold
> brother sleep
> all of that
>   or not
>
> death reminder
> obituary cremation refusal placement
> ganglia warfare in wood neck lace
> panto Plato revives
>
> death bewilder
> wild wolf eye
>   sudden snake eye
> gut button
>   acid
> suds abide in lycanthropic
> fancy tollbridge Amersham
>
> (from *Ode Grey Rose*) [2]

and MacSweeney's career, covering more than thirty years, is full of bewildering twists. A selected poems came out as *The Tempers of Hazard* in 1993[2], and in 1997 another 100 pages of selected poems formed part of Clive Bush's *Worlds of New Measure* anthology[4]; another, posthumous, selected poems, *Wolf Tongue*, arrived from Bloodaxe in 2003. What I am setting out to do here is to provide a simple map of his work, and to point out some of the rules, not necessarily obvious, which organise the text. Some of the information comes from many hours of telephone conversation with MacSweeney, and from a three-day interview in 1996; publication of the interview was vetoed by its subject, but I cannot resist using the results to illuminate his work. I will try to distinguish between what comes from the author, and is reliable, and what comes from my own conjecture. I have already reviewed *The Book of Demons* and *Hellhound Memos*, and made some remarks on *Ranter*, and will not repeat what I have said.[5]

Das Ganze ist das Unwahre. The work of Barry MacSweeney offers exceptional difficulties to the critic, as to the reader, because it is made up of hundreds of bursts interrupted by very fast cuts, where shots from different perspectives fail to resolve. There is a great bulk of work at this pitch of complexity, some 400 pages of it. The name which occurs, after re-reading it all, is Swinburne: where a similar fantastic and glowing ornamentalism, a proliferation and autonomy of small-scale structures, drowns the overall line. Accusations of the imbalance of sensualism and intellect have been levelled at both poets. I feel our poet is temperamentally close to George Barker, in rebellion, excess, and guilt. Both are chronically non-academic types, and this is why little about them appears in print.

MacSweeney, encouraged to write at school, won an award for young Northern writers in 1964, and then became famous in 1968 with a beststeller—in terms of poetry—*The Boy from the Green Cabaret Writes to His Mother*[6]. He then presented the publisher with new and more complex work, which they turned down; so his career ended, at the age of twenty, and he became—the term didn't then exist—an underground and small-press poet. A phase of prolific experimentation followed, typically using his personal genres of Odes, Funereal Elegies, State of the Nation Addresses, female star biographies, autobiography, family history, confessions, history, and Celtic ethnographic forgery. There are great swathes of work in this period that I don't understand. While *The Tempers of Hazard*—a Paladin anthology—is a splendid collection of his fleeting and flimsily-stitched pamphlets, it leaves out books, such as *Ranter* and *Black Torch volume 1*, that are among his finest, and most of *Odes*. It ripples over a wide range: rock, wolves, frills and furbelows, legendary heroes, rebellion, American poetry, broken-up syntax, corruption of the media, alternative history, Celticity, sexual guilt, Northumbria. Around 1985, a period of withdrawal and disillusion followed, along with personal problems. One of the things he said when I interviewed him was that in 1979 he gave up on the possibility of external success in the literary world, or of political change in Britain, and withdrew into himself. He retreated to a fellside cottage to write *Ranter*, and when he had finished he counted seventy empty wine bottles in the cottage, and realised the drink was finding its own level. The project of autonomy in his poetry is inseparable from chemical addiction; the beckoning to excess and revolt instructs the long struggle against sobriety. The dating of the poems, printed with them in *Tempers*, suggests that he stopped writing in 1983, but this is uncertain. He returned to poetry with *Hellhound Memos* (1993), and then *Pearl* (1995), his masterpiece, and *The Book of Demons* (1997). These are straightforward autobiographical narrative, based on self-exploring therapy and on the work of poets such as Anne Sexton and Sylvia Plath, and brought a return to legitimate publishing and the High Street.

Every failed strike raises the possibility of another history, how victory could have been enjoyed in a society with a broader flatter distribution of power, a more collective ethos. The concern with writing alternative histories has largely been confined to interviews and false claims in advertising copy; MacSweeney has actually written a history of coal-mining in the North-east, in *Black Torch*, which floats the postulate of a different history and invests a startling documentary energy to keep that imaginary picture alive for a whole volume, until it is too large and strong to be set aside. This wonderful book was announced, in 1977, in *Poetry Information* 18, as follows:

> *Black Torch*, book 1, a first part of a long projected work, drawing on the political/social activity of Northumberland and Durham miners, will be published by London Pride Editions this autumn. Much of it is in Northumbrian dialect. Book 2, half finished, works around John Martin's diaries—he is the Northumbrian painter— tracts by radical Baptist ministers, and the trial of T. Dan Smith. Book 3 is planned to be based on tape recordings with residents of Sparty Lea and the Allen Valley in Northumberland.[7]

Book 1 did come out in 1978, but books 2 and 3 were never written. 'Blackbird', an elegy for his grandfather published in the Paladin *new british poetry*[8], is book 4. The black torch is coal itself. The evocation of social conflict—something incredibly rare in British poetry—brings us back, of course, to the importance of strength, in all forms of self-possession, courage, endurance, in such contests. It's not enough to have novel ideas, you also have to win at the showdown, or it's all academic, and it doesn't even have psychological interest; it could only be important if it was going to affect real life. His style, subjected to intense elaboration and development, may reflect local speech patterns and life values; but it is not ordinary talk in the pub. There is a large range of documentary about Tyneside in his other work, for example *Ranter* and *Pearl*; he recounted in an interview how the geography of his home town, with near-wild countryside right beside working-class slums, helped shape his work. Such juxtapositions, around large industrial towns subject to stoppages of trade and to periodic conflicts between owners and workers, are common in Scotland, South Wales, and the North of England; he records a geography of the periphery, of decaying palaeotechnic cities surrounded by high wastes. *Black Torch* dares to go back many centuries to explain how social attitudes came about, making the present explicable rather than mysterious. The dialect mentioned is the reported speech of nineteenth-century striking miners, and belongs to the documentary part of the poem.

The groundbreaking study of MacSweeney was by John Wilkinson[9]. 'Pride and pastiche are the key dyad throughout'; Wilkinson fits all of the poetry into his overarching fringe-medical schema, drawn from the—brilliant, but also marginal and non-quantitative—theories of Melanie Klein, where damaged internal objects ("partial objects") bring about fetishism and wildly oscillating affective states, where loved people and things suddenly "become hostile" and are ejected, leaving a state of emptiness. His greatest poem is "Last Bud": 'The poem performs a scorched earth exercise on all MacSweeney's previous writing, and fuelled by the disgust and resentment (. . .) thrusts away friends, patrons, and lovers in favour of a glorious darkness and emptiness, an absolute independence conceding and receiving nothing'(.) ("Far Cliff Babylon", in *Odes*[10], has a similar scenario.) There is a long study of MacSweeney in Clive Bush's book *Out of Dissent*.[11]

Black Torch is political poetry, to go along with *Colonel B*, *Wild Knitting*, and large parts of *The Book of Demons*. Much of his poetry is on a different scale, dealing with mythic artistic figures or with the poet, taken as a heroic myth, or with his lovers, ditto. The key to its construction is simple and omnipresent in pop culture. The moment when I understood it was when Barry phoned me just before a high-profile reading at the Cambridge Conference of Contemporary Poetry and announced his intention to dress up like Johnny Cash and come on stage riding a motorcycle, as Billy Fury had done at Newcastle Town Hall in 1963. Visualizing Keynes Hall, deep within King's College beside King's Street, I was cold to the idea. He described it half a dozen times, and wanted my assent. The next day, I met Jeremy Reed, by chance, and he described how he was writing a novel about Elvis Presley. I think almost all of Barry's poetry is a re-enactment of mythic reality, granting us mobile versatile scenarios, portable objects for reconstitution and imitation. This artistic grammar is popular and comprehensible to all: no-one really fails to understand what it means to walk into a barber's shop and say you want your hair cut like Elvis, even if they disapprove. The moments of failure to share fantasies point to a set of rules for evaluating them immanent in the oppositions and categories of the overall social structure. MacSweeney demands, in an extreme form, emotional projection: he projects onto various Star Figures and the reader projects onto him. Where this projection does not occur, the poetry collapses. Reed has accomplished a long-term project of recording the mythic history of rock stars, fantasy vehicles simultaneously drained and saturated with pure experiences and ideal acts.

These kernel scenes are associative, repetitive, substitutive (you act out what the star did), collective, fantasized but bound by strict rules, populist, clinging to details, domestic, human-oriented, and implement a social structure. Potent objects appear in the poems as properties reminding us of a scene which is overall and enveloping; they are signs like those in a saint's life, who awakes from a vision to find an object, given to him by an angel, still in his hands. They are signals of the edge of real space and the beginning of charged, mythic space; they are visible power, as trophies, the bucrania of primitive temples, were proofs of the hunter's prowess. Their physical qualities are irrelevant, but they have power as symbols of the overall physical and mental skill of the hunter. They do not use sensory realism, because they embody fatidical patterns in personal life experience. The fast cuts are related to the montage of events from different lives. MacSweeney works often from photographs; his poems are not narratives but iconic eulogies which allude to a serial structure; they are chiefly ornaments, glorifying a human person (their whole aura rather than just their "body"), seizing the symbolic world as a set of emanations of personalities. The kernel scene is not one person, but several people in a pattern lit up with a symbolic charge, which can be transmuted and re-cycled in different media because it is clear and finished as a pattern. I believe that all of his poems could be understood if one had knowledge of the scene (even, the photograph) which they illustrate.

> Take this black box, it belonged to my
> son. Glower was where we lived, his face was
> alien. He was not a navy man.
> A corn of skull for Pan. Also take these
> pipes. He was a wretch, they belong to you.
>
> Drift like a lady-in-waiting through the tripe. Open
> the sand, if it was late. My pimp's keener, un-
> surpassed lacqueurs along the baize.
> Deck it, asteroid, ignore the Malaga grape.[12]

The glittering tenuity of structure of the poems tracks real rock stars of the 1960s, such as Dylan and Hendrix: where the perforation of the logical narrative and the song form, respectively, broke through any informational coherence to discharge just such a million globules of meaning, fragmenting and cohering into a hundred patterns we cannot name. MacSweeney took on pop culture, but hip pop culture, and at a particular moment, when avant-garde techniques were flooding the pop genre.

Just 22 and I don't mind dying deals with Jim Morrison; *Brother Wolf* deals with Chatterton, shards of whose pseudo-archaism recur throughout. (The line about "he was not a navy man" probably refers to Morrison, son of an admiral.) MacSweeney takes over Chatterton as the latter took over an imaginary fifteenth-century poet; we remember the Gothic figure, a by-blow of Romanticism, who gets taken over by books and relives them. This is a kind of ghost story where MacSweeney occupies the figures who come alive out of the past. Fantastic greed is the nature of reading when it is taken beyond a little. Temporary and lascivious loss of the personality is the pursuit of readers who lack such screens as academics have. Hugh Walpole was fearfully interested in details of clothing and knick-knacks, knew enough about pricing *objets* to prove Chatterton's fraud. The acquisition of great learning is a displacement. The *objets*, around which the whole apparatus of learning rotates, are meaningless outside the myth: collecting curious information about art is a misdirection of appetite, the real thing is to do art, the rest is just an antique-shop, a thinly controlled form of hysteria. We suppose that MacSweeney's method of mythologizing admired figures is superior to grim and emotionally dulled fact-grubbing.

The occasional loss of lucidity of these poems is not due to experimentalism but to their reliance on pre-existing stories; the poem transcends the magazine stories by being more allusive and less literal. Much of *Odes* is about MacSweeney himself, and here again the lack of obviousness is like a magazine: the hero is cool, is engaged in leisure activities—mainly sexual—and not in bound logical action. The various acts are liberated and casual, like the object-symbols of the good life piled up in an advertising photograph or an album sleeve. They are under-specified because they are over-specified. The work of Jeremy Reed, and Gavin Selerie's book-length poem *Roxy*[13], model the poem on the magazine photograph, as the central site of self-presentation in our time, and so shed light on what Barry is doing in *Odes* and *Jury Vet*—which is partly written directly from photographs of women in magazines.

Wilkinson describes the *Jury Vet* poems[14] (dated "1979-1981" by the poet) as "a personal pathology (combined with) virulent social satire'; MacSweeney 'displace(s) undercover observation to a place outside the body, collapsing the fashion spies of glossy magazines, Special Branch and Security Service operatives, newspaper reporters and the machinery of jury selection for secret trials, into the perverse organising principle of these poems, scopophiliac, coprophiliac, fetishistic, sniffing and prying, unwrapping, smearing and ejaculating. Every sexual perversion is mobilised against the persistence of unregulated love . . .". But the tone of the poems is one of glorification, MacSweeney playing Dick Clark to a hall full of thrilled teenagers: "Your single body's a striking SOVIET." For Bush, "Sexual disgust, the major tone of the poems, bears witness to real hatred (. . .) the actual destructive compromises of marriage in capitalist society . . ."[12] When I interviewed MacSweeney, he gave a totally different interpretation of the poem, which explains every detail of the text in a matching whole. It is addressed to a "You", a real person, whose photograph is attached to the typescript of *Jury Vet*, and whose existence Wilkinson misses. The controversy underlines how obscure much of MacSweeney's poetry is, animated by a drama and situation which are apparent to the author but not to others. There is nothing about jury vetting in the work except a few sly references; it was attached because MacSweeney went to a conference of the National Union of Journalists where details of the "ABC trial" for a journalist's alleged crimes against national security, and the successful attempts of the police to de-select jurors who weren't right-wing, caused a furore. This entered the borders of the poem by a kind of attraction which is indicative of how MacSweeney works, but which may offer problems to the reader. It is not satire.

Jury Vet is not about disgust but about the absence of disgust in a blissful infatuation where the gap between fantasy and reality was levelled, which is why no distinction is drawn between the real girl and the magazine photographs of female punks: the lovers become everyone. It is useful to re-attach the poems to the photographs: of girl-punk groups around 1978, among many others of models and film-stars. MacSweeney was moving from documenting male hero-figures like Shelley and Jim Morrison to glorifying ordinary girls in the punk movement. We know that certain parts of the body, certain angles, don't fit into classical aesthetics; the punk girls deliberately foregrounded these angles, textures, fluids. Barry's passive-receptive capacity is more than most's; it wasn't his idea. He gives an account of the photographs. So the critics behold these non-aesthetic zones, and their reaction chain is "disgust", "alienation", "attack on capitalism". What everyone had in mind, though, was an orgasm of the whole body, the regaining of totality by aestheticising the polluted, the abolition of the gap between femaleness and femininity, between three-dimensional women and two-dimensional glamour photographs. These are learned men who haven't spent enough time hanging out with punk women. *Your single body's a striking SOVIET!*

The contrast between MacSweeney and Wilkinson is striking. MacSweeney rejects any kind of self-criticism, engaging in a kind of lascivious self-promotion up till the points where he collapses into a state of guilt and abjection rarely parallelled in literature; Wilkinson, a student of Heath and MacCabe at Cambridge, has strong rational objections to the presence of the author in the text, as love-object or anything else, and has depleted the text so that there is no recognizable human form. The tension around the star-fantasy method in poetry is that it has low prestige; one definition of middle-class art, or of learnèd poetry, is that it eliminates such projections, tearing away the decorative structures of the ego in order to make someone unhappy and compliant. In order to make the transition out of pop culture, you have to accept that art is not going to work in this way, but instead is about the play of weighted syllables and line-breaks, or the ironic rejection of irony, or the seizing and demonstration of prestigious cultural assets, or something. Wilkinson, for several years a Cambridge PhD student, has more cultural capital than MacSweeney, who left school at 16 to join a local newspaper, but he can't write expressive poetry, while MacSweeney has written great poetry. Some of the vagaries of MacSweeney's career, and of his self-esteem, have been due to the stress between his aesthetic and the critique of subjectivity in which the Left Modernist crews around him were so involved.

We probably need to put *Jury Vet* in the context of cultural beliefs, of rather before 1979, that pop culture out-competed poetry by being more sexual and more egocentric, and that the "real" subject of loud rock music was sexual display—the phrase "cock rock" was much heard in the early seventies. *Jury Vet* out-competes rock culture in both these directions.

The poetry fails when the appropriation of signs is too perfunctory; in *Hellhound Memos*, moments of the poet at the crossroads with Anne Sexton and the blues singer, Robert Johnson, 'swapping licks' on an old typewriter, are embarrassing and unpersuasive. The relational patterns are all archaic, an acquisitive trip where everything means me, and you can take everything home with you; an old manœuvre which works when the language is highly enough integrated. The obscurity of many of MacSweeney's poems is due to his over-identification with the central figures, which means that no scene-setting is allowed, to guide the reader; this is reminiscent of what Basil Bernstein says[15] about explicit code speech, that it has mastery of exophoria, i.e. describing situations in terms comprehensible to outsiders. This explicit: implicit opposition is strongly related to social class, and very contentious; MacSweeney achieves total identification with his characters, fulfilling a Nonconformist, working-class, and old-fashioned artistic ideal, while the "high" poets of the period were busy shunning identification in favour of didacticism, episcopal authority, and exophoria. He is too headstrong to be a natural communicator. Rather than scheme to gain our identification, he takes it for granted.

Ranter (1985)[16], a volume-length narrative poem, marked the end of a phase. The word ranter refers to a revolutionary sect of the Cromwellian period; more religious and less political than the Levellers, nonetheless a proverb for their resistance to the established order of things. The appellation is a nickname—it already meant a vagrant and licentious way of life. This is the meaning which we find often in Burns: a ranting laddie. *The auld ran-dan* is a drinking spree. Alternatively, the name 'Ranter' may have been given in derision of their way of preaching—like rant and rave. Burns' vagrants were also musicians and reciters of ballads; there is a specific style of folk singing in the North-east known as ranting, used for example by the Northumbrian group the High Level Ranters, as also in the well-known Tyneside song, the *Collier's Rant*. It may be coincidental that the Gaelic (both Irish and Scottish) for poetry is *ranntachd*.

Something else we can track down from the outside is the historical references. Some of these are:

1. Diggers. Communist revolutionaries of the 1650s. (p.31). 'King Digger / your burial / first on the list.'
2. Lollards. 14th C anti-hierarchical heretics. (p.31). 'Prince of Lollards / with the very last libel / in every parish / beneath your shoes'
3. Levellers. Forerunners of Diggers (p.30)
4. The Peasants' Revolt ('Working down/ tunnels / of history // Ranter setting / his date: 1349 // Blackheath, Ranter's / proposing place')
5. Viking raids in about the ninth century. 'Would long for the long

cry / as the prow bit your sand, / flailing villages into welts / of widowhood Blood on my blade / in rosehip and fern.'

6. Twelfth-century Kent. 'I am Eadwine / prince of scribes.' (translating 'ego scriptorum princeps').

7. Disturbances of the early Industrial Revolution, circa 1815–30: 'Ranter. Mad & brain-sick, / Captain Pouch, Plug rioter, / verb for rising, knotting ropes / in Spithead, offering wrists / for chains' (20)

8. A mythic Ireland in which the saga of Sweeney Furious (*Buile Suibhne*) is set; a legendary sixth century AD. 'Waiting for Sweeney's / Irish misery / beamed in from a bough' (p.16)

9. The North during its devastation by William the Conqueror's earls after the uprising of Edwin and Morcar: 'Ranter's children / driven out / by D'Aubigny / foster fathers / for orphans / driven on by Mobray / Durham to Evesham, 1069' (p.19)

10. The first century AD. 'Hadrian's leather boot' (p.7)

Clearly, *Ranter* is an extreme example of montage; it can't possibly be tied down to any one moment of history, even for a few lines. This multiplicity was the view of history available to people living in the late twentieth century; it is the way you or I would actually think about Northumbria— although one would also call it 'mythic', which seems to be archaic. If I think of Northumbria, I obviously call up fragments from different centuries, millennia even, and it would be frustrating to pare these down to yield things happening to one person at a single time.

The other line we can check is the place-names. Why does Ranter go from place to place in Northumbria? The best analogy I can find is the outlaw film. A rebel is being chased for his life, and the places figure as stages in the chase; one thinks of *Pat Garrett and Billy the Kid* or John Milius' *Dillinger*; if Harry Dean Stanton can be in both films, then so can Barry MacSweeney star in mediaeval, seventeenth century, and modern outlaw legends. Eventually, we get some explanation of this vagrant life in terms of the Irish romance *Sweeney Furioso* (*Buile Suibhne*). Of course the name is the same. *Ranter* relates to two important themes of Gaelic literature and folklore: the panegyric, and the tales of broken men, outlaws displaced from their land by the defeat of their chief, or later by the seizure of their land by the English; when the whole province of Ulster was cleared of its people in 1610 or so, the uncultivated stretches of countryside were filled with outlaws and caterans for decades. When the Ranter is shown living out of doors, this combines the madman/exile theme of Tristan or Lailoken living in the woods, with numerous traditions of evicted tenants finding shelter in ditches and under trees. In *Black Torch*, the striking miners of 1840 are shown camping on the moors, where they find food from the wild.

The lines about being covered in feathers and living in trees refer to *Sweeney Furioso*; whose plot involves Sweeny being driven mad by warfare, and retiring to live in the trees as a wild thing. He appears as Sweeney on p.16 and Suibhne on p.34. (See the Introduction to O'Keeffe's edition of *Buile Suibhne*[17], quoting a Norwegian text: 'And it is said of these men [*gelt*] that when they have lived in the woods in this condition for twenty years, then feathers grow on their body as on birds, whereby their bodies are protected against frost and cold . . .' A poem within the saga states, 'rowing a rudderless boat/ tis a garb of feathers to the skin/ tis kindling a single fire.') An earlier book of MacSweeney's was called *Pelt Feather Log*. Other Celtic sagas share this plot, notably the *Folie Tristan* romance[18] which gave Ken Smith *Tristan Crazy*.[19] John Arden combines various themes from the Sweeney, Merlin, and Lailoken sagas in part 3 of *The Island of the Mighty*[20] (1974). If MacSweeney adopts this romance, we can deduce that the hero is under stress and at breaking-point. It is 'Ranter's folly' (p.1).

Sweeney is a liminal figure, in the sense of Victor Turner (adapting van Gennep) in his book *Dramas, Fields, and Metaphors*[21], participating in an "anti-structure" where the rules of society, and its benefits, are set at naught. Spatially, this refers to the fells, the uncultivated wilderness, close to the village where MacSweeney lived as a child, and to the cottage where he wrote *Ranter*. Ranter is outside class society, eats only wild food, is unconfined by time. He drifts from one intense experience to another, but has no social identity. If the revolutionaries are all liminal figures, they are there to illustrate the theme, rather than as subjects. *Ranter* starts out by seeming to be a political poem, like *Black Torch*, but resolves itself as an individualistic poem, about a rebel figure and about the failure of his marriage in what one can assume to be the late 1970s. It comes to resemble Ken Smith's *Fox Running*[22]. The bad end of his marriage was already discussed in the last of *Odes*. Re-reading the poem, one sees that the references to history are there as explanations, not as primary sequences themselves: 'Ranter: Leveller, Lollard, / Luddite, Man of Kent, Tyneside / broadsheet printer, / whisperer of sedition, / wrecker of looms / feathered and peltstricken / bound with skin / hung up in trees' (p.6). The bits of history appear almost as *epitheta ornantia* of the hero Ranter, as prestige possessions enumerated in a Celtic praise-poem. The hero feels himself disintegrating as his marriage breaks up, and uses his remarkable knowledge of history to give him reassurance about the survival of identity across time. We aren't going to find out any more about the Men of Kent; the compositional unity of the poem is its depiction of a marriage, although this is disintegrating and is presented as a series of snapshots without explanation. The furniture taken from E.P. Thompson's *The Making of the English Working Class*[23] is not written up as part of a series of events, or a conflict; the antistructure throws away time, which is why the historical figures are all simultaneous.

The last section of the poem is put into the mouth of the ranter's lover, or the poet's wife. The multiplicity of voices falls silent. Where control is surrendered altogether, a new order emerges. Permitting a second voice is one of the signs of greatness in a lyric poet.

Barry wrote Celtic pastiche in the end part of *Ranter*, and in 'Finnbar's Lament' (originally titled 'Glad Wolf Battle Gosling'), whose smoothness and legato make one suspect that *he* regarded Ireland as the home of authenticity and ease, so that his fragmented poetry was the product of an inauthentic society and its broken-up consciousness.

> Opening of her lids was like the rising of larks
> in the blue slowness of a stubble-burning day.
> She would stretch out her arms, disgrace-fetcher,
> and I would lose my identity for hours on end,
>
> displacing my power and delight in power, and my desire
> for the wrecking of other men and the tormenting of tribes.
> We would twinkle to the hearth, bearded one, and
> wrap ourselves in the rags of our fortune.
>
> ('Glad Wolf Battle Gosling').[24]

He has rejected the Irish side of his family; while one can be optatively Irish, he is optatively Northumbrian. Northumbria had a Celtic poetry and society before the region lost its independence and largely fell silent: Irish phraseology would then be an imaginative loan to fill in what never got written down. Topography and antiquities go together, and to both is added class resentment. The word 'flamebearer' (in *Ranter*) translates a heroic epithet *Fflamddwyn* in the early seventh-century Cumbric poem *The Gododdin*. Two commentaries on the poem are in disagreement whether this person was an Angle or a Romano-Briton. Higham[25], in his recent account of *The Northern Counties to AD 1000*, stresses that the Anglian presence in the North was particularly thin, merely an elite which somehow gave its language to a largely Celtic rural society; and MacSweeney, with his local patriotism, was probably aware of this fact, commonly discussed by archaeologists for a long time. Numerous place-names in *Ranter* make it clear that it's happening in Northumberland and near the Thames. The name 'Finnbar' points to Ireland, although it could also be the Highlands. MacSweeney specifies in *Our Mutual Scarlet Boulevard* that Flamebringer is 'Ida', an Anglian king of Northumbria (AD 547–59); this is not too far out, as Ifor Williams remarks in his edition of Taliesin that he might have been a son of Ida; Nennius, in the ninth century, mentions Ida, Aneirin, and Taliesin in consecutive paragraphs. MacSweeney's frequent references to cloakclasps (penannular brooches, nine times in *Ranter*, three times in 'Finnbar's Lament') shows him treating Celtic antiquity in the same terms of personal adornment that he applied to rock stars and female punks. These brooches are some of the most beautiful things to have survived from the Gaelic past, and were still being made in the Highlands in the eighteenth century. MacSweeney's evocation of the Celtic past is based on detailed study. The narcissism, delight in adornment, heroism, and pride of Celtic warriors, the features we find hardest to assimilate, are carefully integrated by MacSweeney; 'A red buckler with stars and animals of gold and fastenings of silver upon him. A crimson cloak in wide descending folds around him, fastened at his neck with precious stones' (from an Irish tale). Even his ornate and centreless verbal style may be based on the rioting ornament of Celtic jewellery and manuscripts.

The version of the Rebel in 'Glad Wolf Battle Gosling' is exceptionally interesting:

Who was my appledawn bride is now the plaintiff
sorely gathered in with her grievance deep.
She'll take me to the Judgement Mound
where for my offences many against the kindred

I shall be rightly impaled or strung by fires.
My own satires shall be turned against me, my courage
Diminished, and magic gone from the streams and wells
My own mead hall forgotten from the songs.[26]

So the outlaw accepts his own lawful doom? *Children don't you do what I have done.* We know outlaws have to die; what brought an end to flamboyance, mythic fantasy, and 'wildness' was the institution of religious guilt, and there are indications that MacSweeney—outlaw, legendarist, fop, parader, ranter, and sometime drunkard—sees this state approaching. But the casualty of Reason and Realism was poetry. I believe that the poem refers to his second wife.

MacSweeney's whole career has been an attack on the line, the sentence, and the rational mind.

The poet who has followed on from MacSweeney, in typography, ornamentalism, and construction in rushes of flakes, is Maggie O'Sullivan, someone even keener on being Irish than he is. The dislocation between phrases is, for her, at least related to political works which suspend and atomize 'official' media statements in order to make them groundless.

Indulgence is either compulsive or disconcerting, so that to be judicious is difficult, but the conservative view of MacSweeney is that the excellent work is to be found in 'The Last Bud', *Black Torch*, 'Glad Wolf Battle Gosling', *The Book of Demons*, and *Pearl*, only; while his assimilation of feminism and popular culture points the way forward for English poetry. For a fan, the whole work is amazing.

Postscript

Barry MacSweeney died in May 2000, a moment which altered British poetry spiritually, murderously, and irrevocably. I took notes during his last phone-call to me, a few days before, to catch the torrent of talk; the projects he cited were *Horses in Boiling Blood* (translations of Apollinaire), *Blood Money: The Marvellous Secret Sonnets of Mary Bell*—slated for Bloodaxe but unlikely ever to be published, for legal reasons—a huge 2-volume *Collected* to be done by Bloodaxe ("the Monty!", he said), *Collection* (God knows what this was), and *Fierce Passion*, possibly a rewrite of a lost work of the 1970s, *Toad Church*. Maybe he passed away from an excess of talent and excitement. A compelling memoir appeared in the *Guardian*, written by Gordon Burn, his contemporary at Newcastle Grammar around 1960–64; while Burn's much-admired books on murderers probably influenced the Mary Bell sonnets, his novel on Alma Cogan, with its obsessive detailing of glamorous women's clothes, is almost an *hommage* to *Jury Vet*. I admit that Barry and I were in bitter feud at various moments, but we always ended up discharging our weapons in the air.

NOTES

MacSweeney texts: *Our Mutual Scarlet Boulevard* (London: Fulcrum Press, 1971); *Black Torch* vol.1 (London: New London Pride, 1978); *Odes, 1971–78* (London: Trigram, 1978); *Ranter* (Nottingham: Slow Dancer Press, 1986). *The Tempers of Hazard*, selected poems of Barry MacSweeney, with two other poets (London: Paladin, 1993). *Pelt Feather Log*. Barry claimed this book existed, but I have no independent proof of this. Even he wasn't sure it had actually been printed. But it may possibly have been published by Grosseteste, circa 1976. *Wolf Tongue. Selected Poems 1965–2000* (Newcastle: Bloodaxe Books, 2003); John Wieners, *Behind the State Capitol, or, Cincinnati Pike* (Boston, MA.: Good Gay Poets, 1975).

[1] Edward Lucie-Smith (ed.) *British Poetry Since 1945* (Harmondsworth: Penguin Books, 1970. 2nd, revised, edition, 1997).

[2] *Wolf Tongue*, p.46.

[3] *Re/active Anthology: The Tempers of Hazard*, together with the selected poems of Tom Clark and Chris Torrance. (London: Paladin, 1993).

[4] Clive Bush (ed.) *Worlds of New Measure: An Anthology of Five Contemporary British Poets* (London: Talus Editions, 1997).

[5] My review of *Book of Demons* is on the Internet at www.pinko.org. My essay on *Black Torch* will appear in a book on MacSweeney edited by Paul

Batchelor. Discussion of *Jury Vet* in 'Sexuality and poetry', unpublished. discussion of *Hellhound Memos* in review in AE 16, pp. 113-116. Essay on *Ranter* in Silent Rules.

[6] Barry MacSweeney *The Boy from the Green Cabaret Tells of His Mother: Poems 1965–1968* (London: New Authors Limited, 1968).

[7] *Poetry Information* 18, ed. Peter Hodgkiss (periodical, London, 1977).

[8] *the new british poetry* (eds. Gillian Allnutt, Fred D'Aguiar, Ken Edwards, Eric Mottram (London: Paladin, 1988).

[9] Published in *Angel Exhaust* issue 11 (periodical, London, 1994).

[10] Barry MacSweeney *Odes, 1971–78* (London: Trigram Press, 1978).

[11] Clive Bush: *Out of Dissent. A Study of Five Contemporary British Poets* (London: Talus Editions, 1997).

[12] 'take this black box': from 'Just twenty-two and I don't mind dying', *Wolf Tongue*, p.21

[13] Gavin Selerie, *Roxy* (Sheffield: West House Books, 1996).

[14] *Jury Vet Odes* in *Equofinality* issue 1, ((periodical, Birmingham, 1981).

[15] Basil Bernstein *Class, Codes, and Control* (London: Routledge and Kegan Paul, 1971), pp.177–80.

[16] Barry MacSweeney *Ranter* (Nottingham: Slow Dancer Press, 1986).

[17] J.G. O'Keeffe (ed.), *Buile Suibhne* (London: Irish Texts Society, 1913).

[18] 12th Century Anglo-Norman poem, extant in two versions. See *Les deux poèmes de la Folie Tristan, édités par Felix Lecoy* (Paris: Librairies Honoré Champion, 1994).

[19] Ken Smith *Tristan Crazy* (Newcastle: Bloodaxe Books, 1978)

[20] John Arden, with Margaretta d'Arcy, *The Island of the Mighty* (London: Eyre Methuen, 1974).

[21] Victor Turner. *Dramas, Fields and Metaphors: Symbolic Action in Human Society* (Ithaca, NY: Cornell University Press, 1974) pp.272–298.

[22] Ken Smith. *Fox Running* (Newcastle: Bloodaxe Books, 1981).

[23] E.P. Thompson *The Making of the English Working Class* (London: Gollancz, 1963)

[24] 'Glad Wolf Battle Gosling' published in *Equofinality* issue 4, (periodical: Birmingham, 1991).

[25] Nick Higham *The Northern Counties to AD 1000* (London: Longman Higher Education, 1986).

[26] *Equofinality* issue 4, *op.cit.*

Tony Lopez: Worrying in Public

The works of Tony Lopez (b. 1950) include *Hide and Seek, Snapshots, The English Disease, Abstract and Delicious, A Theory of Surplus Labour, Stress Management, Negative Equity, False Memory, Covers.*[1] He is a public poet, taking on the shared sites where British people argue about politics and communal life, standing the cost of these sites being rather worn-out scenery, and of the external authority figure dominating the poem because it cannot solve any problems in its virtual world without coming up against the real world, where the problem is not solved. As a Left and critical poet, he differs stylistically from the too benign and unctuous Anglican poet of public welfare, perhaps by the rather cold tone; Roy Fuller might be an interesting comparison, an originator of this optimistic disapproval. Many of the poem-schemes start from the devices of conceptual art, so central to the 1970s; perhaps documentary sources, lists of names, documentation of activities such as walks, official utterances which are 'processed', lexical groupings which may be a window on shared symbolic structures. What seems most interesting in his work is the progression from low-affect editing and twisting to high-affect reliving of experience.

Natural landscape is used, in poems like 'Hart's Tongue' and 'Hill Walkers', as an example of beauty and free living, to be protected from destructive social forces of exploitation. A certain element of his work is close to the Objectivism represented by Pig Press. The sites are not described as if we had never seen them before; we are expected to bring information from the newspapers, news media, or political forums. His poetry is topical, it includes larger events outside itself. It disclaims the superior knowledge of poetry about inner experience and accepts that its account of public events will be controversial, while for us comparing various bits of memory in order to assess what he is saying is a special form of poetic pleasure; after all, talking about politics is one of humanity's more widespread pleasures, and only ceases to be one when the debate is made arid by excess of dread or by the selfishness and partiality of one of the speakers. Thus the title *Negative Equity* was a phrase in common parlance in the 1990s, and refers to home-owners who could not move house because the mortgage on their house was much more than its realisable value: they had bought in before the collapse of housing prices. The phrase implies a condemnation of the whole Thatcher era, when virtually all economic growth was in the increase of house prices; its public acceptance reflected the losses of middle-class property owners in the down-stroke of the "Lawson boom", and it was a major loser of votes for the Conservative Party. It also implies that Lopez accepts that what is in the newspapers is in some sense true. The poems in that pamphlet use details from finance packages and from the new productivity arrangements in higher education.

Lopez's work centres on a shared argument. Staging a political argument is difficult; the opponent is likely to show superior knowledge of the facts, fail to understand what you are saying, disqualify your witnesses as of bad character, and adjudicate victory to himself at the end. The more the poet prepares the landscape in advance, the more we suspect that it is faked, treated with emollients, tilted to one side. A classic move is to exclude the opponent, reduce him to a straw man, erase his lines from the transcript; this produces a straw victory. The poetry readership do not want to come into contact with their political enemies, social rivals, in the poem; the whole ambience depends on certain kinds of people being excluded. One solution to this was poems based on montage, ultimately derived from Brecht, where theses from the other side are pasted together in such a sequence as to expose errors inside them; the speed and quick-wittedness of this manner overlies something not unlike the dialectic. This style can be rather chilling in its incessant irony. Philosophy is hardly possible where one has already a fixed position; which means that epistemological poetry cannot concern the issues most interesting to us, the ones to do with poverty and wealth. On the other hand, arguing about society requires constant huge drafts of information, and the struggle is to preserve the verse from didacticism and greyness. Lopez, cunningly making the concessions necessary to writing a real political poem rather than a private one, has courageously described the surface of modern life in poems of rapid montage, with an absurdist edge. Rather than retreat into some miasma of disconnection where everything seems absurd, he depicts himself as a normal worker with strong emotional attachments, although moving through an absurd life. Montage does not offer a resolution, but leaves us with a zone of doubt; the final irony may be that we leave the poem, convinced of the idiocy of a certain policy, to find that it governs our lives outside the poem.

His most striking poems are certain ones in *Stress Management*, such as 'Northern Lights', 'Way up High', and 'When you Wish', where the brainwashed, propagandised woe of bulimia is linked with the commodity circuit that delivers chocolate to us, and with the history of the commodity and of greed aroused by it. It seems to me that Lopez is not a lyric writer: the landscapes miss the sublime. Instead he can write moral dramas, about real distress and real oppression. 'Northern Lights' takes the polar landscape used by W.S. Graham, on whom Lopez wrote a doctoral dissertation and then a book, and combines it with the biography of T.S. Eliot; but, astonishingly, Lopez refuses to be an acolyte and turns the whole situation round:

> But what if all those incomplete adventures—
> All those expeditions set up with the fetish
> Of gleaming equipment: metal, leather, ropes,
> Straps and fine boots, crampons and ice axes—
> What if the whole project
> Of fractured narratives, of pulp-novel collage,
> Of technical idioms stripped of context
> Is finally an alibi for moral collapse?
> (. . .)
> What if the art itself is a fabrication
> Of actual and terrible guilt; touched up
> With sprayed-on essence of faded photo
> Like a jungle-ad for choc-ice,[2]

It was astonishingly courageous to read this poem to an audience that had so much invested in the belief that real politics isn't politics, but virtual politics, textual engagements, are. A thousand *bien-pensants* pursed their lips in disapproval and denial. Lopez is right.

Related writers might include Peter Riley and Kelvin Corcoran, and Simon Smith also seems to work in this area. The tectonic shifts needed to allow a vision of the communal welfare lead away from intensely subjective expression. But after all it is the strength of his attachments and of his social optimism which makes us admire Lopez.

NOTES

[1] *Hide and Seek* (1973); *Further Snapshots* (London: Oasis Books, 1976); *Change* (London: New London Pride, 1977), *The English Disease* (London: The Skyline Press, 1979); *Abstract and Delicious* (Warehorne: Secret Books, 1983); *A Theory of Surplus Labour* (Cambridge: Curiously Strong, 1990); *Stress Management* (Boldface Press, 1994); *Negative Equity* (1995); *False Memory* (Cambridge: Salt Publishing, 2003); *Covers* (Cambridge: Salt Publishing, 2007).

[2] The poem 'Northern Lights' is from *Stress Management*.

See also interview in Tim Allen and Andrew Duncan (eds) *Don't Start Me Talking* (Cambridge: Salt Publishing, 2007).

From Oracle to Dialectic: Kelvin Corcoran[1]

> "More direct methods may be tempting, but all of them
> enfeeble and distort what has to be said. This statement
> may seem the less surprising when we reflect on how
> many of the important things which the poet has to say
> have to be said by means of paradox . . . Indeed, almost
> any insight important enough to warrant a great poem
> apparently has to be stated in such terms."
> — Cleanth Brooks,
> *The Well Wrought Urn*[2] p.13

> "But the reader may well feel that the amount of attention
> given to the structure of the poem is irrelevant, if not
> positively bad. In particular, he may find the emphasis
> on paradox, ambiguity, and ironic contrast displeasing.
> He has not been taught to expect these in Tennyson . . ."
> — *ibid.*, p. 142

Corcoran emerged into view in around 1985, with the piquantly titled
Robin Hood in the Middle Ages[3], and has produced consistently ever since—
something which is true of no other individual. It is this strength and calm
which have made him a giant figure of the middle generation, placed
between the generation radicalised thirty years ago by the counter-culture
and the younger generation, still only partly visible.

Other members of the class, taught by Ralph Hawkins at Essex
University around 1978, recall Kelvin as being theoretically worked-out
to an amazing extent: he had a position, based on Adorno, which he
could apply to everything. The two key adjectives here are critical and
dialectic. The dialectic unsays what it says—and says what it does not
say. Perhaps this wonderful apparatus is too rigid; perhaps its sound is
too plain, too Midlands, too confident about the alternative we glimpse
behind the existing system; but the rigour is necessary if we are to form
clear apprehensions, and the gamble on the productivity of the reflexive
approach is justified every time. Perhaps awareness is something that
comes inevitably when we are steady, and unsteadiness chases it away at
every second. The dialectic should be as fluent and beautiful as a squirrel
jumping from one tree to the next.

The epigraph to *When Suzy Was* is 'No clear case of disobedience to a
specifically solicited oracular response is recorded' which obviously refers

to the oracle of Apollo at Delphi. The book in our hands is, then, a book of answers. The last poem in the book, 'Catalogue of Answers', is as if the words of the oracle:

> Look: the birdman steps into the green field site.
> All about him the blatant geometry of planning
> cuts in; an ax throws light on the issue. If any
> straight bearing is finally a powerline we should
> leave now. The tectonic plates grind against each
> other at the committee stage. We should leave.

> ★

> Oh Oh I am north, a frozen mapp. Shrunk to
> the core in my tiny house, under a sky of
> ice-floes, tinkling.
> Let the yellow flower rise, let it radiate
> something. Feed me you sub-atomic, half-life
> zoomorph.
> From the door of St Magnus the men of Orkney
> went mad for Egypt, roaring an alphabet of
> hot triangles across the great green.

The composition is in frames, internally consistent and even plain; which are juxtaposed with frames of different axioms, different knowledge status, different silent rules; so that both tilt sideways to reveal something much deeper, partially refuting both of them, and itself mysterious, to be uncovered in glimpses and by leaps of reason. This tilting is disconcerting— and courageous: our comfortable curling up inside the poet's voice is abruptly brought to an end. These are dialectic switches—as insistently favoured by Frankfurt School philosophers Theodor Adorno and Herbert Marcuse. For example, a poem starts out with shared stories, 'myths', about England, and then jumps to similar myths about South Korea. The juxtaposition reveals a superordinate category—allowing thoughts about the nature of culture. These thoughts are not specified within the poem— and we can expect to stumble while making them, because we are falling out of a finished narrative into a dark area which enlightens us.

The sections are not simply opposed—the gap between them is not simply a contradiction. So we have to speak, not of synthesis, but of composition—a constructivist mode. The breaches of context within poems suggest that the division into separate poems is misleading—there is a deeper space, revealed by the angles between individual 'frames' of poetry, which unites all the poems. The quoted section starts with a Bronze Age pictogram (almost certainly)—someone has an axe. They are clearing a forest—which has perhaps never been cut. Europe is being wrested from its forest cover with the new metals technology. But the poet is interested, not only in this access of wealth, but also in freedom—denied by power and straight lines. The next quoted section starts with a northern flower—I cannot work this out very well, although I am sure that the poet is, again, looking at a picture. The link between ice and radiation may simply be that each means a geologically long age of near-sterility. Zoomorph means 'with animal shape', and is often used when describing decorative patterns—often, the zoomorphic ornament of early mediaeval art in northern Europe. The last three lines recognizably deal with a cathedral in Orkney, called St Magnus—and with Vikings going on a (real) pilgrimage to Jerusalem. The triangles are stylised sails—a picture rather than a real sight, and perhaps specifically a reference to ship-graphics by Ian Hamilton Finlay. It is most important to realise that this montage goes on and on, without turning back into a recognizable self-reinforcement—I counted 22 sections in 'The Book of Answers'.

The expectation is that the tilt is not simply the boat disappearing and leaving you in the cold water, but a plunge into a rich medium which is abundant—because embedded in our memories of the world—and which will give a high yield as soon as our habits—of language, of feeling—are interrupted. As if: as soon as we stop identifying with what the politician is saying on the radio, we will 'fall' into a higher awareness. But identification is a source of awareness—so that switching it off is a form of sensory deprivation, and of ignorance. It may closely resemble the attitude of German idealist philosophers, passing legislation for all mankind, and scornful of the meagre consciousness of the unenlightened.

The contradiction which trips off the dialectic is a form of paradox, a favoured figure of the New Criticism. The choice of one of these two forms of contradiction is helpful in classifying British poets. The dialectic style in poetry has the effect of not confirming the assumptions of the protagonists in the poetry—as virtually all other styles of writing do. We are immersed in the life-world of the characters until it seems normal.

Two comments in the book are "My conceit to make the physical condition of language, the arrangement of the struts, curves, and sounds, the form of discovered truth" and "I'd thought to make this book a version of the oracular process, to find out what is always there in the making of the poem(.)" 'When Suzy Was' is a playground song with actions, that goes through the whole life cycle: When Suzy was a baby, she went (wah wah wah). When Suzy was a skeleton, she went rattle rattle rattle. When Suzy was a nothing, she went like this this this (nothing). This is a sort of rustic equivalent of a myth. What I think appeals to the poet is the form: it is the whole life-cycle, in stylised and compressed form. Indeed, it is a kind of archaeology—the variously desiccated, skeletonised, or chemically evaporated bodily remains uncovered by the spade are so many Suzys. When Suzy was a Neolithic peasant, she didn't have private property or a class structure.

Oracles are a dialogic form in which element B replies to and modifies element A. That is, they somehow resemble the dialectic. They are also an oral form—in which each part binds the next, and the turns can be extended *ad libitum*.

South-eastern Europe is not only where Corcoran likes to take holidays but also the gateway by which farming entered the continent; we dig up a civilisation with archaic symbols whose meanings are lost, they dig and Europe emerges under the rim. There is a structural metaphor between the fertile uncertainty into which critical art launches us and the similar uncertainty in which people found themselves as they invented the village and its institutions. They answered "what?" and we ask "why?" Corcoran's primal objects effortlessly reach the plane of myth. I have argued elsewhere[3] that an improvement in the status of women in the 1950s, with the re-orientation of capitalism towards leisure and household goods, led to a redefinition in the 1960s of the male figure as an object of pleasure—a leisure appliance, if you like, a narcissistic move which ironically placed authority in the hands of women, as those most qualified to say "yes" or "no" to these new decorative creatures. The attention then given to the critique of language presupposed that it was the high-powered politicos who were going to have the final say, and not women, conducting a critique of the way a man talks as a way of estimating his character and attractiveness; and was to a large extent a dead letter. The tenuousness of the voice of the male poet is now part of the landscape; who speaks for himself is likely to sound merely self-styled. The external and heroic critique of the power order now has to be combined with a domestic critique of power and goodness within the household. Corcoran shifts between layers of experience like a director cutting between different cameras. What is at stake is not merely the safety of the state—but personal happiness.

The cutting method is based on cellular instability. This dialectic is what I would point to as the link with dancing; nothing is ever asserted, the positions never freeze, the balance of the poem shifts nimbly between opposing points of view. It is hard to depict the cuts without extensive quotation. I am reminded of Jerzy Skolimowski; he began as a boxer, and his camera is never still, never reaches the point of rest (where you can't quickly dodge oncoming blows); this sounds like a jittery way of making the world visible, but the results are astonishing. My understanding is that we improve the readability of two-dimensional light by frequent subliminal movements of the head, picking up anomalies which help to give 3D vision: Skolimowski's teetering camera-dance picks up a stratum of movement control programs which are in fact pre-human. Corcoran never quite lets the left and right planes match: like a man and a woman, like the relationship between the buyer and the seller of labour, like prediction and the event, the two halves always have discrepancies. The function of duality is to provide a schema inside which the two views can be mapped onto each other, and the mismatches picked up; Skolimowski's modelling of space—also a virtual form of eye contact with us, directing attention—is uniquely profound and satisfying. We set knowledge in still frames to control it, and movement of the observer shows the frames; pinpointing the errors in their rendering of recession shows us the cognitive limits of the mind (problems with nine-digit numbers), but also collusion, the construction of social reality.

The breakout into the abidingly valid, from personal & partial standpoints or sources of knowledge, is the opposite of lyric. Because both summate masses of data to extract key patterns, myths and concepts have something in common. The whole tenor of *When Suzy Was* verges on myth—although there are so many different textures in the book. I find this convergence difficult to assimilate. It may be that European idealism drew on Greek philosophy in a form which made them swallow a large dose of myth along with it. That is, when in *Dialectic of Enlightenment*[5] we read the myth of Odysseus and the Sirens, it may be that this is not an external adornment to a sober text—but that the whole text is based on mythical thinking connected by isolated passages of realistic and quantitative thought.

The title of the second book is a kind of pun—tracts means a part of the body (your thinking tracts might be your brain), but also areas of territory, tracts of land, so possibly nations. The less comic implication is that the way we think is conditioned by the society we grow up in—so that the nation we belong to is the raw material we think with, and our notions of politics are predetermined by the rules of the society we were brought up in. This is an incitement to political conjecture—perhaps we can radically change society via an education process. We are immersed in the life-world of the people around us until we seem normal.

The themes continue those in *Suzy*, evolving in a mythical space which is yet critical and rational. It is hard to see a firm border between the books—*Thinking Tracts* is really an expansion of the poetic space opened by 'The Book of Answers'. Much of the language is genuinely primitive—a continuation of the mimed myth of 'When Suzy was (a skeleton)'. Also included are Halsey's illustrations, collages of flat shapes cut out of other pictures and bumped up against each other. The style is after the pseudo-cave paintings which A.R. Penck began in the 1950s—semi-figurative shapes overlaid and jammed together like rock graffiti or a section through an archaeological dig. They are depressing because they lack all recessive space, being obstinately flat and plane; and because they do not involve the expressive hand of the draughtsman, but are simply shapes snatched from other contexts and huddled up against a rigid plane. Deprived of expressive value, the shapes come out of some symbolic system to which we are not privy—and which is disintegrated by the bland method of composition. Grammar is to symbols what space is to visual form, and we are denied both with the same gesture. The idea of illustrations to this text could have been so interesting if a visual thinker had been involved. Fortunately, the illustrations do not detract too much from the text—which sets out from them, and is labelled Pictures one to fourteen.

> I dream arid steppe
> spooked by spring
> they say birdland
> thought door opens
> into the forest dark.
> Peel off sun face
> shine out you Kurgan Nazis
> you surveyors
> you bones in the grave
> with little beads for the kids.
>
> Sweet lens of sacred green
> hold still hold nothing
> but people make it up
> with animals running
> with that new shaping thing.
> The woman underground
> wakes wave on wave
> the wind smacks green sparks
> off the fields her sea
> her trees and rivers running.

The setting is clearly Bronze Age eastern Europe. The steppe/forest boundary is important for the geography of what eventually became Russia. The text refers to a sentimental theory about evil invaders from the steppe, who buried their chiefs under barrows called 'kurgans', and lived on lands too dry to support farming, overrunning innocent and egalitarian peasants.[6] How exactly would we know about the ethical standards of people who lived 4000 years ago and whose words were unrecorded? The judgment does not sound quite right, but the purely mythical discourse sounds very well. The bit about 'surveyors' may point to the same objection to straight lines which we saw with the birdman, and his axe. (Interestingly, he appears in one of the pictures, a kind of graffito.) Surely the surveys would have been done by the peasants, who had fields and boundaries, and not by the pastoralists, who didn't? Does evil have a geographical origin? The equation of the rolling contours of the steppes with waves caused by a fertility goddess stirring, in spring, is brilliant. It also reminds me of a certain passage by Evgeniy Zamyatin.

Just as the transition from paradox to dialectic marks the shift between two generations of intellectual English poets, so the shift from myth to epistemology marks the passing of the baton between two groups with rival conceptions of the sublime. Both represent a breakout into the collective and the transcendent from personal and partial standpoints or sources of knowledge. The basis of paradox, in Metaphysical poetry, was religious—and pointed, as a trope, to the inadequacy of human reason and senses, deceived by a world constructed as a theatre. We can hope that the basis of the dialectic is still, abidingly, an optimistic and heroic belief in the capacity of reason to solve the riddles of the universe—and of the senses to immerse us in the pleasures of the skin and eye.

NOTES

[1] This essay covers the volumes *Your Thinking Tracts or Nations* (Sheffield: West House Books, 2002) and *When Suzy Was: A Book of Answers* (Kentisbeare: Shearsman Books, 1999). Since then Shearsman has also published a *New and Selected Poems* (2004) and the collection *Backward Turning Sea* (2008).

[2] Cleanth Brooks: *The Well Wrought Urn* (originally 1947, quoted here from the 1968 edition, London: Methuen University Paperbacks, 1968.

[3] *Robin Hood in the Middle Ages* (London: Permanent Press, 1985).

[4] in 'Pale Pink Acetate: Self-Adornment in Sixties Poetry', unpublished essay.

[5] Max Horkheimer and Theodor Adorno. *Dialektik der Aufklärung*, (Amsterdam: Querido, 1947).

[6] For an account of the 'kurgan' theory see Brian Fagan, *From Black Land to Fifth Sun*, pp. 82–5 (Reading, MA: Addison-Wesley, 1998).

SIRENS

An inside with no outside: **Foil**[1]

Foil counts 33 poets, and is 400 pages long: CANDESCENT in the glare of omissions, REARED to epic length by monumental errors of judgment, REDEMPTIVELY it is bathed in dazzling rays from the future. Roughly, they are the generation born in the 1960s and early 1970s, excepting those who want to be McGough or Larkin. Or Joni Mitchell. *Foil* is unrivalled, opulent, far gone. It is also a kind of storage warehouse where bales of sleazoid academicism, careerist finger-painting, and avant-garde pastoral are a cartonnage to protect the fabric of brilliant poems from daylight. As a new cultural pattern emerges, an array of 30 poetic arrays, linked to each other by symmetries and oppositions, a debate is opening which, alas, I cannot predict. This will be an ideal-type description, inaccurate for unusual poets—Helen Macdonald's work, for example, sophisticated and three-dimensional.

We look at maybe 15 radiant new poets, and add 15 new years to the curve, to the extent of British poetry. We see their withdrawal from politics, and from exploring emotional experience. After a crisis of legitimation, we find the restoration of a scale of prestige. Above is now linked to below in a stable way. The introduction draws our attention to visual poetry, to 'environments', to the return of the body and the oral, to performance: conceptual innovations of the early sixties. IBM was then, is not now a high growth stock; the new era has no wilderness to stake out, its self-definition is on the fine scale. The canard about the period is that it has seen no masterpieces; it may be that an era of mass higher education and distributed functions does not want language as symbolic power, and so we have delicate chamber poetry. Perhaps we are delicate enough to listen to it?

The tariff structure seems to be that knowledge acquired from speculation, or from philosophers, is superior to knowledge that comes from intuition and from inside. Theories are expensive and exclusive, feelings are commonplace. Personal experience, in relationships and real-world situations, has been reshelved as a kitchen art, less white than white goods. Hmmm. Feelings are Stone Age software but are not the Stone Age of software.

The editor has remarked that the poets don't believe in the counter-culture. Autonomy is not located in a possible new society but in a reduction of scale; a virtual object, a consistency wrapped in a paradox, affluent or ludicrous, programmable and waiting to acquire features. Perhaps we no longer believe in a transformation of social relations, while a transformation of the information patterns by which we produce, amuse our brains, and earn money, is inevitable. The ability to learn (docility) means employment success.

Each folio of poems is the product of a game; each, the application of a procedure which develops a virtual space. The poem game is like an exotic virtual toy, which fascinates by metamorphosing. It contains information, but only about itself; though we explore, there is nothing to explore. Eliminating reference to a self, it is self-referential.

A game is repeatable *ad lib.*, that is, you can always start again at the system origin. It has a non-recursive point; that is, it has a zero or system origin which is not conditioned by any previous moves. Later moves are recursive—that is, defined by preceding moves—and the "richness" of each move is related to the density of its implications for succeeding moves, but also to the amount of effective data which is new and not fixed by previous moves. A good game is, for one thing, one in which the ratio of implication (implexity?) to explanation is high. A game may involve planning, probability, pattern matching, memory, and gaining virtual assets. If it is possible to invent the rules of games, there must be a set of rules by which the game-rules are generated and controlled, at a deeper layer of arbitrariness and compulsion. Inventing games is a kind of game. Niall Quinn, Nic Laight and Nick Macias are poets who have devised geometrical spaces which allow great kinetic excitement, impressively combining transparency and complexity. It may be that we could regard all software as a set of mathematical puzzles; and all poems as mathematical puzzles, local cases of information theory. Imagining the good society was like a game, a sublime zero followed by a cascade of implication.

Idealism has been abandoned as a motive for deep language. The documentary project now seems to have been part of socialism, and the project of self-knowledge and self-expression to have been part of

Protestantism; what was a pleasure then. The relation between signs and any inner processes, has been suspended. Sympathy, attachment, identification, are not on the scene. All this is parallel to the New Generation crew.

Instead of identifying, we are in the poem like mice in a polychrome maze. The withdrawal from the multiplanar cohesion of real-world experience gives the abiding problem of re-building complexity. This was not, always, present in the old, character-based, poetry. One must admit that some poets have very boring personalities; if you read R.S. Thomas, you will notice that the same few ideas occur again and again. So in theory he is free to be diverse, but what he has chosen is a very simple rule-set which repeats itself in a short time and which has been running for sixty years. It seems like more. Artificial rule-sets can easily be more complex, and have more scatter in their results, than "organic" ones. Let's not try to name the winners when we haven't yet worked out the new rules of the game. That someone will be surpassed and destroyed, is clear.

A rule is that the high/low dimension of poetry is now also the depersonalisation: identifying/autobiographical contrast. Sharing is the surrender of distinction. The quality for which poets strive has shifted away from authenticity and towards virtuality. The high prestige of virtuality corresponds to the low prestige of making things, e.g. cars. The admired formula is: arbitrary rules consistently applied. Two match-winners for depersonalisation might be these. First, naïve poets assume that you're fascinated by their feelings, and write poems which just don't stand up on paper, without their composer being present in the room. Better poets write poems which are self-standing, away from the self they refer to. It was easy to deduce that poems which didn't refer to a personality at all were the most sophisticated. Secondly, boredom with identity politics, something which went on for far too long. Alert poets were bound to dissimilate from this central, accessible, sludge. Dissimilation is vital to prestige, while also abandoning territory where, indeed, happiness would have been possible.

American carnivals had a clown called the bozo, whose patter was drawn entirely from reshaping what the audience said to him—an improvisation of precise timing, at risk from the rubes. Khaled Hakim is a bozo on the loose among the culturati, reflexivity on legs, ignoring the rule that analysis is what you do to lower-status people. His work is an act of gratitude for the trauma of having other people demonstrate how well they know your culture. His evocation of overgrown, blown, briar-draggled wild patches of Birmingham is extraordinarily touching.

I also think wistfully of poets who aren't included, points on a bigger and better curve. You can't write D.S. Marriott out of history.

Siren Furnaces Blow Infirm Metals: debuts of the Nineties

Cultural managers lose their looks. One advances into a new decade with a cultural tool-kit formed in the 1970s: I don't have the vocabulary to describe what has changed on the scene with the arrival of so many new poets, unreviewed and uncollected. Yet, there they are, and it's me who's losing definition and wisping away. *However Introduced to the Soles*, by Nic Laight, Nick Macias, and Niall Quinn was undoubtedly the most dazzling debut of the 1990s. Personally, my fear is of missing things, so my wish is to get everything right first time, which precludes writing about first books. My whole critical technique is based on the career review: on recording characteristics made firm by multiple recurrence. But reactions to a first book are a shimmer-chimaera, an aura flickering over the visual field which may turn out to mean that you are falling in love or that you are about to have a migraine. I like situations where I can't talk sensibly. Take *Safety Catch*, by Helen Macdonald, for example. I am quite unable to describe these poems. There are telltale traces from other discourses, such as the linnet in 'Tuist' which comes from an experiment on the line between inherited and learned behaviour where a hatchling acquires the song of another species when played it; the accessibility of such moments should not mislead us into thinking they are central. A passage in 'Parallax' discusses the influence of Newton's *Optics* on how we think, thus moving the latter into the realm of temporal change, as a set of linked cognitive behaviours which we acquire uncritically as children (but can shift consciously as adults), and the "idées reçues ou idées en l'air, lieux communs, codes de convenance et de morale, conformismes ou interdits, expressions admises, imposées ou exclues" which for Philippe Ariès, in an essay on concepts[2], characterise and divide periods; perhaps linked to a passage in 'Tuist' which I believe to be about the 1930s and why they are mysterious; Macdonald seems to regard period-mentalities as a puzzle, perhaps because of a dissociated and detached nature which finds the unconscious rules of the period she lives in difficult to follow. "the beautiful insulatory / qualities of the English Channel" likewise seems to problematise Englishness, seen as a package on offer rather than as "second nature". We could even link this to the linnet in the experiment: we are thrown at birth into a family which equips us with a behaviour set whose arbitrariness we can see but not quite reach. Perhaps this fleet-footed recession explains why the Macdonald poem, full of fascinating objects, is uninvolving, free of silent commands to feel and to identify? But this only covers a few isolated passages within a complex which I find quite elusive. Even these sketches are probably projective on my part, since even if Macdonald is interested in innate behaviour controls she is unlikely to have the same angle on them as I do. Its fondness for subtle, evanescent, and unusual sensations is not the key to this graceful poetry, a fluent and alien sight for which no name or response set yet exists.

If we look at Dan Lane's poem on page 60 of *Angel Exhaust* 15, he says 'soft metallic impression', while on page 133 Kevin Nolan refers to 'clamour of soft metals' (in 'Baion with soft metals to come', quoted from his wonderful pamphlet *Alar*[3]), while on page 27 of *Angel Exhaust* 9 Helen Macdonald refers to "soft / and perfect metals" ('Tuist', since reprinted with two new sections in *Safety Catch*[4]). Clearly we have entered a new dispensation in which hard metals are *pas chic*. I find this phrase quite indefinable, and any sense I do find in it is as a sweet acid blur, something which is like a paradox but yet more ambiguous. It is irresoluble and yet evokes subtle substances, the relaxation of set patterns, delicacy and the removal of strain, the blurring of categories and the lifting of mere functionality. I associate it with *oripeau et clinquaille* (one of Prynne's books in French, and two words advertising pliant and unreliable metals), and with 'A Note on Metal'[5], but mainly with a new era and my inability to comment on it.

There is a faction which freezes out everything which has happened since 1977. This is a mixture of self-satisfaction, historical pessimism, and of projection onto the "counter-culture" so shiny that anything else seems tenuous and unglamorous by contrast. This school consumed, during the 1990s, only books by those who were "on scene" during the 1970s. (Of course, it is questionable whether the radicals of '68 now believe in the counter-culture, which may have been put to sleep in 1975.) This is the kind of purity, and fear of outside elements, which made the political movement of the 1970s unsuccessful. This point of view is past its sell-by date. The publication of *Foil* as an "exhibition anthology" of the new generation, gives us an excuse to argue about the recent past. A few answers to questions about this generation: the London-Cambridge split is meaningless; no-one believes in the counter-culture, and there is very little interest in politics; self-expression and the recall of deep emotional experience are out of fashion; virtuality is the chic ideal; there is no large-scale poetry being written. A lot is happening in the south-west. The overall cultural field has shifted, experience is a poor guide.

Elementarily, it's easier to sell poets who have been doing it for twenty years, and have an acquired audience, than new ones; the competition between someone aged 25 and one aged 50 always favours the latter. It is irritating for young poets that the poets of the 1960s are still around, getting in the way of decisive seizure of montage, Marxism, pop, performance, conceptualism, confessionalism, Jungianism, and so many other things which could be the vehicles of a splendid reputation. It seems to be very difficult to get a book out unless you're a J.H. Prynne covers band—or else in the mainstream. It's strange how people of generous political views can start sounding like workhouse managers when they discuss why it's morally better that young poet X, who can't get their book out, should shut up and stop complaining. The people who make opinion are the same ones who want the few unorthodox publishers to concentrate on getting their books out. On the other side, there is a kind of cultural stalking, where someone becomes a fan of an elder figure, writes like them, pours praise on them, offers to publish them. People without cultural assets must pursue strategies in order to gain them; performance, with its timeless needs for ballyhoo and brass, has produced the most corrupt simulation and touting of assets. To be recognised as legitimate, one has to be recognisable; something really new isn't accepted as new because it is strange and perplexing. Mostly, closer acquaintance exposes what seemed interesting as flashy and short of breath, which I am afraid accounts for some of the other debuts of the decade.

Reviews of the poetry of the seventies placed it all, at the time, in a stylistic map, loosely of American poetry of the 1950s, which gave the reviewers confidence—they'd read the script—but which contained predictions about the future which didn't come true, and which missed everything new about that poetry. Confidence about classifying may be conservatism at the conceptual level.

The negative image of the reader assimilating (and so de-estranging) the poetic line is the poet discerning what his or her true direction is, and focussing a great deal.

I have the habit of deleting what is uncertain, but my problems in saying anything about such poets as Macdonald and Robert Smith are worth setting out, because my state of haze, oscillation, and conjecture is indicative. The new landscape awaits its Greil Marcus. Meanwhile, it might be a good thing if the 'British Poetry Revival' finally kicks the bucket, breaks up, and scavenges itself back to life as multiple autonomous units. The seventies are over.

I suppose the act of consumption to be central to us, and so I offer a list of indispensable books. These are objects, but in fact we cannot discuss ideas unless the evidence is, to some extent, shared. My list runs: Kevin Nolan, *Alar; However Introduced to the Soles,* by Nic Laight, Niall Quinn, and Nick Macias; Helen Macdonald, *Safety Catch;* Adrian Clarke, *Spectral Investment;* Peter Manson, *Birth Windows;* Simon Smith, *15 Exits;* Karlien van den Beukel, *Pitch Lake;* Robert Smith, *Sonnets;* Paul Holman, *Poems 1991–8;* D.S. Marriott, *Clouds & Forges;* David Kinloch, *Paris–Forfar;* Dan Lane, *Stuff Culture;* Michael Ayres, *Poems 1987–92;* Rob MacKenzie, *Off Ardglas;* Tim Atkins, *To Repel Ghosts;* David Greenslade, *Each Broken Object;* Vittoria Vaughan, *The Mummery Preserver;* Scott Thurston, *Statewalk;* Caroline Bergvall, *Glimpses of a Room in Movement;* Grace Lake, *Bernache Nonnette;* David Barnett, *All the Year Round.* We are following *Foil*'s rule of "having emerged since 1986". I appreciate relativising arguments which state that these are not the "best" new poets but only the best within a certain segment of the spectrum, locating which would also locate me, as a partial observer—a hot eye desensitized by its own emissions. I assume that you agree with me—after all, you are an intelligent person.

Foil itself is a book one inevitably has to read. No doubt the limits of the anthology are situated at its limits. Certainly I would like to see a follow-up volume. I was pretty glad to see this one. The Informationists, the Jungians, and the group influenced by *A Various Art*[6] (i.e. *Gairfish*, *Memes*, and *fragmente*, in magazines) are absent. If you read all of *Foil*, you may die. Most of it is rather bad. Thrill to the instantly forgettable New Age kitsch of X, the sloppy, hysterical, Burgerking-Gothic Catling pastiche of Y, the Carry on Lacan sex yibble of W. Bring a thermos of tea and a transistor radio.

Of the poets omitted from *Foil*, we could mention: David Kinloch, Richard Price, Ian Duhig, Patrick Gasperini, Andy Brown, Tim Allen, Robert Smith, Simon Smith, Andrew Lawson, David Greenslade, Vittoria Vaughan, Elisabeth Bletsoe, Norman Jope, Paul Holman, Scott Thurston, Fiona Templeton, Dan Lane, David Bircumshaw, Michael Ayres, Steve Harris, David Barnett, D.S. Marriott, John Goodby, Chris Bendon, David Rushmer. How everyone hates my lists! But the polygon of qualities is too hard to draw.

The reader may well ask what the difference is between *Foil* and the Bloodaxe anthology[7] *The New Poetry*, which covers the same ground but selects not one of the poets who appear in *Foil*. Neither one overlaps with the Stride anthology of younger poets, *The Stumbling Dance*[8] (ed. Rupert Loydell, 1994). Three volumes of *New Poetries*[9] from Carcanet didn't reveal anything you would want to look at twice. The non-overlaps suggest that the dots haven't resolved into a picture. The five books mentioned may represent four vertices of a new literary space. Does this show the abolition of the difference between "underground" and "mainstream"? No, but the oppositions have changed configuration. If we take *TNP* and *Foil* as the significant sites, the difference between them has to do with surface strangeness; the poetry in *Foil* is at first glance puzzling, unsignposted, hard to relate to a self which might be speaking, or to a situation. The poetry in *TNP* is welcoming, has a way in, seems comfortable, even if it sidesteps into originality thereafter. Nick Johnson, although missing some forms of intelligence which other people have got, has certainly scored some successes as a poet.

The gap between the two streams needs to be questioned. My attention was drawn to David Pople and Maggie Hannan as unconventional poets within the mainstream's embrace. Their poetry isn't really very good, but it might develop into something. The gatekeepers aren't as dull as they were; but they do not tolerate the artistically realised originality of a Karlien van den Beukel or a Robert Smith, and so the concept *alternative* will retain its usefulness. Alliance is of little worth unless it is sharply bounded; it is not a binding principle, as alliance at point A implies hostility at point B; alliance means slowing down, the fatigue of identification. There is no alternative "scene". Splits *are* the landscape. Shifts in the site and number of the divisions in the poetic field may be the changes to mark over the last 20 years. They may have changed even though no real horizontal division, and rebellion, is visible within the rather friendly flow of the "experimental scene". The problem of placing the new may be connected to the disappearance of magazines in "my" market segment, which may disappear itself: the erasure of boundaries, the diffusion of its special qualities which could either be expansion or simply dispersal.

There was formerly a polarity like this:

poetry	essay
highly subjective	reflexive & objective

which has vanished as poetry bought into reflexivity. The new polarity is:

poetry	essay
reflexive	reflexive
realisation of	about something and
arbitrary rules	limited to what is true

To this we have to add a spectrum split within poetry, roughly:

culturally "high"	culturally "low" or old-fashioned
reflexive	highly subjective
realisation of arbitrary rules	expressive, reveals character
self-referential	refers to the self

This would, tentatively, explain the omissions from *Foil*. The atmosphere of the 1960s redefined the 50s poets as drab and too concerned by morality. At this moment, we can see that the new set has gone further down this axis, and that it redefines the poets of the 60s and 70s as, relatively, moralistic and concerned with character and duties towards others. They had ideas which were about the world; they used the poet's character as a guarantee of the truth of the poems, which was part of their claim to interest. The poetry which originated in the 60s was hedonistic and relaxed: but the new poetry is tense, striving, status-oriented. There seems to be less leisure for anything except the agreed terms of competition.

Personal politics appear here only in the form of winning status competitions. The "chic charged" procedures carry a whiff of (elite) social contacts, of 'networks', but also of a new version of the good place: the exciting scene where the charging occurred. I don't know where but it takes me there. I do agree that ideas possess prestige, among other qualities. But using ideas except to explain something is somehow ludicrous. The need for poetry of ideas to go to the edge of what the writer understands, to find consciousness, has often meant confusion and hysteria being offered as verbal art. The (brain) pan has boiled over, and that strange sound is the panful burning up on the stove.

The underlying teleology is to cultivate one's ability to concentrate on an abstract idea, which is also the teleology of education. All that perplexes is not complex. Taught performance starts out with the idea that presenting a character whom the audience can recognise and identify with is old hat and un-chic. The figure who speaks has to be denatured. This nullity makes audience inattention likely, so the performer has to project intense concentration and sense of purpose. Non-psychological procedures are applied inexorably. This has produced a certain detachment from the reader's organic waves of attention; a new and uncollected form of boredom. Simply going on for a long time is not cultivated, it reeks instead of dullness and blankness, and heavy going. The pedagogy of the imaginary makes possible a pedantry of the unreal.

The opposition between "art about reality" and "virtual art' can be bypassed if we look at the depth and relatedness of the information encoded in the rules of the work. I have to remind the new poets that new forms of art imply new ways of failing. Even complexity is not interesting unless it has transparency. We can take any work of art as the realisation of a set of rules taking the form of a game. The new term implexity (cf. implicit, complexity, complicit) describes the power of simple rules to generate long series of complex and different game-situations. This quality is found, so to speak, four or five layers deep in the unfolding of the rules, and this is why artistic quality is so shakily related to the "assets" which book jackets and similar propaganda so brazenly bray out. Not all rule-sets have high implexity. Critical classing must surely care for this quality and not for the surface aspects of style.

The modern poet is in effect building a musical instrument in order to find out what it sounds like; each poem demonstrates some of the properties of the formal space thus opened, without flooding it all to the edges. So much follows from the curve in a brass tube. One can produce shapes either by copying them from the world, or by implementing formulae which describe surfaces, corners, curves, etc., and which we could generate *ad lib* or accidentally. Think of the interiors of a thousand buildings, generated by construction procedures rather than by reproduction of a pre-existing reality.

The new poem is desirable above all else. The objects on sale in the shops at the Design Museum or the Craft Centre do have that quality: a kick for the eye. Its structure aims to maximise, in quantity and fascination, information available at any point, in order to throw the reader back into early states of curiosity and playfulness. It is like a shop full of wonderful textiles—268 chenilles. It thinks like a recording engineer, more concerned by textural depth than by the emotional logic of the song. It is more important to suggest this ripple of available textures than to realise them.

Menna Elfyn was recently published in a parallel-text version by Gomer[10]. The Welsh side of the page seems to me lively, dancing, playing with language, altogether charming; in translation, it loses these qualities; she appears merely as a cheerful and kind-hearted housewife. Perhaps a more frivolous translator could do better.

There is a fantasy element in the public perception of Gaelic; an effacing sublimity. Anyway, the Lallans-speaking community is roughly 30 times as large as the Gaelic community. There is an anti-artistic sentimentality now projected onto third-rate Gaelic poets; although, mind you, there is a similar sentimentality projected by and onto pub-level Lallans poets. (There was a joke here about putting low-level Scottish poets onto shortbread tins which my publisher has removed.)

One of Helen Macdonald's poems in *Foil* is called 'Morphometrics', which refers to the grid projections used by the Scottish theoretical biologist D'Arcy Wentworth Thompson[11] (in chapter 9 of *On Growth and Form*, 1917) to demonstrate that all the bones of a certain fish species could be subjected to the same transform to be turned successfully into the anatomy of a different fish species. The graphics he used to demonstrate this give you a "wow" feeling, in fact they are one of the upscale "wow" feelings. Of course, the transform is commutative: you can turn species B into A as well as A into B. He was translating anatomy into topology, giving access to the power of matrices. Part of the reason why he was 50 years ahead of his time is the abiding mathematical under-qualification of biologists; sternly dedicated to observation, recording, and memorising, they were averse to the freedom from reality which makes mathematics (and of course our mathematically-based economic system) so powerful. Grasping the pattern which relates a group of species must be deeper knowledge than factual memory of the visible features of those species: more virtual, more manipulable. You might retort, what kind of knowledge is knowledge of species that don't exist? This is closely related to virtuality in poetry, and constructed poems that describe experiences that don't exist. One of Thompson's remarks was that symmetry in animal bodies may be related to the frequency in physics of symmetries as stable states of dynamic systems, an observation he took from the Austrian physicist Ernst Mach. Mach wrote about mental models and the fictions by which we deal with unknowable reality; he declared both the atom and the self to be fictions[12]. *Das unrettbare ich*, the unsaveable self, was his phrase, a founding idea in Austrian modernism. We might well ask, who is trying to save it? what reads poetry? what writes poetry? Mach's ideas led on, not only to logical positivism (the investigation of mental models as revealed in language), but also to Deleuze and Guattari and their radically atomised and multiple theory of the self, *l'inconscient machinique*[14]. The symmetry proposition tells us that parts of anatomy are not design but results of the laws of physics; the study of how the fertilised cell, with small intelligence, builds an organism which does have intelligence, tells us something about the growth of consciousness. That is, it may be made up of (many) small-scale sealed automatisms, completing processes and so seeming "purposeful", prior to a central self characterised by intention and power. Both the regulation of the growth of the embryo and the nature of consciousness are outside the knowledge we actually possess. Thompson's work is quite close to complexity theory, a part of science which hasn't yet arrived (Stuart Kaufmann even proposed replacing Darwinism with Thompsonian effects. We cautiously propose that, whatever replaces Kaufmann, will be fitter than Kaufmann.)

Mach's scattered and dissolved self is somehow related to ornament, maybe even to the luxuriance of Viennese baroque. Could we relate this to neural Darwinism? She does mention memetics. Doesn't the quality of a picture have to do with its distribution in space, the relative autonomy of its parts? The visual pattern is analogous to the pattern of attention in the brain perceiving it. The balance between dominant and subdued lines in a design, indeed the need for a dominant shape at all, point to the dominance of one "agent" in the brain, and its relationship with other, minor, agents. The relationship of a wrought visual surface to the viewer's ideal of the balance between different psychological agents is a source of anxiety. "Ornament is crime" is related to "the unrescuable self", perhaps a denial of it.

Morphometrics may not be of primary importance to the poem. The poems do not describe "thinking about birds to the exclusion of all else" but a variety of conscious processes in which thinking about birds is common. Actually, bird evolution is only one of the topics which flashes up. Experience is multiplanar; the shifting between quite different planes of experience may be essential to the design of the poems. Perhaps the simultaneity of thoughts about bird anatomy, of the sensation of being in a boat on a lake, and thoughts about another person, is probative of experience which is real and satisfying. A series, then, of singular aggregates of components in several planes which barely resemble each other, which change from second to second, and which are quite different from their parts. This might be a description of the self. The incommensurability of the separate parts of experience may be the heart of the matter. Since they are not attached, the aggregate changes all the time. An *ich* which is real but which serially dissolves. In traditional poetry, the linking of a sentiment to an object, known by touch and handling, by means of metaphor, was essential: the poem existed in two planes at once; it is this principle which we are seeing extended. Judging by some previous Cambridge poetry, unrelatedness is integrity: a quality bespeaking real experience as opposed to fantasy. In this local framework, the sublime is located in uncertainty, and in the projection of a third dimension out of lines on a flat surface.

These poems could be called lyric or documentary, but really both of those mistake what it is.

But there is a complementary faith amongst the damned, which involves their gathering of the stones with which those who walk among the light shall stone them The cover image of *Dogma*, by D.S. Marriott[13] is a reproduction of a Latin inscription within a circular border. *Tene me ne fugia. Et revoca me i domnum evviventium in ara Callisti.* The unevenness of the lettering and the omission of some letters suggest a private commission; the content is certainly an epitaph; the doctrine is pagan, and so probably before the 4th century. *Hold me lest I vanish*; it is the soul speaking, asking to be brought back by the power of the word. Connected with the title, this suggests an eschatological theme: dogma is being used in a neutral sense, as something we believe but cannot reason about; it is presumably a dogma about death and resurrection—first and last things. We find that the poems are about Black history, this is their common theme; so the part about 'hold me lest I vanish' may be the instruction to the poet, to retrieve from oblivion the lives of the obscure (a word which also means *dark*) and the oppressed. The use of Latin may recall the prominence of slavery as the economic support of the cultivated at the origins of our civilisation; probably plays a role in lending symbolic authority to the poet, raised as a Catholic. We may think of birth, into an Empire where your birthright is to treated as an inferior, as like arriving in Hell: redemption originally means "buying (back)", the liberation of those who are property, was borrowed by religious language from its port of origin. I cannot identify *in ara Callisti*; the last word means "of the most beautiful", a Greek word. (It was also a personal name—of Popes and Ally McBeal, we think.) The inscription may be Christian (use of the word dom(i)nus rather than deus sounds Biblical), although the *tene me* formula is familiar to me from pagan inscriptions (for example the Pompeiian ones used by Ekelöf in *En Mölna-elegi*)[15].

The *Dogma* pamphlet opens with a series of wrenching, tragic-lyric poems, and continues with the sequence 'Notebook of a Return', with some formal consistency although scattered widely in time and theme.

> Snow-stars drift away in ashes,
> heat eyelashes down on black divas—their promises—
> and what does it matter anyway
> eyes wide and strong, or weak, sick, cold, castrated?
> Time darkens against the breakwaters
> as shattered bodies pile up, swelling in the stench and heat,
> the rumble of mourning and loss
>
> ('Shot') [16]

The core image is of ashes and snow, whose qualities are scored right into their nature as substances; but which yet are transient, the temporary results of thermal processes. An archaic sense of the self as something small which burns or freezes, in an age before more specialised sense organs or more complex sensations. We could also think of these soul-particles as related to the geological processes which produced the face of the earth—which produced 'Africa' and the seas. The imagery returns constantly to the opposition of black and white: the simplest and yet most fearfully implicative of oppositions. The pattern is fractured but yet reveals such simplicities; *Dogma* can perhaps act as an index to *Lative* (Equipage, 1993).

It is of interest to compare Marriott's version with the original, in a passage of James Baldwin—who also wrote my initial quote for me. 'When we re-entered the streets something happened to me which had the force of an optical illusion, or a nightmare. The streets were very crowded and I was facing north. People were moving in every direction but it seemed to me in that instant, that all of the people I could see, and many more than that, were moving towards me, and that everyone was white. I remember how their faces gleamed. And I felt, like a physical sensation, a click at the nape of my neck as though some interior string connecting my head to my body had been cut. I began to walk'.[17] (from *Notes of a Native Son*) "I shall take one specific case. I am on my way to an uptown movie theatre. The trip takes me through strange neighbourhoods. Walking, I sense I'm being watched. Behind me I can see blood, my blood, marking the way I'd come, collecting in puddles where I'd either stopped or lingered. I pass a knot of white men who stop speaking when they notice me, their eyes full of malevolence. I reach the movie house and go in down the rear stairwell. As I am shown to my seat all eyes are upon me. I wait, expectantly. A shadow begins to fall across the screen. My anxiety begins." (from 'Photophonics'[18]). Marriott's version is much more dramatic—it goes much further. My belief is that several of the passages in the *Notebooks* are based on found texts—Black classics, in fact, but that a transformation process has also taken place. (Hence traces like the non-English vocables *movie house, uptown*.) The freedom of the language is based on this familiarity—the rules of a genre. The exact relationship of the texts to each other offers particular difficulties, but we can recognise the gestalt—they are scattered over a cognitive field which we can see to cover three continents and three millennia, therefore a wide subject, and therefore (as all the segments tell us) the history of Africa and Africans. The overall title clearly refers to *Cahiers d'un retour au pays natal*, by the martiniquais Aimé Césaire (perhaps the greatest of all the surrealists). 'A dream, called Lubek' clearly refers to the ship *Lubeck*, the first English vessel known to have carried slaves from Africa to North America. We can consider the Eurybates section as a treatment of the cultural history of Africa—specifically, of the arrival of the Greek alphabet in North Africa. This would tend to make us think in terms of incompleteness—Europe became the hinterland of the primary civilisations of Egypt and Mesopotamia, sub-Saharan Africa, with marginal but fascinating exceptions, did not. The sand was a sea cutting the rest of Africa off from Egypt, just as the Atlantic cut off the *involuntary colonists* of the American lands off from their stems in Senegal, Benin, or Angola. "Return", on its own, reminds us of the *nostoi* (the returns) of the victorious Greeks from Troy—like Odysseus, who appears here; bloody, labyrinthine, wrecked voyages which are the basis for so many of our staple narratives. The poems relate to this African history—scarcely over our horizon, however broad its dimensions—as a hymn might relate to a body of sacred history: an intensely emotional outcry alluding to shared knowledge. They are inexplicit, free in handling, traumatic, frightening tales of seizure and becoming. The casting of much of the work in prose is slightly surprising.

Marriott uses these texts—classics of Black literature—as tunnels through which to enter a far wider reality. The cult of the individual in poetry relates to the possessive individualism which is so close to the heart of capitalism and empire. As we know, the North Atlantic maritime economy also relied on the possession of individuals. This is why thinking about Black history involves a minimum of three continents as scenery— shattering the frail verbal fabric of the English poem about continuity. But of course these *are* English poems about continuity. A quote, at the head of a passage by Amiri Baraka about the saxophonist John Coltrane, another strand of Black experience, claims "New Black Music is this: to find the self and kill it." (He refers to wholly improvised jazz, the stream which began around 1960 with Ornette Coleman's *Free Jazz* album, an improvisation with a "double quartet".) This points to the wrench which is the first commandment of this extreme poetry: the exit into the superhuman or subhuman. We do well to think of the Coltrane of the 60s when reading this poetry although, because of its anguished quality, I think more of Paris in the 40s and 50s (specifically in the forms of Fanon and Baldwin). The 'Photophonics' section mentions Bion, who is in fact the psychoanalyst W. R. Bion, one of the most significant (and uninfluential) thinkers of the 20th century. The work denies the pre-eminence of individual experience, since it deals with these broad horizons; mentioning Bion perhaps redirects us to the depths (*Tiefen*) of the soul, as in fact these poems sing at a level of emotional urgency which realist-mundane personal poetry is incapable of. However, their theme is anxiety—something individual because it is internal.

There is a stratum of folk language in the poems. This would be the most identifiably Black part of English, and is of course low prestige. The line "Me, I got it writ on the tail of my shirt" means "kiss my arse", an obscure rustic joke found in the rockabilly classic 'Rockin' Chair Daddy', by Harmonica Frank Floyd, and in a Tudor joke-book, the *Merry Gestes*, credited to Will Kemp. (Floyd, incidentally, was the first candidate in Sam Phillips' search for "a white man who could sing like a Negro": *Told her name was on the tail of my shirt, Rockin' chair daddy don't have to work.*) The line quoted may be something like "white education, black ass". The Latin text has *fugia* (for literary *fugiam*), another example of the vernacular—the loss of final –m, as in almost all Romance languages.

The cover picture is about fragility but ends with sublime optimism: *call me back to the lord of the living, in the altar of the most beautiful one.* (Long after this was published, I went to the British Museum and saw the dog-tag with the *tene me* inscription, BM Bronze 902. The British Museum says it probably belongs to a dog, not a slave. Their translation is quite a lot different. 'on the estate of Callistus'. dominum eu viventium=dominum meum viventium, my master Viventius. The dog bit is drawn into the title, *Dogma*.)

Addendum. I don't think Thompson was using matrices—I was wrong. I'm not sure if matrix geometry was available when he was writing. His morphometrics were not based on number sets but on drawing—manipulating the ratios of body parts by hand, using squares.

This work so far has been conceived in terms of the oppositions of the 1970s, which have indeed persisted undamaged among people surviving from those days. Fortunately biology pushes culture forward. In 2004 we were discussing why X would not go to gigs by underground poets promoted (by underworld leaders David Miller, Sean Bonney, and Jeff Hilson) at the Poetry Café in Betterton Street, London. Someone explained that the cafe belonged to the Poetry Society, from which the avant-garde committee members had resigned in 1977, and therefore that boycotting any event there was perfectly reasonable. So was this man X a cultural saint who rejected bourgeois compromise and upheld archaic virtue? No, he was a complete fucking idiot. The people who populated the poetry wars look obsolete if they are still fighting the same secret wars thirty years later. They empty pubs by repeating the same verbal riffs they have been spouting for the past 30 years. They are conservatives sucking on a grievance as if they couldn't afford a new one. The cultural field for people born after 1960 is not clear; it is certainly not something I can set out in definite or convincing form, but it certainly does not involve re-investment in the rusty barbed wire on the demarcation lines of the 1970s. (The people engaged in that world were born in the 1930s, the 1940s, and to some extent the 1950s.) The new field may involve oppositions more rigid, more embittered, and above all more numerous than the ones beloved of Mottram, but it certainly will not involve the same oppositions. At this juncture the project of studying the older cultural field can be offered as a way of understanding the recent past. The recent past has, however, collapsed. The merry go round has run down. There is no need of an apocalypse which destroys great structures and leaves only harmony. This has the advantage of making the system visible—it is almost a theme park you can wander round all day, almost a warehouse of bankrupt stock which you can study at leisure. It's not as simple as thousands of books being available, dozens of interviews—it's also endless evenings I've spent with people slowly getting to know how they think. Enough time has passed for the literary pattern to become clear, even as it fades away.

NOTES

1 This essay covers *Foil: defining poetry 1985–2000* (ed. Nicholas Johnson. Buckfastleigh: Etruscan Books, 2000); *However Introduced to the Soles,* by Nic Laight, Nick Macias, and Niall Quinn (Aberystwyth: DKNY, 1995); Helen Macdonald, *Safety Catch* (published as part of *Etruscan Reader I,* Buckfastleigh: Etruscan Press, 2001); D.S. Marriott, *Dogma* (Cambridge: Barque Press, 2001); Kevin Nolan, *Alar* (Cambridge: Equipage, 1997).

2 from *La nouvelle histoire* ed. by Jacques le Goff (Paris: Editions Complexes, 1988), p.188.

3 Kevin Nolan, *op.cit.*

4 Helen Macdonald, *op.cit.*

[5] collected in: J.H. Prynne *Aristeas* (London: Ferry Press, 1968).

[6] *A Various Art* (edited by Andrew Crozier and Tim Longville. Manchester: Carcanet Press, 1987).

[7] *The New Poetry* (edited by Michael Hulse, David Kennedy, and David Morley. Newcastle-upon-Tyne: Bloodaxe Books, 1993).

[8] *The Stumbling Dance* (edited by Rupert M. Loydell. Exeter: Stride Publications, 1994).

[9] *New Poetries* (ed. Michael Schmidt; Manchester: Carcanet Press, 1994); *New Poetries 2* (Carcanet, 1999); *New Poetries 3* (Carcanet , 2002).

[10] *Eucalyptus: Detholiad o Gerddi / Selected Poems 1978–1994* (Llandysul: Gwasg Gomer, 1995).

[11] See Chapter 9 of *On Growth and Form* (Cambridge: Cambridge University Press, 1917); Ian Stewart and Martin Golubitsky, *Fearful Symmetry* (Oxford: Blackwell, 1992).

[12] Mach's essay from 1895 in Gotthart Wunberg, ed., *Die Wiener Moderne* (Stuttgart: Philipp Reklam Jr, 1981).

[13] *l'inconscient machinique*: see Gilles Deleuze & Félix Guattari, *L'anti-Oedipe* (Paris: Editions de Minuit, 1972).

[14] D.S. Marriott, *op.cit.*

[15] Gunnar Ekelöf, *Dikter* (Poems) (Stockholm: Bellman, 1960).

[16] D.S. Marriott, *op.cit.* p.3.

[17] James Baldwin *Notes of a Native Son* (London: Michael Joseph, 1964).

[18] D.S. Marriott, *op.cit.* p.19.

IN ARTICULO LINGUARUM VITAE: BAM, BAM, BAMBA
or, Uncoded Sound

Reflections on Imagining Language *and* Russkie futuristi *(illicit tape bought at Compendium Books, of unknown origin, with reminiscences of the Futurists and readings of their poems).*[1]

The fact that the tongue has no joints does not mean that there is no distinction between phonemes.

Not everything which has no dimensions is immense.

Part of *Imagining Language* deals with a kind of language which I will call uncoded, because its strings of sounds do not bear any relationship to a set of meanings. However, the most interesting poems here, by Velimir Khlebnikov and his close associates, are in *zaum*[2], which is meaningfully coded, although it builds words which do not exist in "natural" Russian.

When Little Richard sings "Awopbopaloobop alopbamboom", the meaninglessness of the phrase is not meaningless, instead it means exultation and freedom from constraint. I will skip the case against nonsense sound, because surely everyone likes Schwitters and Little Richard. When he sings "from the early early morning to the early early night", this also signifies freedom, and inconsequentiality. It means everything and nothing, a lack of dimension which brings it close to some moments of religious language. Even Richard was sober compared to The Rivingtons, strangers to reason; even "Papa Oom Mow Mow" ("is he serious or is he playin'?") was dusted by The Trashmen—merest myrmidons of the Goddess Gaga—and the ineffable "Surfin' Bird". Truly, they had seen the abyss looking back at them and asked it for a date.

Futurist *zaum* language was not wholly new, and indeed owed something to Jakobson's work on the ecstatic language of the *Khlysty*, a Russian sect, which he communicated to Khlebnikov while he was still a student. None of the words meant anything in Russian. This technique bears structural resemblances to words used, in Late Roman times (and probably earlier), for curses and spells; and to the *Ephesia grammata*, prayers in a language not understood by the priests but supposedly agreeable to the gods. The diverse values of these uses of the same phonological rule, of losing any coded meaning, imply that the device itself is underspecified, and its psychological effect is decided by the social semantic which frames it. That is, codelessness is codeless and requires coding in order to acquire a precise value. The only signal which is self-specifying is one which specifies itself, that is, it is fully coded language. This might mean that the context of this book, i.e. the prose content and the trappings of design, weight, paper quality, etc., affects the impact of the poetic content very deeply; and that the pieces would appear wholly different in a different context.

The book proposes other anomalous forms of poetry, with restricted rule sets. I do not propose to talk about these. But they come in the package.

The fund-winning and Rousseau-esque proposal behind sound poetry is that there is a state (or process) of infantile bliss, which coincides with an uncoded stratum of language, and that this bliss is recoverable in adult life, as a neurological-biochemical pattern, and that the exposure of adults to uncoded language triggers this regression or recuperation. My belief is that this is true; but that the stimulus-response chain in question works only under very special conditions, and probably only for short periods. We could call this oral state Lala-land.

This book is awesome in length, and any attempt to grasp the laws of poetics and brain behaviour involved needs a collection of texts like it. A number of types of text, important for the project of finding out rules, are wholly excluded.

If a flush of new information is what tosses us back into the blissful play/learning state, then un-coded language, which is poor in information, is weakly able to restore us to this bliss, and structurally complete, adult, language is powerfully able to do it.

There is a custom of going into psychology with the spirit of a museum-keeper hunting for trophy objects, with no interest in the societies which produced them, and their meanings. With sound poetry, it is not enough to babble of "infant bliss" and ignore everything else about psycholinguistics, and, indeed, about being a baby. Real babies are capricious and have short attention spans: casting the reader back into babyhood will reproduce these qualities, to be applied to your poems.

I've already written about sound and poetry in reviews of Michael Haslam, Grace Lake and the *Gododdin*[3], and about cursing forms in a number of others. I was originally asked to write about this area using a philological approach, as a fan of historical and text-based linguistics; but this is, I feel, the wrong way to get at something general, species-wide, unchanging, and based in brain physiology. For the first eighteen months after birth, the brain is still growing, and of course learning; the biochemical implications of this are quite strong, and if the seat of consciousness is in the brain then it is very likely that consciousness and the self are flooded by this growth and learning process. Much less certainly, the biochemical "taste" of learning make us partially recur to this protean state when we learn something new in adult life, and there is a state attendant on learning, almost a colour, whatever the kind of thing we are learning. The activities, both specialised and complex, of play and learning, are not peripheral to art: information handling is indicative of the boundary of art with non-art. Because learning and play are most important in early childhood, art which is like play must seem, or be, regressive.

We frequently find in song meaningless syllables, fitted to tunes, often repetitive and also repeated, for example as refrains. This is not quite universal in vocal music, being, for example, banned from hymns. (*Alleluia* is such a melopoeic run.) There is no history of the refrain, but the link to the ahistorical babbling or lalling of infants is palpable. One could argue that this babble or chirrup is simply due to laziness in finding proper words, and that its uncoded quality has no specific psychological effect, but these hypotheses are extraordinarily unlikely. It seems, at least to me, that such babble is vital to pop music, that it is all around us on the radio, that it relieves and relaxes us and makes us playful, and that we respond to sound poetry because we recognise this quality, and agree about its value; and that listening to scat records is a necessary preparation for talking about uncoded "sound" poetry. To our opponents we say tralala tirralirra rumti tum. Yip yip yip yip mm mm mm mm. Lesebesebimbera.

The co-existence of "meaningless variation" and "explicit formed discourse" in art suggests that there are two levels of message of different psychic ages: ornament corresponding to infantility, and "discourse" corresponding to middle childhood, when one has a grasp of grammar, of spatial separation, and of the reality of other people. In poetry, recurrence and ornament obey a different set of rules from the rational minimalism and precision which govern the logical layer. These two layers are not quite stable in their relationship. A third, inexplicit set of rules dictates when one gives way to the other.

The problem with babble is its licentiousness, its endless repetitiousness. The objection to seriousness is that it continues one theme of attention for too long. So both modes are repetitive; the difference is in the pattern of their internal variation.

What interests me is the distinction between melodic line and ornament. How do we know which is which? are there really two channels in music, or in poetry, following different mathematical rules and even using different parts of the brain?

Lowell George sang "I've been from Tucson to Tucumcari / Tahachapi to Tonopa", and "Smuggled some folks and smokes out of Mexico".[4] Futurist theory tells us why these lines are so great, and tells us how to look for "smokes" curled up inside "Mexico", where the reversal of the sounds is as potent as the doubling. We also notice that the use of foreign place-names, with their alien phonetics, is one of the most potent devices of poetry. *Hustled some force of dwarfs out of Düsseldorf.*

The modernist theology is that sound poetry is a break which cuts horizontally across time, but the principle seems to underlie texts almost as old as writing itself. They flag as their competitive attraction the newness of their techniques, but simultaneously accumulate texts from each of the past three millennia in order to acquire hereditary legitimacy as a second line. We look for something fast, chic, and detached, and find a museum being dumped on our heads. He who justifies the arbitrary would look for a straight edge in a dumpling.

Anglo-Saxon, like certain other Germanic languages, has a double series of personal names, with different phonetic rules, so that *Offa* corresponds to *Uhtferth*. The simpler series [Tammo Lubbo Otto Ezzo Ubba Aella] are felt to be hypocoristics (i.e. pet names), which would have been used by children (with constancy, i.e. later than the babble stage) to refer to siblings.

Their phonology resembles, in features like reduplication, simplification of clusters, assimilation, etc., child speech. That is, we know what Anglo-Saxon children sounded like although we only have formal, adult texts. Note that reduplication includes double consonants.

For Osip Brik, phonetic repetition (*zvukovoy povtor*) is the basis of all poetic language. But not all repetition is poetry.

A certain Appalachian ballad, recorded by Hedy West, has a refrain "splattimer lattimer lingo". There is a transcription of one of the legendary outburst-hymns of the Khlysty, completely nonsemantic: *nasontos, lesontos, phurtlis, natruphuntru, natrisinphir, Kreserephire, Kresentrephert, tscheresantro, ulmiri, umilisintru, gereson, drowolmire, tschesondro phorde, kornemila, koremira, gsdrowolne, korlemire sdrowolde, kaniphute, jeschetschere kondre, nasiphe nasiphont, meresinti, pheretra.* (Sound values here as in German!) Conybeare[5] cites similar (perhaps) strings of rubbish recorded in Greek and Egyptian magical papyri. The words are mostly grouped in rhyming pairs, but some are also "reversals': kresentrephert / cheresantro (where "tsch" stands for "ch", in frequent phonetic alternation in Russian with "k"), kresentrephert / pheretra. Owing to phonetic shifts before the written record, Russian has no -nt- or -nd- clusters: compare Latin *sunt*, Russian *sut'*; English *thousand*, Russian *tysyacha*; the frequency of the -nt-cluster in this text acts therefore to signal exoticism, "ringing" a missing place in the matrix of syllables. It would be quite erratic to connect this pointed use of a non-string to borrowing from real languages, say Finnish or Greek. We find another reversal in Hugo Ball's 1916 poem 'Caravan', which has 'jolifanto ambla o falli bambla' (so olifa / ofali) then 'wulubu ssubudu uluw ssubudu'. This was published in his novel *Tenderenda der Phantast*. A Venetian counting-rhyme favoured by Zanzotto starts "enkete penkete"[6]. The Cramps sang "I'm the most exalted potentate of love / The celebrated Hottentot of twine".[7] Nonsense language operates by doubling. So in poems, we could find pairs of words which double each other, but simultaneously have a logical meaning. But in fact we could redefine all rhyme as a case of this. In Milligan's *Greek Papyri*[8], no.48, we find a spell (in Greek, *praxis*) with an Egyptian magical incantation: kata toutou tou theou [by this god] sabarbarbathioth sabarbarathiouth sabarbarbathioneth sabarbarbaphai. (Theta as syllable terminal is impossible in Greek, although of course it is possible in Hebrew and Egyptian, and may be imitated from those languages.) Scheerbart's impressive sound poem of 1897 runs in part 'Zepke! Zepke!/ Mekkimapsi-muschibrops (...) Lakku-Zakku- Wakku- Quakku- muschibrops (...) Lesebesebimbera."[9] This phonetic construction does not seem to be tied to any particular language. We should hypothesize that it therefore belongs to infancy, to vocalising before acquiring a particular language.

I recall my mother frequently bringing up the names Misterton and Mosterton, nearby villages in South Leicestershire, as absurd and touching (and possibly as evidence of the low credibility of South Leicestershire in general, as seen from North Leicestershire); evidently they reminded her of a pre-existing structure, which is in fact already semantic; the names are funny for a simple reason. Rhyming is a way of forming new words suitable to a rustic area where people cut bread with garden spades, sleep in trees, and look the same from the front as they do from the back.

Learning a new language is likely to switch on the play circuits, if this theory is right; and curious poets can test this by learning one. Does learning put the brain into a temporarily different state? does language-learning stimulate phonetic play? *Zaumnik* poetry presumably has a lot to do with the atmosphere of certain language faculties, where adults such as Jakobson, Khlebnikov, and Shklovsky were carrying out the "infantile" task of language-learning full-time. The more unfamiliar a language structure, the more you have to regress (and abandon "reason') in order to acquire it. The study of non-Indo-European, perhaps Turkic or Finnic, languages, is a more radical step than studying, say, Romanian or Norwegian; but Khlebnikov's decisive experience was studying Sanskrit and Old Church Slavonic, discovering the common roots, and sliding into a world of roots.

Tsvetayeva's "Poloterskaya" must be the greatest poem ever written about housework; (the name is the form used for names of dances, like the polonaise, and so means "Floor Polisher's Dance", and indeed there is a lot about floor polishing being a gliding motion like dancing); it contains, but does not mention, a low-grade but popular Russian joke linking pol'ka

(Polish woman or kind of dance) and polka (a shelf, but also the diminutive of pol, 'floor', which was originally made of wooden planks). The poem is full of the kind of dream doubling and coupling of words which makes mummy into mummery: Kolotery-molotery, / Polotyery-polodyeri,/ Kumashniy stan, / Bakhromchatiy shtan. This quatrain is pure dream, but we could say something like:

Ripple-skimmers-moth-skinners / Flashwipers-floorwhippers /
Red cotton flock / frilled trousers.

I am not quite sure about the frills, but perhaps we could say:

Red cotton-rag strips
Gleam stripes-flounced bottom.

Where mop meets georgette, the Poloterskaya combines unmotivated phonetic association with full-scale natural language. Unfortunately, such mixed poems don't get indexed by impoverishedly consistent academics, and, however interesting they are, it's hard to collect them. Carried away by prose, I never read much Russian poetry. How many such poems did Tsvetaeva write? Most of her poems don't use this technique. How many other poets used Futurist sound technique within conventional poems? Pasternak may have been the most successful in doing this. Hans Arp also seems a likely candidate. Such mixed work is not included here. Unmixed work seems to me, relatively, single-track and uninteresting.

The search for phonetic patterning (of the type kolotery-molodery) in the structure of all Latin poems was Saussure's later project, which you may have read about in Jean Starobinski's *Les mots sous les mots*.[10] It was unpublished because its results were negative; in a way which the phantomicity of the presence of "jakobson" in "jean starobinski" may point out to us; but Jakobson's uncovering of Futurist-style phonetic echoing in all kinds of poems is reported throughout his *Questions de poétique*.[11] It may be a basic principle of great poetry.

Some English critics believe that the level of sound is the place of authenticity, sturdiness, reliability. But it belongs to arbitrariness and delirious inconstancy.

Repetition and reversibility are marks of infant speech, applied to syllables and words. But when applied to larger linguistic units, such as entire clauses, they are signs of rhetorical sophistication. We could see the paradox as a reversible sentence.

Nowadays we locate the liminal close to the everyday, just handy: the wilderness turns out in practice to mean the woods a mile outside town. Or, the beginning of time turns out to be the twelve days of Christmas, when shapes go blank, shaggy kallikantzari roam the village, and the shift from shapeless to shape is re-enacted. Boundless and dimensionless substances like light, sex, god, the ocean, are inside poems, and there supply a vital contrast to the unfolded and specified elements of the poem. Every syllable starts out as a blank ur-syllable. Babble is composed of such archisyllables, before individuation. There is no point siting the transcendental out of walking distance.

"Infant bliss" may relate to being allowed to play all day, to the spring-like sensations of growth, to non-specialisation of which babble is a form, or to the total attention of a mother waiting on you hand and foot. Distinguishing between these seems to be beyond our knowledge. But this question is vital for aesthetics.

Kitzinger has described[12] how in the decaying Roman Empire there was a revival of provincial visual traditions, without perspective, involved rather in magic, and ascribed value by ethnic narratives. This is for him the origin of mediaeval art. Such stelae, jewels, etc., correspond to the language of magic. So the position of ordered grammar in poetry corresponds to geometrical perspective in art, and possibly to legal procedures in the running of society, and medicine, as opposed to magic, in the care of the body. It seems that in our time the collapse of external space in poetry, and the rise of subjectivity, have brought about a rejection of syntactic structure and a resort to certain magical and infantile forms.

Babies learn to walk. They become much less dependent on their mothers. Walking offers a new access to space, and so anticipation, movement planning, a new concept of time. This makes the coding of sound into language, to express the new cognitive complexity, appropriate. Babble belongs to a world which may have infant bliss but which is cognitively poor. But even after the emergence of an autonomous outer space there is still a capsule of subjective space, within our bodies and within the grasp of our hands. However much you geometrise art, the perspectiveless space is still there, lurking and archaic.

The Futurists' tape includes reminiscences of Mayakovsky by Kornei Chukovsky, a gramophone recording of Mayakovsky reading his own poems, reminiscences of Khlebnikov by two women, readings of Khlebnikov poems, Kruchenykh reading his own poems, and readings of poems by obscure futurists Iliazd and Vasily Kamensky. This is really a great delight, a reward for turning over Compendium's tape counter. Mayakovsky's voice is quite pleasant, if stagy; a surprise since I have always imagined that, if I met him, I would want to hit him over the head with a saucepan. Semyon Kirsanov reads Khlebnikov much better than Jakobson. Chukovsky has an absolutely wonderful radio voice, ornamenting every potential "drop", exquisitely varied, and yet discreet. I have never read anything by him, but his daughter, Lidia, used to write for the dissident magazine *Kontinent*. Could we compare Kirsanov's shift into children's poetry to the large-scale adoption of avant-garde techniques by advertising?

Para-musical sidestep

I tried to find a historical comment on the meaningless words (fol de rol, sha na na, rumbelow, etc.) which appear in song texts, but was unable to do this. Certainly these uncoded syllables have a lot to say about what we have found in sound poetry, ecstatic utterances, magic spells, and so on. Although I am not a musicologist, I did try to find out what musicology had to say about wordless vocal improvisation. My approach was through a musical encyclopaedia, and was handicapped because I could not find a headword which corresponded closely to what I wanted to know about. The word *melisma* does not mean exactly this, but is rather variations on a single syllable of the set words for a church service, and is not wordless, and is bound to a specific period of Western musical history. *Vocalise* is a variation on a specific vowel, perhaps designed as a singing exercise. *Eiapopeia* may be the kind of uncoded creativity we are looking for, but is a historically bound word, not one which is ever applied across cultural boundaries. I couldn't find an exact word for singing in phonemes but without words, as in doo-wop (indeed, *doo-wopping* might be such a word). I may say that I was looking for research which would prove that uncoded vocal improvisation was a human universal, and a constant in musical history. Since I couldn't find any such research, the question of universality will have to be spiked. I did find a lot of interesting material in the article for 'improvisation'. An issue is the effect of written music: in Western music, literacy, written scores, the dominance of the composer over the performers, and polyphony, notoriously all go together. Curious scholars, and in particular those associated with the early music movement, have been re-assessing early scores, and the less learned music which was displaced by the literate and academic onsurge. They are very keen to point out the role of unwritten ornamentation in performance of early scores. From my point of view, this simply means that uncoded vocal creativity, which we obviously don't have mechanical recordings of until the late nineteenth century, is not recorded in written form either. Improvisation, rather than being something *universally* available to the untutored folk musician, may have been distributed in a much more limited and interesting pattern; which is what field study of folk music has recovered. The most interesting moment of improvisation is something recorded by critics in periodicals: the practice of opera singers of freely ornamenting their own parts, prevalent up until the 1830s (perhaps), which was purged by Rossini, fighting on behalf of the composer. We are told this was a great reform. Of course, we have Rossini's scores, but not the flourishes of the sopranos, which vanished as soon as they fell silent. The Italian opera was dominated by stars; which I take to mean that the right to improvise was confined to the star singers. Further, I doubt that most singers (especially folk singers) had the necessary ability; and we may doubt whether this licence to trill applied in other countries, or, for example, to church music. It is an open question whether the written ornamentation of Mozart, Rossini, etc. differed from the spontaneous ornament of the singers, or whether it observed the same patterns (while fixing them).

Everything tells me that jazz was a unique cultural moment, a revolutionary break with tradition which benefited from the thwarted talents of an entire nation that was blocked from achievement in other areas. There was no Charlie Parker in the thirteenth century.

*

Note on *The Gododdin* and on Richard Caddel's phonic version of it

In the 1960s, Louis Zukofsky tried to transliterate Catullus into an English version which had the same sounds:

> O th'hate I move love. Quarry it fact I am, for that's so re queries. Nescience, say th'fiery scent I owe whets crookeder.[13]

The earliest example of this technique known to me is by Ernst Jandl, from circa 1957, "oberflächenübersetzung" (Mein Herz liebt zapfen eibe hold)[14]. Caddel's poem, which is the third part of *For the Fallen*[15], is a similar exercise based on Neirin's early seventh-century Old Welsh poem, *The Gododdin* (or as the colophon has it, *Hwnn yw e gododin. Aneirin ae cant.*). Ifor Williams' introduction to his edition points out the nature of the text as we have it, where phonetic drift and association have taken over parts of the original text, as written by a named individual, and reduced it to sound; he quotes three variants of a certain couplet:

> cret ty na thaer aer vlodyat
> un axa ae leissyar.
>
> caret n hair air mlodyat
> un s saxa secisiar
>
> cleu na clair air uener
> sehic am sut seic sic sac

These do not resemble each other, nor any known kind of Welsh. Language here has gone all the way back. Forfeiting its nature as a string defined in several dimensions at once, it gains by falling into a world of unbound association. There is no text of the *Gododdin* which is wholly meaningful; that is, more than mere sound. The verbal ornaments of the poem, as described by Williams, supply, moreover, a compositional principle which is phonic before, or beside, semantic: the verse structure obeys the rules of *cynghanedd* as well as those of rhyme. Each couplet is preceded by an acoustic shadow of definite structure, into which the words, when they arrive with their specific sounds and their burden of meaning, must fit; the nature of such poetry is double, and its quality depends on the interaction of these two sets of actions, one organised and semantic, and one phonetic, based on simple principles of repetition and alternation, and nonsensical. The poem contains its own, old, babble score as something folded inside it, like an animal cell containing captive plant DNA. Caddel makes association the foreground factor of poetry; clusters of words without syntax orchestrate a shadowy and indefinite experience; sound flows follow a pattern of memory which flows rather than stand upright, rolling along a surface which offers no depth of coding. Caddel's poem is admittedly unreadable, but is a genuine curiosity. He produced an English poem by listening to the sound of Welsh words whose meaning he did not know. Memory is stimulated indirectly, by a mere *nominis umbra*, like the wires of a piano trembling to a sound from the next street; this abolition of the keyboard may resemble Tom Raworth or Adrian Clarke. I suspect that a principle of phonetic echoing of entire lines is also present in early Welsh poetry:

> Kyn mynet or byd bryd breuddwydawl
> kein vynwent brouent bro gorfforawl
> kyn maynved diwed bwyf dwywawl gyffes
> (Bleddyn Vardd, 13th century?)

In the same poem we find "yny may mawrway heb ymeiriawl / Yny may mawrwall eneit marwawl", where the highlighted words are lexically quite distinct (respectively, "great woe, intercession, great want, mortal") but Bleddyn is making a dazzling play on the similarity of their casing.

Williams' hypothesis[16] is that Neirin composed his poem around 600 AD, but the thirteenth-century manuscripts that we have are copied from a version in 9th century spelling; this copy, partly effaced by thirteenth-century forms, must have been considerably adapted from the original; Williams reconstructs one couplet as follows:

> ac cin guo-lo gueir hir guo-tan ti-guarch
> derlidei med-cirn un map fer-march

while the manuscript form is:

> a chyn golo gweir hir a dan dywarch
> dyrllydei vedgyrn un map feruarch

Clearly, there is no authoritative text from which Caddel's sound-shadow could have worked. We do not know the pronunciation of seventh-century Welsh. However, the original form persists, puzzlingly, in the shape sketched out by the rules of alliteration, although the words have vanished. The earliest form of the poet's name is Neirin, which later evolved into *Aneirin* (cf. the shift from Latin *scutum* to Welsh *ysgwyd*).

The other two parts of Caddel's *For the Fallen* are composed on quite different principles.

Appendix on uncoded language

Jakobson. I am now totally unable to find this essay. However, I believe it was written in about 1920, that I read it in about 1986, and in Russian. It may have mentioned the Khlysty texts in passing, and said about them that their construction was not random, because it systematically avoided any syllables which were meaningful in Russian, and because it included so many examples of syllables which were impossible in Russian. This proof of purposiveness qualified the supposed irrational and inspired nature of the ecstatic texts. The migration into the uncoded area resembles rules which mean that certain phonemes only appear in sound-words (*tsch* in German), or that certain words are taboo (as described by Jakobson's collaborator Bogatyrev). I believe the texts he used were similar to the ones printed by Conybeare[17].

The 'ecstatic' texts demonstrate—and I cannot remember if I got this from Jakobson or if I worked it out myself—a remarkably low proportion of syllables which are meaningful in Russian. Low—that is, much lower than random. The texts are structured by a rule of avoidance. This means that they are not ecstatic, but highly controlled. This rule of avoidance can be compared to rules which govern poetic language, in various cultures, and differentiate it from everyday discourse (or from prose). Poetry is produced from the pre-existing linguistic mass by a mixture of generative rules and negative rules.

The texts are organised around their syllabic inventory. If we drew a matrix of the syllables possible within Russian phonology, and blacked in the syllables which are actually used by Russian words, and then coloured in the ones drawn on by the Khlysty texts, it would be clear that they did not overlap with the 'blacked out' area of the matrix. Indeed, we could predict the syllable inventory of the religious texts by considering the unused syllables.

The texts involve strings which are meaningless but which repeat. If we imagine a line in a poem being followed by an acoustic shadow of itself, on a principle of repetition, we can also imagine this shadow as then being given lexical content and a meaning. It is then a line which rhymes with the previous line and repeats its rhythmic pattern. We can guess that the composition of poetry relies on an irrational acoustic creativity.

Jakobson was interested in these "uncoded" texts already as a student, but apparently never published on them. He remarks on them in various autobiographical notes. Notably, his sister heard a sect member, around 1913, utter a sentence in what turned out to be a private language of the sect. This was meaningful and so coded, but did show several of the (nasal + dental) clusters which are so unusual in Russian and so common in the ecstatic texts.

I had better give a route-map of what will follow. It consists of two interrelated essays, about emptiness and the connection of the avant-garde to the world of Hellenistic cults, both of which are closely connected to this essay on uncoded sound. You will recall the connection drawn, a few pages ago, between sound poetry and a type of 'ecstatic' religious language. Along the way, we will talk about heightened suggestibility, about the uncoded imagery that emerges in this heightened state—and about how to lower the threshold of response so that one can emerge into this state.

NOTES

[1] General sources: *Imagining Language*, (ed. Jed Rasula and Steve MacCaffrey, Cambridge, MA: MIT Press, 1998); Allison Elliot, *Child Language* (Cambridge: Cambridge University Press, 1981); George Milligan, *Selections from the Greek Papyri* (Cambridge: Cambridge University Press, 1910); Vladimir Markov, *Russian Futurism, a History* (London: MacGibbon and Kee, 1969). Records: The Silhouettes, *Get a Job*; Richie Valens, *La Bamba*; Little Feat, *Sailin' Shoes*; Cab Calloway, *Minnie the Moocher*; Little Richard, *Tutti Frutti*; The Rivingtons, *Papa-Oom-Mow-Mow*; The Trashmen, *Surfin' Bird* (brilliantly covered by The Cramps); The Cramps, *Smell of Female* (on *Live at the Peppermint Lounge*).

[2] Sometimes translated as "transrational language".

[3] In *Angel Exhaust*, issues 12, 13 and 16 respectively. A version of the last is included at the end of this chapter.

[4] Both are from the song 'Willin'.

[5] Frank C. Conybeare, *Russian Dissenters* (Cambridge: Harvard UP, 1920), itself quoting from a work by Karl Konrad Grass.

[6] A child's counting-out rhyme. An internet check suggests that this opening phrase is also found in South Slav rhymes.

[7] The song is 'The Most Exalted Potentate of Love', from the album *Live at the Peppermint Lounge*.

[8] Milligan, *op.cit.*

[9] available in Klaus Peter Dencker (ed.), *Deutsche Unsinnspoesie* (Stuttgart: Reclam, 1978).

[10] Jean Starobinski *Les Mots sous les mots: les anagrammes de Ferdinand de Saussure* (Paris: Gallimard, 1971).

[11] Roman Jakobson: *Huit questions de poétique* (Paris: Seuil, 1977), especially 'Structures subliminales en poésie'. These texts are available in other forms.

[12] Ernst Kitzinger, *Byzantine Art in the Making* (London: Faber, 1977).

[13] Louis Zukofsky, quoted from Martin Seymour-Smith, *A Guide to Modern World Literature* (London: Hodder and Stoughton, 1975), vol. 1, p.52.

[14] in Ernst Jandl *sprechblasen* (Neuwied: Luchterhand,1967), but dated by the

poet "28.11.57"; since gathered in the poet's collected works: *sprechblasen, verstreute Gedichte 3* (Luchterhand, 1997).

[15] Richard Caddel (1949–2003), 'For the Unfallen; in *Angel Exhaust* 16 (1999); subsequently collected in *Magpie Words* (Sheffield: West House Books, 2003).

[16] Ifor Williams, *Canu Aneirin*, 2nd ed., (Caerdydd: Gwasg Prifysgol Cymru, 1961).

[17] Conybeare, *op. cit.*

EMPTINESS, THE INFINITE, AND THE SPIRAL

There is a wonderful article by the Australian cultural historian Tom Gibbons entitled 'British abstract painting of the 1860s'.[1] He is writing about spiritualist paintings—in particular those of Georgiana Houghton[2]. The paintings were made in trance states by an "inner light". Often, they were painted in the dark. They are not all abstract—some show meetings with higher beings (aliens?). He says that spirit drawings are 'generally at first in spiral forms'. It is virtually an obligate shape of non-representational imagery.

Theosophy, an offshoot of Spiritualism, picked up on this kind of art, and there is a book called *Thought Forms*[3] (by Theosophist satraps Leadbeater and Besant), which is often quoted as a source for abstract art. I am a sceptic—but Houghton's paintings (which Gibbons found in the store of the Victorian Spiritualists' Union, in Melbourne) are extremely beautiful, and fully abstract. Gibbons has uncovered the fact that Houghton was friendly with a whole family of Varleys—descendants of a close friend of Blake's. There is a whole line of interpretation (favoured by the editor of *Modern Painters*, the late Peter Fuller) which says that the absence of Modernism in England was linked to the prominence of sectarian and prophetic religious groups, and which may hold, further, that the correct line for an English artist is to follow the visionaries—Blake rather than Picasso, Jones rather than Pound. Maybe we should set aside the problems of Modernism and study the problems inherent in Vision—figures like Raine and Michell are not exactly free from ambiguity. Anyway, there is an obvious link between emptiness in poetry and abstraction in painting—and sectarian visionaries seem to have been in on the start of both.

The occurrence of spirals in someone's pictures may simply be an indication of lowered thresholds of suggestibility—spirals are a typical form of spontaneous imagery. The lack of impinging light might expose to sight the structural constants of the visual software. Automatic patterns may be flickeringly there all the time, although they are hidden by normal visual activity, the response to external light and the information it is so rich in. One such pattern may be the spiral. If a brain sees one obsessively recurring pattern in a wide variety of visible scenes, the pattern may be a part of the brain's activity patterns, rather than something which could be found (by someone else) in the visible world. It may be that this condition of spontaneous generation of imagery is really the goal of art, and that artists tend to obstruct it by injecting their tedious personal problems into the work of art.

Against reason; poetic "magic"

The rejection of realism, and hence of discursive writing, virtually defines the avant-garde—but they are not the only anti-realist group.

Sensitivity is a charged word in the way we talk about poetry. To say that a poet is insensitive is virtually to say that he is no good. Oddly, the same applies to readers of poetry. They all want to be sensitive, and quite probably most of them are. This would be different from, say, rock musicians or rappers: the same test would not be applied to them. The concept sensitivity brings us close to the notion of lowered thresholds of response, and of skill at dealing with situations where inhibitions are removed and very delicate stimuli may matter a lot.

> (When we dream) "The substantial stuff of day, that pressed its claim with the insistence of crude fact and harsh reality, dissolves into a fumy vapour, that heaven's own winds hurl into an inconsequential past. We leave behind the armour of our mortality [. . .] The verities of the unknown are richer and profounder than the half-stolen evidence of creed and cant; for they have eternity on their side [. . .] We see the troubled water beaten by the wind; the cool air floats past us, but we cannot turn back and so deny the soul-instinct within us. Beauty has caught and taken us for her own; and neither denial nor doubt can take from us our homage to her undying power. The now faint forms that time once limned upon the parchment of our memory, are well forgotten in their shapeless filmy impotence; their hold upon us lost in this greater quest where future treads upon the past with all unseeing speed. Around us the heart-beat of humanity's multitudes throbs to the pulse of our own, and draws our dream into the one infinity that folds us all. Do we take our little minds and weave around them the coarse thread of modern reality, with its sly sophistry and eager quest for the vain bubble, pride [.]"[4]

191

This is all about sensitivity. It adds, of course, the overlay of a class of extra-sensory perceptions which (only) the sensitive can see. I am not wholly in favour of this; but it is not actually untrue. It is subjectively valid as a description of dreams. It is hard to remember any concrete details of it afterwards. Let's just imagine this being written as an answer to an A-level question. That wouldn't go at all. It is not too much to say that the whole Practical Criticism project was designed to oppose this kind of writing, and was aroused by pupils and undergraduates producing writing like this as essays and exam papers. This points to a basic opposition in modern poetry. There was, from the 1920s, an academic line that favoured precise observation, compactness of phrasing, avoidance of lush and emotive imagery, etc. Among readers, and especially among poets, there is a counter-current which feels that the dominant academic method, i.e. of questioning reactions and analysing everything, is simply anti-poetic. Being exposed to challenge and marking lowers the threshold of suggestibility and makes you less able to respond to art. This polar opposition between the credulous and the sceptic has not necessarily surfaced very often; it is just one line of division among many, and alliances or sympathies push it to the back of the stage almost all the time.

There is a basic ambiguity in the project of Practical Criticism. It may be intended as a way of exploring human reaction to pieces of poetic language, and thus advancing human knowledge. Alternatively, it may be a way of ensuring that the pupil offers the knowledge which she or he has acquired, in such a way that it can be tested. It would then be a support for administrative decisions, a way of demonstrating value for money, of segregating people into grades. It would aim to thrust the act of being observed into the heart of the poetic experience. It would tend to substitute the relation between the student and the assessors for the relation between the student and the poet; the student gains assets and legitimation by an act of self-display. You may choose whether you see reading poetry as like dreaming, with access to the infinite, or like sitting an exam, and demonstrating your knowledge to people more powerful than yourself.

The spiritual version of poetry appreciation did not simply climb into a weeping willow and cast itself into the heartless river. It was defeated in the universities, though. Perhaps the yearning for intimacy, suggestibility, for the release of involuntary images, is a feature of uneducated taste, and emerges wherever the sway of the academic system is weak. It is the naive taste, and for that reason is common among second-rate poets. This fact of distribution hardly clinches the argument. The whole line of verbal organisation which makes the poem clearer, i.e. more open to rational attack, is rejected by this taste. Its partisans reject rational accountability in favour of passive and welcoming openness to images from the unconscious, the imaginary, or wherever else. The group is the screen on which involuntary images are projected. A key statement on this issue is Yeats' *Oxford Book of Modern Verse.*[5] Yeats gathered the heritage of the Occult Revival, of Theosophy, Swinburnian paganism, and spiritualism. He leaves out the realist line. He selects poems which support the idea that the material world is gross stuff which hides eternal and impalpable Ideas:

> But why embody the unknown: why give to God
> anything but essence, intangible, invisible, inert?
> The world is full of solid creatures—these
> are the mind's material, these we must mould
> into images, idols to worship and obey[.][6]

The term 'inert' refers to an argument about the non-perceptibility of God, who does not interact with the material universe; the argument over the priority of what can be detected by the senses over spiritual ideas has been central to twentieth-century English poetry. Virtually all the poets whom Yeats picks out for praise, in the Introduction to the *Oxford Book*, vanished from the view of later anthologists. However many people the schools train in Practical Criticism, which I have said was aimed to prevent teenagers from writing like James S. Marshall, there is still an obstinate current of opinion for which the whole rational method is leading in the wrong direction. They are enthusiastic about sensitivity.

The Quest was edited by G.R.S. Mead from 1909 to 1930, and was the magazine he started after resigning from *The Theosophical Review.* Yeats wrote for it. As soon as someone gets over-enthusiastic about the line of sensitivity, they start to migrate towards supernaturalism, spiritualism, and occultism. There is a book, known in Europe as *Picatrix*[7], reportedly written in Harran (Syria) by eleventh-century pagan Arabs believing in an ancient star religion. Ronald Hutton's recent research seems to show that the text may refer itself to Harran only as a self-validation—purveyors of occult knowledge cannot say 'I discovered this by experiment', so need an authority, as legendary as possible. *Picatrix* was written in eleventh-century Spain. The evidence for post-seventh century pagans in Harran seems to dissolve on examination—but there was certainly a legend about them. In *Picatrix* there are useful instructions for how to pray to Saturn: "Take some artemisia, some grains of bericus, juniper roots, nuts, old dates and some thistle in equal parts. Crush them and mix them with good old wine (that is, which is numerous years of age)." It also advises: "When you wish to speak to the planet to which your request is properly assigned, clad yourself in clothing dyed in the colours of the planet; undergo its fumigations and pray with its prayers." "You shall address yourself to Saturn for requests which have to do with old people, generous men, heads of cities, kings, hermits, men who work the earth, the administrators of cities and of inheritances, with remarkable men, farmers, builders, slaves, thieves, with fathers, grandfathers and great-grandfathers." In this version of the cosmos, influences roll down from the stars to influence earthly events. Knowledge of shapes and decans allows you to deal with this universe; most of the content of *Picatrix* is vast numbers of practical details about the rules of analogy and how to use them and win. God was inert, but, for the Sabians of Harran, the stars were receptive to *suggestion*: chains of links between colours, stones, sounds, plants, etc. broke down their inhibitions and inclined them to bring about what the magician wanted.

Fairly obviously, the immense fields of analogies deployed by *Picatrix* resemble the analogies used by post-*Symboliste* artists, and early programme statements of *Symbolisme* copy their sets of analogies directly from occult texts related to *Picatrix*. Equally obviously, a large proportion of the poems in Yeats' Oxford Book have a formula of "capturing" a spiritual idea by means of vivid sensory and pictorial data, which are psychologically linked to it and call it down. The magician collects and brings together appropriate objects, and so does the Yeatsian poet. Defining the exact relationship between modern art and the Neoplatonic occult will take rather more patience. I don't want to resolve the contest between sensitivity and academic sharpness, but can shed light on the occult background. Along with Edwin Muir, Kathleen Raine was the most consistent follower of the line of Yeats' anthology during the 30 years after Yeats' death. She spent the 1950s in large-scale research into Western occultism, undertaken in order to reconstruct the intellectual world of Blake. She drew her concept of how the universe is constructed from the writings of occultists, which you are not likely to find in university libraries. Raine was a literal believer in Neoplatonist physics, as this passage from one of her poems reveals:

> We do not see them come,
> Their great wings furled, their boundless forms infolded
> Smaller than poppy-seed or grain of corn
> To enter the dimensions of our world,
> In time to unfold what in eternity they are,
> Each a great sun, but divided to a star
> By the distances that they have travelled.
>
> Higher than cupola their bright ingress;
> Presences vaster than the vault of night,
> Incorporeal mental spaces infinite [8]

This comes from the same verbal world as the passage by James S. Marshall. It's also a beautiful poem, from a beautiful book. It is hard to work out exactly what it means, but clearly it belongs in a world of natural magic where Platonic ideas have an influence on our mundane world which is identical with that of the stars, so that ideas also are the stars. She is describing the ingress, or entry, of influences from the stars into the world of humans. 'Scala coeli' means the ladder of heaven—which the star-seeds are presumably climbing down, on their way to us. The influence of the stars on human affairs is a doctrine which is very widespread in Asia, as René Berthelot explained. What the passage tells us is that the stars are the physical appearance of eternal forms; that their influence flows into our world in packages too small to be detected by the senses (unlike light, which is more crass); and that our experience of beauty is part of a relationship with those influences. Neo-Platonist texts explain all of this.

Astrology is the most familiar example of the spirals of influence, and is a good example of Neo-Platonist thought. Much of it was allegedly developed by Sabians, the pagans of Harran. The use of allegory, in the art of the Renaissance, may owe a great deal to astrology, with its richness of imagery; Spenser's imagery around Astraea (the starry one) adapts the theory of influence emanating from the stars. It seems very unlikely that the huge numbers of poets and painters who used this imagery believed in its literal truth, any more than they admired the monarchs as much as they pretended. It may not be accidental that the peak of allegory was associated with the peak of natural magic, as Bruno promoted it. The printed textbooks of emblems used during the sixteenth and seventeenth centuries were directly related to the *Hieroglyphica* of Horapollo, a work on Egyptian picture signs which gave the pictures distinctly Hermetic readings.

Allegory has declined, and is scarcely available to a modern poet. It relied on very detailed knowledge shared by a community. Poetry rides along on the intellectual skills developed in any society, and history shows bizarre over-development of skills by sedulous training, florid summits of virtuosity which were abandoned because they proved fruitless or were replaced by an easier method. Science wiped out its rivals, as did alphabetic writing. People who spent long days pondering Bruno and his congeners developed intellectual skills which we do not have. The problems we have with Spenser may be because he was part of the "deep" sixteenth century and we are not.

The new scientific world-outlook does not give a prescriptive rule for writing literary works. If you depart from a simple documentary account of some events, you cannot be either scientific or, probably, unscientific. Meanwhile, there has been a general collapse of the genres on which poets formerly relied. The modern poet has to create a set of rules for getting from one page to the next. Poets need large-scale frameworks within which to move as they write, focusing intently on individual frames of the verbal creation. The whole world of the Occult Revival of the nineteenth century has proved productive as a framework in which to create art. Many thinkers have contemplated an "Egyptian Reform" in which scientific thought would dissolve away, to be replaced by a set of intellectual practices based on Hermeticism and allegory.

It is singular that the association which meant that the word *mathematicus*, for Romans, actually meant astrologer, still held around 1600 AD, when the mathematical knowledge of John Dee and Robert Fludd was associated (as Frances Yates has recovered for us) with occultism, including knowledge of the stars.

If you repetitively add one to any number, you can create a series of numbers extending to infinity. Numbers exist even when no-one has written them down yet. Random and infinite are two of the most powerful concepts in mathematics. It is not surprising if they are also some of the most powerful concepts in verbal art, or in sound. Nonsense is not merely the absence of meaning—it draws on these awesome waves of blank energy.

If we imagine a device which translates numbers into musical sound, we have an infinite array of sounds. The Neoplatonist conception of space filled with sound is a sensuous equivalent of the infinity locked in number. If we imagine the numbers as vocal sounds, made of phonemes, we have an endless array of uncoded words. There is a Greek term for these: *ekhos*, a word made of formed sounds with no meaning. Perhaps the uncoded strings of the Khlysty and others are a pointer to this universe—a way into it.

Platonic influence is a form of determinacy. Thinking of this fictional mapping of cosmic shapes into the events of the earth allows us to see meaning as a determination of language; it gives us the category of mappings of which meaning is one instance.

Because an infinite number of poems is made possible by the rules of the code—Greek as much as English—the poem you are about to write already exists. This is a fundamental condition of the poet's life, and bears a resemblance to the other domain, of words with no meaning, defined by *arreta onomata*, the unspeakable words. Any lexicon occupies a set number of places in the matrix of all sequences possible within the phonology of a given language, and this number defines the complementary set of sequences which do not represent words. The mathematical properties of this second set may say something fundamental about the brain.

This poetry works if everything resonates, so that links do not need to be laboriously spelled out. It does in fact work, and this fact teaches us something about the nature of the universe—actually about the nature of the brain, which works by associating things with each other. However, it is bound to remind us of the Neoplatonist view of the physical universe—with influences flowing everywhere, governed by analogy—so that shape is the lens by which astral energies are focused onto some point on the earth, to bring about the events which occur in the visible world.

The Neoplatonist universe is permeated by sound. The calls, if made correctly, bring down the gods. The gods, too, speak through the throats of the possessed: the vibrating reeds, and this is how the Chaldaean oracles were revealed. The interstellar spaces are filled with voices. We now have to pursue the strange links between modern art and the practices of the world of syncretistic cults.

I agree that suggestibility is a key element of the poetic experience, but when a poem fails there are other things to investigate than the sceptical and instrumental bias of the whole of Western civilisation. The latter cannot be averted. Suggestibility can be achieved in many ways, and the outright attack on Western values—on science, manufacturing, trade, the Enlightenment, I.A. Richards, or whatever—was an emotional reaction which prevented practical experimentation. Personally, I think that Gestalt psychology and the investigation of those radar operators produced a great deal more than the squadrons of the Occult Revival.

NOTES

General sources:on sensory deprivation: Jack Vernon, *Inside the Black Room. Studies in Sensory Deprivation* (London: Souvenir Press, 1965); Wieland Schmied, ed., *Zeichen des Glaubens: Geist der Avantgarde* (Stuttgart: Electa/Klett-Cotta, 1980); *The Quest* (periodical, London)

[1] Tom Gibbons 'British abstract painting of the 1860s' in *Modern Painters* (periodical, London, 1:2, 1988).

[2] It is worth looking for Georgiana Houghton on the Net. The paintings can be seen at www.vsu.org.au

[3] Annie Besant & C.W. Leadbeater *Thought Forms*, as cited by Gibbons, *op.cit.*

[4] James S. Marshall in *The Quest*, volume 17, 1925, p.398.

[5] W.B. Yeats (ed.) *Oxford Book of Modern Verse 1892–1935* (Oxford: Oxford UP, 1936).

[6] by Herbert Read, 'The End of a War', from Yeats (ed.), *Oxford Book, op.cit.*

[7] Quotations here taken from *Picatrix: un traité de magie médiéval*, traduction, introduction et notes par Béatrice Bakhouche, Frédéric Fauquier et Brigitte Pérez-Jean (Turnhout: Brepols, c.2003). My translation.

[8] from the poem 'Scala Coeli', in Kathleen Raine, *The Hollow Hill and other poems 1960–1964* (London: Hamish Hamilton, 1965). For more on Raine, see my account of *Temenos* in *Origins*, and pages 68–81 of this volume.

The Avant-garde and East Mediterranean Cults

One of the themes of this chapter is the links of the modern avant-garde to Hellenistic and Imperial cults, of roughly 300 BC to 300 AD. This is something I found quite alienating, but the links are undeniable if you look at the primary evidence. Drawing this connection may not help you to understand Modernity, unless you have an expert knowledge of a rather obscure area of Greek culture. Nor is it a kind of proof that avant-garde poetry is superior—comparison is not an argument about quality.

It may be helpful to trace how I stumbled across this idea. After reading Ernst Kitzinger on magical representation in late Roman provincial art, I had written about Roman curses in the late 1980s, and then recognized the same material when writing about Maggie O'Sullivan in 1993.[1] In 1989, I read in Greil Marcus' classic *Lipstick Traces*[2] a comparison of Lettriste sound poetry (a French movement of the 1950s) to Gnostic vowel chanting. In about 1994, I wanted to write a commentary on *Suicide Bridge*[3], by Iain Sinclair, and discovered the paranormal section of Swiss Cottage Library: a whole wall of books, and, as I stood before them, I seemed to spot about ten sources of Sinclair's weird cosmology just from the spines. When I eventually dug up accounts of theurgy and magic, I was surprised at how detailed the links were to the recent avant-garde. There is something about that complex of ideas which makes it tenacious through millennium-long winters of darkness. Mead pointed to this in 1913 and other writers picked it up from him.

The return to these artistic techniques points to the return of a similar vehicle carrying them, and this is no doubt the cult structure, as a fraction which emerges in cities, where old and communal religion has broken down and a kind of free competition of ideas is taking place, inside or outside the law. The affinity of avant-garde groups to sects is fairly clear. The crisis of myth, as the traditional central content of poetry, is still an open question in Western art; one response to it has been the Occult Revival—to use James Webb's term—which shows, rather consistently, a return to the creations of the cults of Syria, Egypt, and neighbouring areas. These cults grew in a milieu with considerable erudition and access to written lore, they were not folk tradition but involved innovation and named, personal, leaders or founders, and they had to co-exist with other sects (inspiring competition, re-conversions, and synthesis). Their remarkable mythological creativity—if compared with 1700 years of dogmatic and governmental Christianity—invites comparison with the avant-garde of the last two centuries.

Trying to work out the relations between the Greek intellectual tradition upheld by Proclus, the Egyptian traditions embodied in the various redactions of *The Book of the Dead*, the late Egyptian material of the *Corpus Hermeticum*, the star-worshipping traditions of Syria and Mesopotamia, and the nether strata of folk magic, is a task which could take up someone's entire life. All of this material composes a *world*—one distinct from the Christian cultural current, and the current of Classical polytheism and philosophy, which we learned about at school. The flavour of this world derives from the urban nature of its setting: sect leaders living in the large and ethnically mixed cities of the eastern Mediterranean had access to different religious traditions, and because they were literate they could acquire great knowledge of the sacred texts. The word *syncretistic* is applied to describe the cross-fertilisation of ideas in those cities; which means both plagiarism, and individual creativity, as sect leaders broke away from tradition and constantly wrote new sacred texts. Part of the reason why Christianity won is that it had organs of discipline, which meant that dogma was petrified and enforced; whereas the Gnostics, for example, had a decentralised intellectual and mythological creativity, doctrines evolving wildly and without restraint.

Here I find utterly beautiful poetry and myths, as a kind of niche product within a mass of religious writing which is tedious, obscure and pedantic. To take one example—

> Submit not to thy mind earth's vast measures, for that the plant of truth grows not on the earth, and measure not the course of the sun by joining rods, for that he moves in accordance with the will eternal of the Father, not for the sake of thee. Let go the moon's sound; she ever runs by operation of necessity. The stars' procession was not brought forth for sake of thee. The wide-winged aerial flight of birds is never true, nor yet the slicings of the victims and of other entrails. These are all toys, lending support to mercenary fraud. Flee thou these things if thou wouldst enter true worship's paradise, where Virtue, Wisdom

and Good-Rule are met together.[4]
(Oracle, as quoted by Psellus, translated by Lewy)

Insofar as these cults tried to explain the nature of the physical universe, they were utterly wrong, and the details of their arguments are wearisome as well as inherently worthless. We should also mention the music, which is of great interest although of course it has disappeared, and the ritual acts, which may have had a beauty of their own. This approach of picking up what is beautiful while leaving the bad science behind may strike some people as frivolous. However, it is surely better than throwing out what is beautiful while picking up and preserving the bad science.

Richard Reitzenstein has evoked for us, in a classic section of *Hellenistische Wundererzählungen*[5], the crowd-pleasing *aretalogi* who were the carriers of portable cultic ideas. Their name clearly indicates that they originally narrated the wonderful deeds (aretai) of gods, vouchsafed to them in dreams; but the way in which the noun is used by Roman writers shows that they were seen as popular entertainers, as fluent tellers of lies. Clearly, these people were the forerunners of hot-gospellers, fortune-tellers, and daytime TV, as well as of the avant-garde. Were the verbal wares they were peddling similar to what we have, still surviving, in the rare manuscripts of Hermetic, Gnostic, and Neoplatonist works? This is unanswerable, since the Roman satirists did not record the patter of the aretalogi. We have a clue in the theme of astrology—this certainly is something which came to Italy from the Near East, and which embodies the ancient knowledge of Syria and Mesopotamia, as well as the fundamental ideas of Neoplatonism. It may be that they related to the great texts as the sermons of friars relate to Christian theology. Alternatively, it may be that the ancient Mediterranean was so rich in religious ideas that the aretalogi were quite unrelated to the mages of Alexandria, Harran, and Antioch.

It may be worth dwelling briefly on the operative stratum of this world of cults—the magic which was supplied on customer demand, and which adopted the delicate intellectual structures to a lower end. The figure of the fortune-teller may be illuminating here. The doctrine of influences allowed the thought of influencing the fates by appropriate actions here on earth. The apparatus of talismans, curses, spells, etc. travelled much more easily than the difficult ideas of Gnosticism (for example), and it is at this humble (and illegal) level of operative magic that we find traces of the cults in Europe—and even in Roman Britain. It is worth pointing out that talismans, inscribed curses, etc. are part of the very earliest by-products of literacy—and a way in which the literate could extort revenue from the illiterate.

It's easy to forget that most people in that old Mediterranean world were illiterate, and that there was an ocean of spoken creativity, flowing over everyday life, which has foundered, leaving only what was written down. The image of all those charlatans competing with each other is what encourages me to enjoy the surviving syncretistic writings, bizarre and ill-founded as they are. If the imperative of attracting people was written deeply into the rules of the game, this explains why so much of this cult discourse is so striking and even beautiful. This would also nudge us towards thinking that its revival over the last 150 years has had to do with aesthetic charm and formal fertility, as opposed to some religious conviction. Perhaps illiterates didn't think they needed the written word— they already had everything they needed to know, from the talkers in the market-place.

The cults may answer a puzzle, to do with the abdication of the primary urban communities of the old Near East as the intellectual centre of the world. A rapid-fire version of history has them simply switching off as the Greeks switch on. The Greek intellectual breakthrough had to do with alphabetical writing, meaning that a far higher share of the population could learn to read—it was like the invention of printing, changing the basic economics of knowledge. Criticism and scepticism were made much easier. The Greek world includes South Italy, and so Europe starts, circa 500 BC, to arrive on the scene. But maybe the diagnosis is different—the urban centres of the Near East continued to be creative, and to produce texts and readers in abundance, only that there was an essential loss of continuity, perhaps a leap forward, which means that we don't recognise the ethnic-geographical basis of the new writing—and don't read it, because it is not on our syllabus (aimed at rapid results). The arrival of an alphabet may have undermined the older writing forms, syllabaries and hieroglyphics. Cuneiform, after a 3,000 year history, came to a catastrophic halt. This shift may have disrupted the handing down of ancient knowledge, and encouraged new forms of recording and disseminating knowledge—new structures. The gnosis which preoccupied so many people may have been a projection of the "old" knowledge—a legend of secrets kept by the priests of the old cult centres, now in eclipse. One of these may have been the secret of eternal life—as claimed by the Egyptians. The Egyptian hieroglyphs were wholly forgotten, and an entire corpus of knowledge, going back to 3,000 B.C., vanished with them. There was, in all these countries, a twilight, where old-fashioned groups preserved the old knowledge—and could sell it. Gnosis was not thought to be found in Greece and Italy, the homes of a later, disenchanted, alphabetically based system of learning. In the end, the whole Near East migrated to alphabetical writing. Mostly, this was Aramaic, followed by Greek. Mani (3rd century AD, founder of Manichaeanism) may stand as the type figure of an Aramaic-writing creator—whose work has mostly vanished, due to systematic purging by the Christians, but has also spread as far as Mongolia (to which the Aramaic alphabet, *estrangelo*, also spread). Clearly, his work is not "art" in a secular sense, but Manichaean poetry is beautiful.[6]

A satisfying account of the transformation of the traditional Egyptian world into the "late" world of Roman times, and the bulky textual series which we call "Hermetic" is supplied in the Czech scholar Jan Assmann's *Ägypten. Eine Sinngeschichte*.[7] He has given solid reasons for linking the *Corpus Hermeticum* with the ancient, pre-Greek traditions of Egypt. Not all its parts belong together. The whole *Corpus Hermeticum* is attributed to Hermes (=the Egyptian god of writing, Thoth). Thoth was the author of the *Book of the Dead*. So the whole Hermetic literature may be a translation of the salvation knowledge of the *Book of the Dead* into Greek letters and vocabulary. I said translation but, as far as we can tell, it is mainly a weird transformation or affabulation, somewhere between a new creation and a hoax. In Hellenistic times, the whole region must have been full of books nobody could read.

The great rock critic Greil Marcus compares the sound poetry of the Lettristes to 'Gnostic vowel harmonies'. He does not give details, but, drifting around the darker reaches of Mediterranean culture, I stumbled across bibliographical references to surviving traces of these lost and occult arts. A key quote is from a book on music by the Pythagorean Nicomachus of Gerasa: "hissing and lipsmacking and inarticulate and discordant sounds they call 'in code'". (I quoted this in a previous book, and I apologise for the repetition.) This does seem like an exact match for the Lettristes and for their offshoots in England. Key sources—I can only give a sketchy account—would include Hans Lewy's *Chaldaean Oracles and Theurgy*, Dornseiff's *Das Alphabet in Mystik und Magie*, Höpfner's *Griechisch-Ägyptischer Offenbarungszauber*.[8] Detailed recovery of these oral practices is impossible without direct recordings of sound, but the snatches we do have recorded using letters of the alphabet point to creations clearly anticipating modern sound and concrete poetry, and to a cultivation of autonomous sound, perhaps entirely in the sphere of working magic, conjuring up the gods, and evoking trances. The Neoplatonist cosmology had outer space filled with sound, so that not only did sound come down from the stars (moving in spirals, *heiligden*), and the gods could speak through human throats, but also the gods could be called down by calls (*epikleses*), a practice called theurgy. In 1909, Aleister Crowley and Victor Neuburg went into the Algerian desert and used some of these calls to summon up spirits, with results which remain controversial to this day. A body of poems revealed by the gods through human vessels was available to Proclus, and known as the Chaldaean Oracles. It describes the structure of the universe. The whole cosmos was supposed to be full of sound, and worshippers could chant meaningless syllables which corresponded to these *arreta onomata* (unspeakable names). Uncoded sound thus played a major role in this religion, where the structure of the universe corresponded to unreasoned sound (*asemous ekhous*) rather than reasoned sound (or *logos*). The relics we have of these words show the same sound structures which Jakobson identified in the Khlysty. Special roles are played, in this scheme, by repetitive and wordless sounds pronounced by humans—and also by sounds chosen automatically by devices, such as spinning-tops with characters written on them. The use of randomness is another preoccupation of the avant-garde.

Although the key texts as we have them are in Greek, part of the interest of these heterodox ideas is that they come from other East Mediterranean cultures, and preserve elements of ancient and rich cultures, which are not part of the mainstream of "our" cultural past. Proclus had oracles in a Greek text, but knew they were Chaldaean.

One of the incantations printed by Preisendanz[9] is described as *pterugoeides*, in the shape of a wing: a tapering form, like a wing understood as tapering continuously from base to tip:

> akrakanarba
> kanarba
> anarba
> narba
> arba
> rba
> ba
> a.

This well evokes the design principle of these things, without meaning but with a high degree of formal elaboration and symmetry. Another group is sets of vowels, known as the heptaphthong or 'seven sounds' because there were seven vowels in Greek. These are shown in repeated clusters which, in recitation, surely anticipate sound poetry. For example: Iaeo aeeiouo ouoieea khabrax phnesker phix phnurophokhobokh ablanathanalba akrammakhamari sesengenbarpharanges. These are the rigmaroles which Greil Marcus was thinking of. For lack of letters I have obscured the distinction between long and short e and o in Greek—the clusters of seven vowels are actually seven distinct vowels, i.e. the heptaphthong.

To understand how these practices came about, perhaps we have to think of the economics of the intellectual. Suppose, in the first century BC, you learn how to read and write in the Mediterranean. You acquire a formal education, reading the classics—and also, perhaps, the scriptures of certain cults and sects. A philosophical education is rightly the apanage of a land-owner's son, suited to fill his life of leisure; but many people acquired an education who had no estates, and no serfs. They had to apply their knowledge to putting food on the table. What we see in the magical papyrus—collected by d'Anastasi around 1820—is full of theatrical show. If a spell has to be written in a special ink (made with the soot from a goldsmith's workshop and dragon's blood, juice of a plant called dragon) that impresses the customers, but do we really think that the gods are pleased by such things? The Oracles are beautiful in themselves:

> 'Rush to the centre of the roaring light.'
> 'Cast in the mind the watchwords of the manifold universe, and move with a firm step towards the fiery rays.'
> 'But there is a long path of the fiery god, winding spiralwise, sounding. Whoever has touched the ethereal fire of that God, cannot tear his heart away from it; for it has no power to burn.'

Raine believed in the Ancient Knowledge to such an extent that she felt her own poetry must be great if it corresponded to it; passing over the notion that the reader could become bored, and had to be shown something continuously interesting. She didn't appreciate the basic theatrical values of the world of cults and so failed to adapt these wonderful, if highly archaic, resources into a poetry which was exciting rather than pious, credulous, and dogmatic. At some phases of her career the dogma caught fire, or loosened its grip, and allowed her to write genuinely persuasive poetry. The thought does occur that modern poets have seized on these flashy, exotic, but ultimately meaningless lumps of language because the poets are as excited by flashy effects as the demons were supposed to be. This is perhaps saying something about modern poetry. Maybe there are no deep or abiding structures in the universe, and the specious and exciting is all that art has to work with.

The Neoplatonism which Giordano Bruno believed in is really a form of magic, not a kind of philosophy. It was practiced by people who were also Platonists, notably Proclus, but most of it derived from non-Greek religions of the Middle East, sometimes very ancient ones. As Frances Yates pointed out in *Giordano Bruno and the Hermetic Tradition*[10], great parts of the systems of Bruno and Tommaso Campanella were taken from the astral magic of

*Picatrix.*This had a great deal in common with the ideas which Proclus absorbed in the fifth century AD. (Yates had previously written a study of *Love's Labour's Lost*[11], a parody of a group now labelled The School of Night, where a link between occultism and innovative poetry may already be observed.) A starry sky is an unresolvable and endlessly complex visual pattern, and it is not surprising that star-gazers see spontaneous patterns there. This may be a clue as to the foundations of Neoplatonism.

It would be incorrect to consider the Neoplatonic universe, filled with sound, and governing itself by sound, without grounding this in real sensory experiences of formless, boundless, and apparently infinite sound, heard here on earth as part of theurgical rites. The music described was recognisable by reference to actual sense-experiences, not plucked out of nowhere as a tenuous speculation. The theology may actually indicate to us that these musics, overwhelming in their impact, were the undoing of reason. In fact, we might guess that a musical breakthrough was the primary thing, and that the theology was a later attempt to explain the effect it had on people. Allen Fisher writes:

> there is a sonorous architecture
> overlapping the outline of streets
> and buildings   field and centres
> re-enforcing   counteracting
> the attractive or repulsive tone of
> this place
>   (from *Place* XX)[12]

The idea of a resonance of ideas, of linkage through similarity of form, haunted the twentieth century. Allen Fisher has described the central concept of *Place* (the central work of the English underground during the 1970s) as the acausal asynchronous principle described by Jung, which Jung saw as a break with western science. Allen could have attributed these links to the associational threads of the brain, sticking then inside the materialist world-view and fathering complexity and simultaneity on the anatomy of the brain. I must admit that the brain seems well capable of this kind of link. But, Jung wanted a breach with materialist science. His principle, which I don't think anyone believes in any more, belongs inside a Neoplatonist view of the cosmos, based on analogy and on the abolition of distance as a limit on interaction. It was expounded in a paper given to the Eranos gathering in Ascona—about which I have written in an earlier book.[13]

Olga Froebe-Kapteyn, organiser of Eranos, was a friend of G.R.S. Mead (1863–1933), not only the pioneer translator into English of a great deal of Hermetic and Gnostic material, rich resources of Near Eastern occult lore, but also a Theosophist and a Spiritualist. He represents the continuity, possibly unwelcome to other types of Modernist, between a late Symboliste milieu at the end of the nineteenth century, and the 1930s. He edited, 1909–30, a magazine called *The Quest*. We may not *like* to see small-circulation occultist magazines as the forerunners of small-circulation poetry magazines, nor to see Modernism as an offshoot of *Symbolisme*, loaded with magical, Spiritualist, and hermetic beliefs—but we should make sure of our facts.

Another major figure of Eranos, over the years, was Henry Corbin, who wrote two fascinating evocations of the meetings. He was the subject of a 60-page paper by Eric Mottram, in an issue of the magazine *Talus*. Material from Corbin's writings on Iranian religion (Sohravardi) found its way into a little-read Mottram poem ('Peace Project 4')—along with a poem, *The Pearl*, which had been published in translation by Mead in 1908. (He produced a second translation of it in 1926, and it would seem that *The Quest* was linked in Mead's mind with the quest which takes place in this poem.) Corbin was also the elective ancestor—he died before it was started!—of *Temenos* magazine, edited by Kathleen Raine. It is a little surprising to find this point of contact between a figure devoted to progress and reason, like Mottram, and a group decisively influenced by neo-occultism. It surprised me because I had the wrong map. Corbin studied the Neoplatonist elements which passed into Islamic mysticism, and was very well aware of the parallel Neoplatonist elements in submerged Western thinkers like Bruno, Boehme, Swedenborg, and Blake. I personally have often under-rated the Blakean elements in the English and American avant-garde, because they don't suit my view of the universe.

It is easy to see Bruno's trip to England in 1583 as a failure, with his obvious successors, Thomas Vaughan and Robert Fludd, as vagrants on a by-way of history, an eccentric path which led nowhere. The advance of science was rapid, and led, after the founding of the Royal Society, to the creation of powerful and coherent institutions for sharing accurate knowledge (in which Bruno played no part). But maybe it's not that simple. Maybe there has been a current of anti-scientific thought, nourishing to its pupils, which preserved the ideas of Fludd and Vaughan, nourished Blake, and was never interrupted, all the way up till its appalling flowering in the 1960s. If you start looking for rejected knowledge—maybe there is an awful lot of it. The by-way doesn't just lead you nowhere—it leads you there again and again and again and again.

Frances Yates looked at the kinds of device described in Fludd's work and observed that they were mostly useful for theatrical machinery and that their use would make possible something very close to what Inigo Jones really did for successive Stuart kings. At that time high technology was associated with Courts rather than with corporations, with theatrical illusion rather than with manufacturing production. If we go forward two centuries, we find a similar link of occultism and optics in the work of William Fox Talbot, inventor of the photographic print. Chemistry means, historically, the Egyptian art (from Kemt, the 'black land'), a reference to its connection with the arts of Hermes Trismegistus. Talbot's trapping of light in silver glaze could be seen as a capture of Platonic radiance flitting through the universe, a visual proof of the geometric influences which are the real fabric of the apparent world. Talbot produced a book of photographs showing *The Talbotype Applied to Hieroglyphs*.[14]

James Keery's research on *The White Stones*[15] turned up a Bible scholar who compared the "white stones" (*psephos*, in the original, *Revelations* 2:12–17) to Gnostic amulets, sometimes inscribed with spells which allowed the owner to penetrate the seven walls of death and reach the New Life—which is indeed the theme of *Revelations*.

Part of section VIII of Allen Fisher's *Place* series goes:

> who are the dodmen   the snails   the surveyors
>   no longer with horns   or dowsing wands
>   no longer tracing the earth in lung-mei & ley

stretching the globe
or as Manzoni   encircling the earth
who are you now that would draw the St.Michael line

from Avebury circle to the extreme southwest[16]

Considerable light is shed on this passage by two books published by
Abacus at the end of the 60s: *The Pattern of the Past*, by Guy Underwood,
and *The View over Atlantis*, by John Michell.[17] Both books were preoccupied
with spirals—and a spiral is the organising concept for the movement of
Place. The Chaldaean Oracles twice refer to spiral movement: of Time,
heilicoeides, of influences from the stars, *heiligden*,—both adverbs meaning
'spirally' (and deriving from *helix*, literally, a snail). Snails play a large role
in Michell's iconography, following Watkins' crazy suggestion that the
name Dodman Hill (snail hill) compared a Neolithic surveyor, holding
two staves, to the horns of a snail. It seems possible, then, that there is
a Neoplatonist element in Fisher's work. *The way hill serpents slept/ on
religious spins of force* (from *Place* VII) is more specifically based on Michell's
beliefs in a completely man-made Neolithic landscape, in spirals connected
to the dragons of Chinese *feng shui* theories—as he explains, *lung mei*
means dragon current. Underwood was a dowser and saw the spiral as
part of the unidentified 'energy field' which made dowsing work. *Picatrix*
talks about an ideal city whose geometry is in line with the stars and so
channels the influence of the stars in the most beneficial way. This idea
was copied in some detail by Giordano Bruno and Tommaso Campanella.
Michell took this idea of universal fluxes of energy, needing *lenses*, but
he or his predecessors adapted it to an English ideology, removing the
city and moving it to a rural setting. H.J. Massingham had—in his 1926
book *Downland Man*[18]—looked at the artificial hill, 130 feet high, at Silbury,
and decided that the whole landscape of the Downs was the product of
deliberate engineering by Neolithic peoples. The political urge behind the
cult of Neolithic, pre-urban monuments was to exalt the village and make
out that everything wrong in history derived from urbanisation. This idea
was welcome to a large audience, and can be found in a wide sector of
English cultural thinking during the nineteenth and twentieth centuries.
Massingham was a believer in Diffusionism, a kind of New Age delusion

of the 1920s, and thought that all civilisation had diffused from Egypt, while Silbury Hill was "a perfect replica in earth" of the Pyramids of Egypt. Belief in the magical powers of the Great Pyramid was the source of 'sacred geometry'. Both Underwood and Michell are dealing in broken-down Neoplatonic concepts.

Michell's evocation of the British countryside as a spiral showing the flux lines of a force-field is the projection of Neoplatonist theory into the landscape. The detection of zodiac signs in features of the landscape is a give-away. The transfer of interest from cities (as in *Picatrix*) to the whole countryside was led by ley lines, a false concept invented by Alfred Watkins in 1925.[19] Watkins' original vision, however, parallelled ideas about prehistoric trackways being developed in the same year by Massingham, and published in *Downland Man*.The belief in the occult powers of buildings (now called sacred geometry) is simply the natural magic of Bruno, and was common in the milieu which produced Michell— for example, in the publications of RILKO.[20] For Michell, all the hills are artificial power stations for channelling this energy (and were also built by use of it). There is no evidence for his theory—but, if your reason gives way and you accept it, the existence of hills becomes evidence for it, and their shapes show the wavelength of the vibration which shaped them.

Underwood and Michell have in common a preoccupation with spirals, and this is possibly what drew their work into the ambit of *Place*, which was already about a spiral. Both movements I and III of *Place* have a great deal to do with the rivers of London, and obstructions to them, seen as analogies to obstructions in the flow of various things within the body—the poet's migraine, for example. This concept of analogy and the restoration of harmony harks back to *Picatrix*—the sidestep into the way rivers and springs flow is owed to Underwood. However, tracing a lot of possible leads has convinced me that Neoplatonism is only one strand in Fisher's work, and that his interest in geometry is not occultist in origin.

The sects had access to the secrets of the universe through oracles, but did not conduct experiments or otherwise seek for evidence supplied by the senses. There is no reason, then, to believe their account of what happens in outer space. If these energies cannot be shown to make toast when required, it may be they did not shape hills.

Both the void and the irrational excess of pattern play key roles in modern art. Defining these roles would take a long build-up. I have listed a number of spiral visions, which suggests to me that the presence of spiral themes points to spontaneous visual imagery. By 'spontaneous' I mean detached from impinging light, a visual form of the void. Paisley patterns are the product of free imagination, not copying from natural forms. I would suggest that the pervasive and repeating patterns which Watkins and Michell "saw" were not there in the visible world, but were part of the cognitive structure with which their brains dealt with the world. The fact that Watkins saw straight lines everywhere, while Michell saw spirals, suggests that what they "saw" is not there in the visible world. Visual phenomena, in the area where *visual* has stopped overlapping with *visible*. The reason that you see one pattern everywhere is that the threshhold at which your pattern recognition response is triggered has dropped—perhaps due to fatigue or perhaps to elation. This can be a beautiful moment. An archaeologist who sees things which aren't there has been defeated—but a poet who can make his readers see more patterns and respond more easily has won.

At another level, if you look from a hill at a wide stretch of landscape, you do see lots of repeating patterns—both spirals and straight lines, in vast quantities. But you can also see equally vast numbers of all the other shapes in the pattern library. What went wrong with the para-archaeologists was not their eyesight, but in the software in their brains which deals with pattern recognition.

So, what do we have?

Removing the scaffolding of discursive structure shoots us into a different world of unstructured association. This relies on a state of suggestibility. The emptiness of certain poems may be necessary to draw on this state— just as the noise of rational, instrumental, business language may be enough to numb it and kill it.

The emptiness is linked to powers of boundlessly ramifying association—which we find worked-out in vivid detail in pictures such as the Neoplatonist image of interstellar space, aswirl with sounds. We can easily imagine a universe of swirling shapes—or sounds, endlessly spinning out new forms, and only disappearing where they are blocked and overwritten by solid, realistic, representational forms. Reason lives in the devastation of what came before it. Conversely, most of the methods of poetry may have as their goal the removal of functional thought patterns and the lowering of resistance to suggestion and association.

All this is not an argument able to prove the merits of the avant-garde. The reader will have to decide whether they like modern-style poetry, like that of Tom Raworth or Adrian Clarke, or not. Talking about the state of high suggestibility and free association is irrelevant to someone who is blocked off from entering that state, and simply experiences frustration and numbness when faced with abstract painting, or non-discursive poetry. I do want to point out, though, that this associative poetry is not hard work, it actually involves switching off the part of your mind that does the work. Free association is what follows the abandonment of effort—as effort meant the repression of all associational paths except the most orthodox, authorised, and production-oriented ones. There is an argument that poetry which is the most dissimilar to tax law (say the Tax Credits Act, 2002) is the purest poetry, and more likely to achieve the proper effects of poetry than poetry which is still 50 or 60% similar to tax law. Realistic poetry is just unable to lead you into a state of visionary well-being.

The parallel universe of free association is there all the time, but we cannot get access to it all the time. The poem does not bring it into being, but only opens a door into it. The door is not there every time we come to look for it. It is as if it were hidden underwater—we have to dive to find it.

There is an implicit question which we need to resolve: is Modernism a branch of occultism? It is hard to deny that Mondrian was influenced (at one stage) by Theosophy, but almost impossible to assert that most of the thousands of abstract painters who have created since Mondrian have had any involvement with Theosophical doctrines at all. For this reason, it would be disastrously misleading to leave readers with the impression that avant-garde poets and abstract painters in general draw their inspiration from any esoteric doctrines—or even know what these doctrines say. But, we have to go one step further down this path in order to realise why the resemblance exists. I believe that the key is this: hyperassociation induced by emptiness. In the world of modern art, any two ideas are adjacent, and jumps between physically remote things are normal. However, there has to be some kind of shape analogy to trigger the associative jump. This principle of things of similar shape having an occult connection obviously resembles the Neoplatonist idea that the heavens influence the earth, through the principle of similarity of shape, and that shape is then the lens by which rays of influence from infinitely far away are focussed. Since the brain associates disparate things of similar shape, links between similar things, however remote, are present in every human mind, and it is superfluous to suppose that there is a physical link. Any living human brain is capable of free association. It is not something you have to learn. Modern doctrines of association, based on *Symbolisme*, have nothing to do with physics. Physics just supplies a metaphor. The influences are taking place in inner space. It is futile to think that by disproving Neoplatonist ideas of physics you invalidate modern art.

A different place belongs to poets who certainly cultivated the occult, such as Kathleen Raine and Peter Redgrove. The distance between them and modern poets in general is part of the common sense of the poetry community. They were not respected by their colleagues as thinkers. Much of Raine's poetry demands a literal acceptance of Neoplatonist theories of influence from the stars. Redgrove's description of a comet, in his last book, includes a phrase about 'vibrating reeds'. The idea that anything in space vibrates is truly bizarre. I am still wondering if this echoes the Chaldaean phrase about the throat as a flute (*aule*) when it vibrates with the words from outer space. Raine's poetry is based on Neoplatonist concepts.

There may be moreover a whole cognitive procedural set needed for creating verbal art, that is departing from simple recording of observations in a rigid and agreed framework. One can be talented at subjective action, or untalented. This procedure set need only detain us insofar as it offers explanations helpful to the reader, who is presumably capable of reacting subjectively once inside the poem. Neoplatonism may have been, back in the 2nd century AD, a brilliant, philosophically informed and as it were rationally post-rational, interpretation of this set of procedures. Which is why it keeps cropping up. Its relationship to an archaic, illiterate, and magical world of the Mediterranean Bronze Age or New Stone Age is tantalising but need not preoccupy us at this moment.

Maybe we could see Eric Mottram as a modern syncretist—his awesome lists of "resources" seem to support this. His use of *The Pearl*, a Syriac poem from the Christian *Acts of St Thomas*, is an example of this. This was the subject of an extensive essay by Reitzenstein[21], shortly after being translated into English by G.R.S. Mead. The poem is labelled as the hymn sung by the Judas Thomas, the twin of Jesus, while in prison in India. Mottram's quote from the poem is in 'Peace Project 4', published in *Angel Exhaust* in 1986, and goes like this:

> I saw my stature had grown to sit the way it was made
> and in its regal movement it spread over me
> simplicity in bi-unity
> a robe of light inexpressible
> in categories of language
> Poimandres speaks here
> daimon paredros protector
> lamb over his shoulders
> head haloed by seven planets
> sun and moon at his sides
> syzygies of light

The "stature" is the external self of the narrator, a feature of Gnostic-Manichaean beliefs. *Paredros* is another name for this double. In fact, the last 70 lines of the poem are an adaptation of *The Pearl*, along with some commentary on the technical (Manichaean) vocabulary used. Poimandres (shepherd of man) was a spiritual leader, and the name of a treatise in the *Corpus Hermeticum*. We are already outside the realm of 'The Pearl', and 'Peace Projects 4' is a syncretistic work. Mottram's source must be a work of prose, probably by Corbin (two of whose books he gives as 'resources' in the book version of *Peace Projects*). Syzygy translates into Latin as *conjunction*, and refers to the conjunction of two heavenly bodies, for example as creating a high tide; but also to the marriage, specifically of two doubles (self and paredros), the end of their separation. (This concerns the relationship of Jesus to his twin, Thomas, in the text.) Light is the symbol of pure being, what the soul is made of; an idea shared by many different cults. (I suspect that Froebe-Kapteyn—a friend of Mead, according to Eliade—had been a member of the Quest Society.) Coincidentally, I produced a version of 'The Pearl' at one point—using an existing English translation; which is why I recognised Mottram's use of it. It is really a very beautiful thing. Mottram's account of it is typically obscure, awkward, and too fast to follow—he destroys the wonderful surface of the text in favour of violent jump-cuts (or, as we must now call them, syncretisms).

The history of *The Pearl* is a strange one. It seems to be a Christian poem, although using a mythology we hardly recognise. Mead identified it as Gnostic and by Bardaisan, but Han Drijvers' work on Syrian religion has shown that the *Acts of Thomas* are not Gnostic in any distinct sense. Drijvers relates both the *Acts* and the *Pearl* poem to other Christian texts from the same city (Edessa) and of around the same date, and shows that the central imagery is common, and not heretical. Mani took the imagery he used for his Syriac poetry from the Syriac Christian texts—and considered himself to be a prophet of Christ. The maximum view of *The Pearl* is that its quest theme is the original of all Western Romance quest stories, and especially the Quest for the Holy Grail. In any case we are bound to admire thinkers who are dedicated to the search for the unknown rather than to the peddling of fixed and static knowledge.

NOTES

General sources: Hans Lewy *Chaldean Oracles and Theurgy* (Paris: Études Augustiniennes, 1978); Franz Dornseiff, *Das Alphabet in Mystik und Magie* (Leipzig, B.G. Teubner, 1922); Theodor Höpfner, *Griechisch-Ägyptischer Offenbarungszauber* (Leipzig, H. Hässel Verlag, 1921); H.J.W. Drijvers, *East of Antioch* (London: Variorum Reprints, 1984). Be warned that these ancient texts have survived without much context, so that terms like 'Gnostic' and 'Neoplatonist' suggest a degree of systematic understanding which we do not have. For example, Lewy's definition of the 'Chaldaean oracles' includes many texts which other scholars would keep separate. Sect leaders produced syncretistic theologies—i.e. massively plagiarised other sects. See Peter Green, *Alexander to Actium: The Historical Evolution of the Hellenistic Age* for the historical background (Berkeley: University of California Press, 1990).

[1] A revised version of this is included in this book, pp.266-275.

[2] Greil Marcus *Lipstick Traces: A Secret History of the Twentieth Century* (Cambridge, MA: Harvard University Press, 1989).

[3] Iain Sinclair: *Suicide Bridge* (London: Albion Village Press, 1979); reissued with *Lud Heat* as *Lud Heat and Suicide Bridge* (London: Granta Books, 2003). See also my commentary on this book in *Origins of the Underground*.

[4] Hans Lewy *op.cit.*

[5] Richard Reitzenstein *Hellenistische Wundererzählungen* (Leipzig, B.G. Teubner, 1910).

[6] for a text of 'The Pearl' see http://www.gnosis.org/library/hymnpearl.htm

[7] Jan Assmann *Ägypten: Eine Sinngeschichte* (Munich: Carl Hanser Verlag, 1996).

[8] Lewy: see note 4.

[9] Karl Preisendanz *Papyri Graecae Magicae. Die Griechischen Zauberpapyri* (Leipzig & Berlin: B.G. Teubner, 1932).

[10] Frances A. Yates *Giordano Bruno and the Hermetic Tradition* (London: Routledge & Kegan Paul, 1964).

[11] Frances A. Yates *A Study of Love's Labour's Lost* (Cambridge: Cambridge University Press, 1936).

[12] Allen Fisher: *Place* (Hastings: Reality Street Editions, 2005), p.72.

[13] The *Eranos-Jahrbuch* (periodical, Zürich: Rhein-Verlag). Some further information about the Eranos, and related topics, in my *Origins of the Underground* (Cambridge: Salt, 2008).

[14] On Fox Talbot & Neoplatonism, see Mike Weaver, *The Photographic Art* (London: The Herbert Press, 1986).

[15] J.H. Prynne *The White Stones* (Lincoln: Grosseteste Press, 1969).

[16] Allen Fisher: *Place*, p.51.

[17] Guy Underwood *The Pattern of the Past* (London: Abacus, 1972). Paul Screeton, *Quicksilver Heritage* (London: Abacus, 1977); John Michell *The View over Atlantis* (London: Abacus, 1977). If you find yourself agreeing with these books, seek psychiatric help.

[18] H.J. Massingham *Downland Man* (London: Jonathan Cape, 1926).

[19] see Richard Hayman, *Riddles in Stone* (London: Hambledon, 1997).

[20] Research Into Lost Knowledge Organisation.

[21] Reitzenstein *Hellenistische Wundererzählungen, op.cit.*

CONTAMINATION CHAMBER
OR, THE PROBLEM OF DEPOLARISATION

Following excerpts from an email conversation with *Argotist* editor Jeff Side about the possibilities of dialogue between parts of the poetry spectrum:

"God, I'm so sceptical about bulletin boards. And yet the structure of threads and dialogue is so organic. It makes essays look monolithic and (maybe) authoritarian.

I found it distressing. I would like mutual understanding. But these people get asked to think theoretically for ten seconds and they say "I have to go and feed the rabbit". Without attentiveness a shared dialogue is strictly a waste of time. As for whoever it was demanded that you read his book and then prove to him that it was populist, this is arrogant—why should anyone have to go and read his stupid book.

The reason I would not get stuck into a thread like this is that if people are thinking about different books of poetry when they speak, then no dialogue takes place. The idea of a court in which different judges have access to different and non-overlapping sets of evidence is simply ludicrous.

The idea of a dialogue between mainstream and underground, intellectual and downdumbed, Left and Right, English and Welsh (etc.) remains attractive. The preconception that such a dialogue would lead to greater mutual understanding seems quite unconvincing. The key is not in the generosity of the competitors *(sic)* but in the procedures followed. Using shared texts is essential here. A and B must be talking about the same thing. They must both have read it, have access to it in memory, etc.

The fan-out of the market offer is a wonderful thing. It's hard to conceive how few books there were around even in the 1950s. But when people can follow a line of "lifestyle choices" and head off over the horizon it's no good thinking that they can then talk to other poetry fans who haven't shared those experiences.

I think there might be a project of devising procedures so that a public debate could be held.

I could argue that everyone is 'self-realised' and has nothing to gain, but we have to ask whether anyone could find their way through the market without knowledge of the goods on offer. It seems then that we need a consumer's guide which overarches the cultural divisions. Proper debate would be a process which should reach fruition before such a guide could be assembled.

These botched dialogues are a model of how the poem itself can be botched and fail."

Jeff and I were talking about a discussion thread in a web forum for mainstream poets. Communication in this 'open' forum was just making them more extreme and less self-aware. As they acquired group cohesion, their stereotypes of every other group just became more and more distorted. Jeff Side uttered one or two deviant views and was subjected to group bullying. The more the forum flowed, the more unfriendly it became to anyone else. Group narcissism was stifling any intellectual process.

Let me quote something Ted Hughes said—"It was even worse bad luck for Shakespeare's language that the crippled court-artifice of Restoration speech should have been passed on to the military garrison of the Empire, where the desirable ideal of speech for all Englishmen became the shrunken, atrophied, suppressive-of-everything-under, bluffing, debonair, frivolous system of vocal team-calls, which we inherit as Queen's English."[1]

This is obvious rubbish. The phenomena he describes may actually exist, but they are wholly separate from each other. The 450 years of social history he is apparently describing have no unity; fashion changed all the time and groups not dominated by fashion spoke in extremely varied ways. Besides, the majority of Shakespeare's plays take place at courts, and among the entourages of kings, and his general style is courtly and full of artifice. All the same, I think this is indicative of how teenage poets think—driven by panic, the primitive levels of the brainstem bypassing the cortex to produce rapid, synthesizing reactions of flight and lust.[2] Presumably all poets go through a stage before they have written any good poems and before they have a style of their own. Readers, no less cogently,

221

form confused, over-excited, imperious, irresistible fantasies about the meaning of style. At least, that is how I remember it. These give the terms of the primary response to poetry—the tier which is motivated enough to read new poetry, the zone where the legends are formed. Such reckless irrationality is energetic enough to shout down the evidence and burst out into a self-validating authority. What Hughes is describing is really his anxiety fantasy about a reader rejecting his poetry. Ideas about style are a precious residue separated out from personal, overheated, and confused over-experiencing of being rejected. Hughes was as it were ejected into deeply exotic space by his horror of writing in a moderate and cultured way.

The anxiety fantasy is counterbalanced by dreams of splendour. The same book by Keith Sagar which gives us the Hughes quote I used above has a positive statement about Hughes, reading in part:

> It is a return to an alliterative poetry that, pounding, brutal and earth-bound, challenges the latinate politeness of artificial society with ruthless energy and cunning, and so drags the latinate words into its unruly, self-ruling world that even *they* come to sound northern and Germanic. [...] by asserting the naked, deeper rhythms of our Germanic [...] heritage, Ted Hughes is taking the English language back to its roots.[3]

This is from an unpublished essay by A.S. Crehan, and gets to the heart of the matter. This is the fantasy of Hughesian poetry. Further, Hughes' work is much more totally the realisation of the hughesian fantasy than other poets are the realisation of any vision whatsoever. Crehan is saying that, by reverting to a prosody based on consonantal harmonies, Hughes is vaunting the Saxon or Danish way of thinking (of the eighth to fourteenth centuries?) and rejecting everything—cultural, political, or linguistic—which arrived later. (Of course, the Renaissance, with its Italian and Spanish sources, was associated by English people with Machiavelli and with ruthless energy and cunning—this was the commonplace opinion of the time. The king most associated with the Renaissance was Henry VIII— the incarnation of ruthless energy and cunning.) This move of negation was very generally understood by the poetically concerned in our period.

If you can grasp that leaving out the latinate words is the key to a style, you can also grasp that eliminating classificatory systems of knowledge can be the key to a style. If there is a style which you find puzzling, it is always worthwhile to look and see if it is ejecting tiers of vocabulary and cultural or behavioural assumptions as a negation of the institutions which go along with them. I do not recall ever seeing a critic point this out. I suppose most critics have a big investment in getting critical poetry off the stage.

A key concept here is contamination. We could refer to this by the Greek term, miasma. Style is supposed to wash the poet clean of all the crimes of society. Meanwhile, the good substances of the English past and present are supposed to leak in. You can be 'brutal rootal Saxon' or 'latinate and courtly' and give the miasma to someone else.

What we quoted Hughes as saying, above, bears an interesting resemblance to an essay by L.C. Knights on Restoration drama[4]. Knights' argument contrasts Shakespeare very sharply with the language of the drama of roughly 1660 to 1690. (The extrapolation from 1690 to 1960 is Hughes' own.) We can tentatively reconstruct the laureate's thought processes as having set out from Knights' devastating Marxist-academic critique of dramas by Congreve and Dryden to formulate something, by reaction, which joined his own poetic processes. This is conjectural. What I am suggesting is that unformed poets encounter prescriptive literary critical essays, at school and as students, and are plunged by them into intensive reactions which push them towards a poetic style which solves the problems. Hughes must have read hundreds of critical essays. Full-time students had such academic tasks. He must have thought intensively about all of them in relation to his own (future) poetry. The point here is not that any single critic had much influence on the scene—I'm sure they didn't—but that essays like those by Knights contained convincing generalisations about poetic style which had an impact on would-be poets. I suppose another issue is that while people who had done the A-level and read *The Well-Wrought Urn* and so on could easily understand what the contemporary poet was up to, someone else might find it baffling.

The mention of Knights allows us, of course, to open the curtain on another zone of insecurity, guilt, and high emotion. His classic *Drama and Society in the Age of Jonson* is described on the cover and in the Introduction as an attempt to test the Marxist theory of literature. This transcendental and redemptory theory of history opens the possibility of a different and better state. More depressingly, it opened up a *miasma field* where experts (there was always one of these on hand) could interpret almost every line you wrote as a symptom of some social disease or other. Three particular areas of fantasy, during those hard years of style development, are history (e.g. everything since Shakespeare is corrupt), class (everything intelligent about poetry is middle-class and so contributes to the oppression of the masses), and character (where every syllable you write leaks out your inner nature and other people might detect disastrous flaws). Such is the energy of this field that young poets get excited about all three together, flailing at them all at once. The heats of adolescent revolt can become heroic in this way. The Seventies may have seen a shift away from preoccupation with economics and class and towards the way men behave towards women (and women behave towards men). However, all contamination theory seems to be Marxism at one remove.

Anthony Thwaite wrote in 1974: "I may seem to be contradicting myself here, but I think not: I'm in fact reinforcing my argument that we're in a state of deadlock, and that soon the camps may be so divided that one side won't be able to communicate with the other—indeed, won't even want to communicate."[5] I was given a proposal (in about 1996) for a dialogue between different parts of the poetry world. After a while, the proposer admitted that he thought my underground magazine, *Angel Exhaust*, would be a good venue for the material to be published in. I was very sceptical. I thought about it seriously, and I had a clear vision of dozens of poets being asked to clarify the scene and simply talking about themselves. The conditions of the business mean that someone asked to write for a magazine can only see it as a chance for exposure. If you challenged this, they would be indignant and say that this *was* clarifying the scene, and that the key problem in the whole literary world was people not reading their work enough. As for promoting rival styles, they would be averse from that. So I turned down the proposal—which, surprisingly, seemed unable to continue without my resources.

I suppose the programme for reducing balkanisation has to be a social one. A conference would be suitable, and obviously one where many of the rival factions would be present and take part in dialogue about the key disagreements. People would actually shift their ground, and shed some of their phobias and dislikes. They would come away and read books from the other factions.

We spoke earlier of the wealth of poetry available—more than 2,000 new books in a year, according to the only comprehensive count I know of. Since you couldn't conceivably read all of these, rapid judgements are the only possible ones. This encourages the use of reductive criteria—surface features turn into the basis for deciding whether to read something. This problem could be addressed by systematic reviewing—but the reviewing workshop is totally inadequate to evaluate all those books, or even five percent of them. Further, reviewers are under acute pressure, and a widespread feeling in the public is that reviews are unreliable because they partake of the same factional loyalties which Thwaite was talking about.

Experts seem convinced that if you had extensive dialogue between all the factions, a détente and depolarisation would follow, and the scene would be transformed. I cannot see any evidence of any dialogues having had any such result. I may keep a reserve of doubt that a conference about détente would do anything but increase hostility—and indeed whether the hostility and incomprehension we see now are the result of long persisting social processes *including* dialogue and close knowledge of each other. Indeed, where there is pressure for mutual definition, for finding the edges—this is the very topic most likely to incite competition and cause dialogue to break down. At a conference about mutual misunderstanding, everyone would explain the virtues of the faction they belong to—as if the problem were other people misunderstanding *them*. This self-justificatory material is already available. It is not a shortage.

These events would necessarily involve critics and cultural managers being criticised for presiding over the bad polarisation and *nurturing* it. This would mean most of the event being wasted with them justifying their own past bad decisions—forbidding someone from defending themselves is a breach of natural rights which could not be thought of.

My suspicion as an editor is that if you got thousands of pages of raw material from such a conference you would only end up with half a dozen pages that would truly advance the debate. That is, finding the unshared assumptions and exploring unconscious blocks. I do not think people are highly motivated to carry out those tasks. Arranging a debate that would really enhance inter-factional understanding would be very delicate, and would probably have to be a long-term project: it would go badly at first, but by observing the positive results and following those up, you could gradually enhance it. You could develop rules of speech that would discourage people from endlessly reverting to themselves and making propaganda for the position they already held ten years ago. The protocol of the event would have to make sure that people shared the objective, of depolarisation, and were not treating it as a personal appearance and an opportunity for self-promotion.

We have a theory of prejudicial stereotypes, with an information content A; of reviews, like the ones I compile books of, which contain more information, so $A \times B$; and the information to be gathered from a reading of someone's entire book, so $A \times B \times C$. $A \times B$ may be more information than A, but it may not be a huge amount more. Anyway, why would there be a line where as you expand a simplified account it suddenly changes from unfair to fair? As for pre-judgement, there is a whole mass of knowledge of art which in its entirety amounts to connoisseurship, and which is embodied in classifications and terms which record the classifications. This body of knowledge is a huge asset for the reader, allowing them to find their way through the labyrinth of art; and reviews are also a key asset, making shopping more efficient. To put it bluntly: unless something is completely original, judgements based on past experience are fairly effective. People are equipped to recognise what they want or don't want. At the end of the line, if a reader dislikes a certain book of poetry, you can't just write this off as bad polarisation: this is their subjectivity, a civil right. The ideal of equal distribution has never applied to art. Does randomness amount to fairness? Would depolarisation mean I have to read books I dislike *all the time*?

The point of poetry is to be enjoyed. If you don't enjoy something, you don't have to read it. If duty is taking that right away, pleasure will take wing and vanish. So can we 'depolarise' without legislating for aesthetic numbness?

My feeling is that the degree of factionalisation across the scene could be reduced by people straying outside their home range and making the effort to challenge their own prejudices. To clarify that: even if you have a feeling of horror and asphyxiation on looking at the cover of a book, reading the first poem, etc., it may be that on prolonged reading you could react totally differently and even get to enjoy it.

The proposition is that you can switch off prejudice without attacking subjectivity.

The path to depolarisation is redemption through repentance. This may sound unlikely in itself; it is surely very unlikely at a public event. Repentance is too much to ask. Perhaps a more likely way forward is to redefine modern poetry as a legacy, a collective asset. It would then be natural for conservatives to cherish it and inventory it. This process would reach fruition by making people able to understand the whole range of modern poetry.

We spoke earlier of a process of emptying out and of a sealed chamber, a ganzfeld. At this point we can clarify that by saying that what is emptied out of the modern poem is contamination by collective guilt, and what is being sealed out of the emptying chamber is the collective representations which carry the guilt. At that moment, it might seem that everyone undertakes that emptying out and that the avant-garde is innocent—and, it follows, must be the best kind of writing. At this point we can say that the way symbolism works is that poets attribute a specific meaning to it and then readers assign it any meaning they damned well want. Unfortunately, the value assigned to purging by the poets is not the same one assigned to it by large parts of the art public. To start with, you can't put on the mantle of revolution without sweeping up some of the dirt left from bad actions by past revolutions. In England, the modernist project is linked, in most people's minds, with modernist architecture in its local form—of tower blocks. I can't quite dissociate the revolutionary project in English poetry from the sight of huge sixties council-owned tower blocks of the 1960s being demolished, round about 2003, in Edmonton where I used to live. Strong sensory memories—sight, sound and dust. They were the biggest features on the landscape, in Edmonton.

English people have quite an effective set of links that runs between abstract theorising, monotonous and featureless cellular spaces, removal of individual rights by arrogant intellectuals, abolition of the past, abolition of the neighbourhood, geometric purity, modern materials, rational planning, general solutions. It goes on to include continental tyrannies, Marxism, idealist philosophy, centralised planning, psychology labs, brainwashing, sensory deprivation. This sounds more like a dream sequence than an argument. I set it down here just to point out that the reading public may see experimental and 'emptied' art as just as contaminated as any other style. I should underline that crimes committed in a dream, especially someone else's dream, are not real crimes.

We spoke earlier about contamination as part of a pre-rational reaction. The proposal here is that people evaluate poetry *before* they decide whether to read it, and that this evaluation is highly subjective, rapid, fragmentary, dominated by feelings of identification and contamination. This is where social reality permeates the poetic experience—a leak so big it feels like an immersion, soaking, staining or enriching the poem. The line between prejudice and social memory cannot be drawn at any specific point. And the poem is made out of social reality. If people identify conservative poetry with evil Tory governments and theoretical-abstract poetry with evil continental Marxist dictatorships, you can't argue with them—and the identifications are not subject to rationalising reform. Actually, the tangled helices of memory and fantasy that produce negative reactions and shutdowns must be extremely similar to the ones that produce intense and spontaneous aesthetic reactions.

I feel bad because I haven't set out the case for organic, personal, traditional type poetry—not within this book, anyway. Let me point to a section within a book edited by Peter Abbs, *The Symbolic Order* (1989). This was part of a project involving ten books in all, but I haven't seen the others. The book I did see is about the role of arts in education, rather globally. The section of interest is about modernism—against modernism, actually. Without suggesting that generalisations about the arts are ever true, I can point to these essays (by Arthur Danto, Ernst Gombrich, and Peter Fuller) as clear statements of positions against the avant-garde of the past few decades.

I can also point to two magazines which are genuine examples of depolarised activity. *Terrible Work*, edited by Tim Allen and Steve Spence, in Plymouth, is no longer published. *Fire*, edited by Jeremy Hilton from a village in Oxfordshire, is flourishing—and is a shining example to all of us.

NOTES

[1] Ted Hughes (ed.); *A Choice of Shakespeare's Verse* (London: Faber, 1971).
[2] see review by Chris Nunn of Nicholas Humphrey in *New Scientist*, 28 June 2006, p.58.
[3] Keith Sagar: *The Art of Ted Hughes* (Cambridge: Cambridge University Press, 1975).
[4] L.C. Knights, *Drama and Society in the Age of Jonson* (Harmondsworth: Penguin Books, 1962; originally 1937).
[5] Anthony Thwaite, 'The Two Poetries', in Poetry Dimension 2, ed. Dannie Abse (London: Abacus, 1974).

HYPERLITERATE; OR NOT QUITE

Friedrich Heer remarks that Peter Abelard, in the 12th century, was a modern kind of philosopher, and wrote a book called *Sic et Non* (Yes and No). How frightening this paradox must appear to the nervous reader: a book which denies what it asserts. Apparently the writer is hiding the meaning of the text from us. But new distinctions cannot be made without splitting the old ones; we recognise that an old category can be divided in two—the parts are, and are not, the same. No point expending rage and fear on this denial-assertion; breaking down the code does not mean the code breaking down. New poetry is bound to make new distinctions, and therefore to use doubt and paradox. The existing vocabulary is temporarily suspended, and becomes opaque; it ceases to function while it is being changed. But, didn't we spend the whole of our childhoods learning new words? why should we have lost the ability?

There is no adequate word for summing up the unconscious rules, emotionally salient to those in the know, which determine what is allowed to appear in a magazine like *Angel Exhaust*, and which purchasers look for in such a magazine. The rules are fairly simple to master; the editor of a "modernist" magazine can tell amazingly quickly whether a poem belongs in the magazine, even before working out its conscious meaning. Hyperliterate is a suggestion to describe this poetry. It is so called because it calls for more exploitation of reading skills than simpler poetry, which already exploits reading skills. Simple texts reinforce the meaning by restating it many times at various levels. This is helpful for the reader who is not certain of the language. But as skill increases we experience this repetition as redundancy; the more grasp we have of the code, the more virtuality we want. Relative clauses, and hypotaxis in general, offer this in a simple way. Once you virtualise the instructions and signals, you produce modern poetry inevitably.

The proposition calls virtuality, speculation, avoidance of fact, flouting of conventions, paradox, attenuation of instructions and scene-setting, complexity of information, dense use of abstruse ideas, cultural allusiveness, lightness of rhythm, ambiguity, indeterminacy, lack of demands to identify emotionally, lack of autobiographical motivation, addiction to play and variation, consistent results of a single factor, i.e. hyperliteracy. This cluster asks for greater literacy than mainstream poetry, and this explains why it has a smaller audience; it uses greater literacy than mainstream poetry, and this explains why it is more prestigious. It is an overfulfilment of tendencies which already separate writing from speech, and published poetry from amateur.

One of the rules is that, once you find a poem easy to understand, you don't want to read it. This may not be true in all societies, but it is true in ours. There is no rule saying that I, as an adult, cannot enjoy poetry accessible to 15-year-olds, but in fact this is a rule which I apply; and it stems from a disengagement in favour of poetry away from popular music and cinema, because the latter are totally aimed at teenagers, and do not advance as the consumer's skill with the code advances. Can we really separate the scorn, irritation, tribal pride, officiousness, and self-congratulation with which the devotees of the avant-garde treat anything which is not avant-garde enough from social hostility in general? Is this not the glacial sense of authorisation with which a sixth-former brushes off the attempts of a fifth-former to speak to them?

The artistic modernity of the twentieth century seemed so alien to the people experiencing it that they were stunned. Perhaps it was a unique feature of the twentieth-century West, or perhaps we can find analogies to it in other cultures. While searching for historical analogies to the "avant-garde", we should notice that most of the official and public channels for publishing British poetry completely ignore its existence, and realise that the same block may be applied to past poetry, and may have applied in the past. Modernity relies on small-scale differences which an indifferent gaze may simply fail to notice. In selecting poems for translation, you unthinkingly de-select the ones which use language-specific features as central; as these vanish in translation. Any reading of literature from a past culture is translation; the more embedded a text is in the specifics of the culture which produced it, the less comprehensible it is to a "foreign" reader. Because the transmission of ancient literature depended so much on its use in education, classical texts unappealing, or incomprehensible to schoolchildren were not copied and so did not survive until the Renaissance. Hocke's classic statement of the thesis that modern literature is a form of Mannerism appeared in a book where he demonstrated the systematic neglect of Mannerism by nineteenth and twentieth-century taste. The reliance on nuance must appear as lightness to a reader who is not part of the in-groups, and a living person cannot be part of an in-group of the 16th century. Long-lived corporations, such as the Catholic Church or the University of Oxford, provide partial exceptions to this. A text which is about itself, and so self-referential, must seem slight; if it refers to itself and simultaneously contradicts itself, it must seem quite meaningless. Yet this is the condition of learned literature.

The reliance on cultural knowledge is not confined to high artistic forms. There is an account in the biography of Henry Irving of an act parodying Irving; he objected in law, and the verbal part of the act was removed, as infringing copyright; but the imitator simply went on stage and imitated Irving's walk, and the audiences got the joke and found it very funny. Such a mode of meaning must seem recondite to anyone from "outside", but is not truly sophisticated or intellectual. The television comics rely to a great extent on take-offs of characters from other television shows, jokes incomprehensible to someone who does not have a television, but hardly exclusive or intellectual. Component no.1 of the avant-garde is mimicry, i.e. reproduction of external form while emptying out the intentional and sincere meaning, and parody is the door by which formalist art entered. The cabaret milieu in which modernism originated was dominated by parody, as contemporary accounts indicate. Later, we have Miró "reproducing" a Dutch painting by repeating all its masses and their location in space, while effacing their object nature; he broke through into the geometrical and went on to do his own designs.

Moments when something like our avant-garde may have come into flower are Hellenistic Alexandria, the Empire of the 2nd century, Italy in the Mannerist era; a search in China, and perhaps Thailand or Bali, would also be fruitful. The international Latin-based culture of the high Middle Ages, say from 1180 onwards, may also have produced some uninterpretable works which may resemble our avant-garde in particular ways. Difficult and apparently slight and joky Latin works do not attract much academic attention; the Alsatian poet Jacob Balde produced, to celebrate the peace treaty ending the Thirty Years' War, a work[3] *Poesis Osca* in the Oscan language, known by fragments, spoken by a culture regarded as rustic by the Romans: peace and prosperity were associated with the peasant, as opposed to the warlike and unproductive aristocrat, so the choice of Oscan reflects the theme in the deepest choices of form, a modernist trait. Since no-one can read Oscan, the original print was accompanied by a facing translation into Latin. Surely this is reminiscent of the avant-garde of the 1960s? This work—never reprinted as far as I can determine—is ignored because it seems slight, bizarre, and remote from a social basis or from daily speech; but a modernist might recognise precisely those features. A recondite poet of the seventeenth century would inevitably have written in Latin, and been missed by the labours of nationalist historians of literature in the nineteenth century. I came across *Poesis Osca* by chance, on a shelf in an eccentric London library; no-one ever writes about it, unlike his more orthodox and sensible works. How many more formalist Latin works of the Mannerist or Baroque periods are there, perhaps included in the bulky handlists of this literature, in which there are no courses and for which no university departments exist? When I compare the non-expressive, non-realist formalist poetry of our times to neo-Latin, I am neither being sarcastic, nor cutting a cudgel to beat the former about the head with. Our learned elite is not the first to have existed, and neither are its "insider" texts with their brilliant "unnatural" language.

Learned poetry requires an audience, to experience its reactions, i.e. it is not merely private reading; competition with closely similar people not divided by acquired status; rewards from above for conforming; rapid personal change, including insecurity; new positions are not barred off by formal disqualifying rules; the book is central to the preoccupations of the group. All this sounds very much like higher education. This is the site we have to study to seize modern poetry, as the noble household, the court, or parts of the Church, were the sites in previous ages. Higher education is stabilised by induced high anxiety. It is a diffuse, low-level, social anxiety which polices taste. The interfaces between universities and schools, the media, and non-academic poets, are fault lines where structures become visible.

The increase of fineness of scale of the medium creates immediately an excess of information. As a comparison, a map of 10 times the scale has 100 times as many points within any of its squares as its smaller-scale rival. This surplus of data may cause special problems. Perhaps it is the role of fashion to ensure that the reader and the writer do not miss each other altogether, and the fanatical fashion-consciousness of this group is an elementary imperative to keep sociality in existence.

If we imagine symbolic communication as forming its messages in a virtual space, it follows, in this metaphor, that mapping is taking place continuously, and that two players using different scales to divide up their symbolic space are faced with non-compatibility. A shape in symbolic space A may be a line drawn through a number of points which, in symbolic space B, either have no equivalents, or many equivalents, or are non-contiguous. What arrives as a message from A is then not a shape in B; not executable. Paradox is either a trick or a breakthrough into the place where rules are formed.

The effects of increasing intellectual level are paradoxical and discontinuous. "Intellectual" poetry does not seem normally to mean a more complex pattern, or one with more involved symmetries, or with more members. Complexity of information is not the same as bulk. We are not talking about a string 100 pages long being more complex than a string one page long; but about a string 30 lines long being more complex than other strings of 30 lines. This distinction has necessarily to do with being less declarative and invoking more implicit knowledge. It is only imitated by piling up words, use of polysyllables, and dropping of the names of philosophers and physicists; this imitation is crudely true, but refinement is the heart of the matter. For a reader who cannot read the sentences, the amount of information getting through is small, so that 80 complex lines may be less data-rich than 800 simple ones; the reader either wants poetry to be like this, or does not.

References to *modernism* and *innovation* are misunderstandings, although they are, let us say, 80% or 90% accurate. If we shed the word *modernism* and disengage the usage rules by which we decide whether a text is "modernist" or not, we realise that these rules also imply hyperliteracy. The poetry in question is assimilating towards a shared aesthetic ideal, not merely dissimilating away from a (conservative) one. This poetry is the result of "progress", in the sense that it is reached after acquiring more basic reading and compositional skills, but not in the sense that it was not there 80 years ago, or that in 10 years' time it will be mainstream.

As a learner of foreign languages, I have spent much time with texts chosen because I could understand them. Hyperliterate poetry is always difficult to understand, and seems paradoxical, secretive, and slight when one does not understand it. All languages have this kind of poetry, and it is always inaccessible to the learner. Difficulty and modernity are structurally related, and the former is our guide to understanding the latter.

The received wisdom is that poetry in any language is always more difficult than prose. It is striking that this applies to Greek of the fifth century BC as well as to Norse of the thirteenth century AD, as much as to twentieth-century languages. Anything we say about poetry and complexity has to accommodate this fact, or be disqualified at the outset. The received wisdom does not cover the whole field: some poetry is very simple. Although song lyrics are poems, they are expected to be simple and clear. Anyone trying to get a feel for Gaelic culture will realise at a certain point that there was folk poetry as well as bardic poetry, and that the latter died out with the Gaelic nobility; various travellers said that ordinary people could not understand bardic poetry.

Certain features of "high" poetry in illiterate societies resemble hyperliteracy, which therefore does not depend on the written medium. It is impossible to get close to the true mannerism and complexity of Old Norse and Old Irish poetry without being reminded of the twentieth century, and without realising that complexity and ambiguity have an abiding appeal to the human mind, satisfying its structural drives. Troubadour poetry (*trobar clus*) and Greek tragedy show the same ornate difficulty, without necessarily being of oral composition. Much mediaeval poetry is very simple; the distribution pattern between formalist and simple poetry is not transparent to me, but is of the highest historical interest. Sung texts, and narratives, tend to be simple; but this rule is unreliable. It may be that elaborate poetry appeals to audiences who appreciate self-conscious elaboration in other forms of behaviour, so that courts, universities, and monasteries—of the learned kind—favour it; this also does not get to the bottom of the matter. It may be that elaboration in poetry is associated with appreciation of high verbal skill in other contexts, such as conversation and political or forensic debate, but possibly this is a feature of all societies, including the ones whose poetry is simple.

A simple catalogue check tells us that not all poetry is complex; I prefer not to pile up several thousand works of this other kind and try to diagnose them, but suspect the influence of a didactic function of poetry, which puts clarity of exposition, and consistency with dogma, above expressive values. This genre seems to exist in Buddhist cultures as well as Christian. One can either equate this tedious manner with an audience of low education or, more convincingly, with the education process itself, with the implication of a corporate body of priests qualified by control of dogma, and the non-availability of the "truths" to the mass of the population being an indicator that they were not, in fact, true. My impression is that there was a shift all over Europe to a simple, fluent, prolix, narrative style lasting from AD 1100 to 1500 (at least), and that the older, "Dark Age", complex style became archaic, for reasons I do not currently perceive. The cessation of the skaldic style in Scandinavia (replaced by dull chivalric romances in the style of Western Europe) is a crux where study might start; the bardic style continued in Ireland, Wales, and Scotland, which tellingly had their centre inside themselves. The shift may be linked with literacy, and with its corollary, i.e. that the "top style" was taken over by Latin—the primary medium of literacy—with all spoken Western- and Central-European languages becoming "low" in a dyadic pair sensible to the culturally trained.

Because the ability to criticise the utterances of a politician presupposes sufficient command of the verbal code s/he is using to uncover what it is covering over, there is a necessary resemblance between the skills of hyperliteracy and the activities of critics of the political system. This skill level is also owned by the politicians within the system, and their speech-writers, the politologists, etc. The association between hyperliterate poetry and political radicalism is close, but not straightforward; traditionally, the most elaborate poetry was paid for as eulogies to members of the ruling elite, or as the text for ceremonials of the State. This relationship with politics has dictated the course of hyperliterate poetry as a cluster within

British culture, which gets sold, has a market, gets reviewed, provides up-and-down careers for the individual poets, is embraced or spurned by institutions, etc. Someone who perceives the ambiguous relation between reality and political language can either react by writing ambiguous texts or by writing committed but unambiguous texts, which assert X and also assert that X is reality, thus closing up the gap again. The cultural managers, structurally obliged to please their political paymasters, could take on socially critical poetry written in low-prestige language, because this did not sound like power; but they reacted violently against Marxist poetry written in hyperliterate and high-prestige language, because it did sound like power; it sounded like the transvaluation of all values, starting with the erasure of all existing assets. For this reason, it was not allowed into the anthologies or the textbooks. So that conventional poetry can be presented as a revolt, it is necessary to pretend that radical poetry does not exist (or is "not poetry").

NOTES

[1] *Angel Exhaust*: completely wonderful magazine edited for most of its life by Adrian Clarke or myself.

[2] See Gustav Rene Hocke, *Manierismus in der Literatur. Sprach-Alchimie und esoterische Kombinationskunst* (Hamburg: Rowohlt, 1959).

[3] *Poesis Osca* is now available online at www.uni-mannheim.de/mateo/camautor/balde.html

Objects, Abstraction, and a Head for Heights

The contrast between French and British ways of integrating abstract thought with physical data seems to go back to certain contrasts between the conventions of Protestant and Roman Catholic spiritual writing, and this if true would confirm the significance of books three or four centuries ago, i.e. the raw material disseminated by the arrival of printing, of mass literacy, and a national distribution network, to the "deep" layers of poetic taste today. The operation of this linkage supplies one of the diagnostic differences between high and low writing.

Lawrence Stone discusses an obstinate plainness as a feature of the first half of the seventeenth century:

> In analysing the Court versus Country conflict, as much weight must be placed upon imponderable factors of feeling and emotion as upon purely financial considerations. The conflict was one of *mores*, or religious and political beliefs, as well as one of economic interests. In the early seventeenth century England was experiencing the full stress of the two cultures, those of the Country, and of the Court: Decker against Massinger, Milton against Davenant, Robert Walker against Van Dyck, artisan mannerism against Inigo Jones; suspicion and hatred of Italy as vicious and popish against a passionate admiration of its aesthetic splendours; a belief in the virtues of country living against the sophistication of the London man about town; a strong moral antipathy towards sexual licence, gambling, stage-plays, hard drinking, duelling and running into debt against a natural weakness for all these worldly pleasures and vices; a dark suspicion of ritual and ornament in church worship against a ready acceptance of the beauty of holiness advocated by Laud; a deeply felt fear of Papists and Popery against an easy-going toleration for well-connected recusants and a sneaking admiration for Inigo Jones' chapel in St James; and lastly a genuine admiration for a balanced constitution, as opposed to the authoritarian views of Charles and Wentworth.[1]

The plain / showy opposition echoed the opposition between the Country and Court parties—not quite "parties" but currents of opinion or alliance *within* the gentry and aristocracy. There was for the opinion of that time a telling linkage between Italian classicising art (seen as pagan and lascivious), and the supposed immoral sexuality of the Court, and Catholicism (seen as anti-constitutional and autocratic). This is now obsolete, but a vaguer suspicion of high culture has survived, partly because it was structurally favourable to lower strata of the dominant group, who commanded "lower" cultural assets. Traits, pointing to inferiority, such as caution, flatness, lack of conceptual fluency, lack of verbal beauty, were sanctified as proofs of "seriousness". The resistance to high language was sustained by the Nonconformist tradition from that point, and the later history of that tradition has a lot to do with the thread of "plain" or "flat" poetry in this century, said ludicrously by John Lucas to be the "English style". One of the features of English society since the 17th century has been its continuity; another, the unhalted rise of the Nonconformists.

English poetry must appear to foreigners, if they possess literary culture, as one where people have forgotten how to express their feelings; where the linguistic arena is so fraught with mutual hostility that everyone is scared to speak subjectively; and every verbal gesture is a displacement activity. This hostility is no doubt a legacy of the war between classes; resentment between the different races, ruling or subjected, of the Empire, and between men and women, probably adds new industries to it. If you are politically defeated, you can console yourself by acquiring objects; as the Dissenters, in the eighteenth and nineteenth centuries, consoled themselves for being excluded from public office, and from ecclesiastical government, by business success; but you cannot console yourself for political failure by writing poems about objects.

The book *Essays Catholic and Radical*[2], edited by Rowan Williams and Kenneth Leech, consciously speaks for a faction in the contemporary Church of England which is ritualistic, is high-flown and intellectual in language, and is left-wing. It structurally resembles the hyperliterate current in British poetry, fulfilling a crossover between Left opposition and the high-flown. It has a head for height. Where height meets radicalism, the cultural limits often clung to by the Left, as a hangover from its origin in Nonconformism and in a lower class with no grasp of the higher cultural codes, were transcended. The benefits to the intellectuals are clear, too: self-confident intellectuality exploits its (geometric) links to the hegemonic group by developing assaults on the hegemony, which cannot easily be dismissed because they use legitimated language to frame democratic and subversive messages. Williams, a Welsh-speaker, Bishop of Monmouth, promoted since I wrote this essay, is an interesting poet[3], slightly in the style of Geoffrey Hill. *Essays Catholic and Radical* was the product of a conference held in Loughborough. Loughborough, apart from being my home town, is known as a hotbed of post-structuralist theology.

Like most terms in the English critical vocabulary, "empiricism" is a coded term, and different groups read this encoding in different ways. The use of the term indicates an opposition between *high* and *flat* poets, where the former are happy with ideas, and the latter are not; the former use high-flown language, and the latter use coarse and awkward phrases; they can detach themselves from ideas, acquire new ones, play with ideas, and the latter are stuck with whatever traditional attitudes they learnt at school. The sociological approach proposes that dogged empiricism is an approach favoured by those with less symbolic capital, occupying lower niches in the system of government or the education industry, and possessing more resentment of privilege, central government policies, academic theories of poetry, etc.; and simultaneously that the low:high opposition is a continuation of a series of such oppositions which go back at least to the seventeenth century, and that the pattern of alternate erasure, preservation, or revival of these stored relationships is of great interest. It is clear that many individuals with (relatively) low symbolic capital write high-flown poetry.

The relationship between "ideas" and "experience" is central to modern British poetry, and because so many thousands of people have grappled with this relationship it is not possible to give a summary of it which describes all the variations fairly. Primitively, we can trace this split back to the home environment, where there are two streams of information reaching the child, one from physically present people who interact with them, and one from books, radio, pictures, etc. Reducing the number of those enfranchised to delegitimate you is a kind of endogamy, confining the available resources to a tight network; it is circular, because it necessarily implies that those whom you have authorised to invalidate you are validated by you, own the same cultural assets as you, and so are unlikely to invalidate you.

The poetry in *Ladder to the Next Floor*[4] avoids effects; it is unhappy with ideas or emotions; it is happy with objects; it is blunt, dogged, realistic; it regards language as a set of demonic traps which can only be mastered by arduous plainness and literalness. Subjective experience is thus inferior to external, physical, sensations. (It is close to the poetry in *The Stumbling Dance* and *Completing the Picture*. I discussed these anthologies in *Fulfilling the Silent Rules*.) Part of the interest of this production is that the poets involved are not aware of English literary culture, and their linguistic models come from elsewhere, perhaps from speech or magazines.

These virtues (of scepticism and empiricism and cutting back) could not be more common, more central, more average, in British intellectual life. If we find them in poetry, they may add nothing to the set of ideas familiar to us from any other field of writing, or indeed from the conversation of educated people. They cannot represent an alternative to the present system, because any alternative to what is already there must be speculative. Comparing poetry and philosophy points us towards a third set of linguistic events, namely the conversation of the country: a huge body of evidence, unfortunately transient and inaccessible, whose characteristics may underlie not only poetry and philosophy, but all formal discourses in general. Some of the rules of self-presentation applied in English speech might be:

do not draw attention to yourself
do not talk about yourself
use irony and self-deprecation if you do have to talk about yourself
don't get emotional
emotional exchanges are lapses
don't make personal remarks
don't talk about people behind their backs
conceal unhappiness

These values make for a successful collectivist society, where people are trained to use their conscious energies, not to aggrandise themselves, but to restrain their base appetites and attain love and understanding for others. Where such values appear in poetry, and I think Wales and Scotland are quite similar to England in this, we can attribute them, not to any literary influence, but to the shared values of the society in which speech occurs. Hundreds of such speech rules might be found. One of the unwritten rules of contemporary poetry is that the poet writes about first person experience, while other people, sharing equally in shaping the situations within which the first-person lives and moves, are depicted only as shadows or listeners, not as conscious agents verbalising their consciousness. This collapse of the poem to the dimensions of the self certainly has a tangled history, longer than one lifetime. But, practically: you cannot put yourself in the centre of the poem and also be unable to dramatise or aestheticise yourself. Or: either find another subject for poetry than your personal experiences, or devise a certain dramaturgy of the self, which is exciting, and also sufficiently externalised and depersonalised to allow the reader to identify with and take it up as their own, a floating experience that is not somebody's property. Some social practices might make for an egalitarian and non-violent society while also reducing the scope of poetry almost to zero: because we have the two rules, that poetry must be about the personal feelings of the writer, and that a speaker must minimize and understate whatever they say about themselves. These two rules *in combination* simply erase poetry.

I feel that this issue of dealing with objects is one of the diagnostic keys which let us distinguish between high poetry and low. The line of division is vexed by persistent waves of anxiety about betrayal, exclusion, conspiracy, and missing the point. The zone where writers are free from mere physical details is rife with collusion—this is the problem. Fundamentally, art is collusion, the participation in shared symbolic structures. Someone who fears that this game leads to his exclusion is paralysed, unable to play the game effectively. He then regards the game as wicked. Recourse to objects is a fatal error—a diversion from the enchanting possibility of starting up a new game which does not have the same constraints as the old one. I suggested, in an essay on anthologies in my previous book[5], that there was a fundamental gap between poets who were trapped in memories of actual objects, scenes, and action sequences, and poets who were able, by imagination or free association, to recombine the sense-memories and form new and unique combinations. This is the prerogative of those who have a strong grasp of the material of knowledge, as well as of the verbal code; they can create new combinations without being afraid of losing their way or forgetting the original sequence. They are inevitably the better writers, and anyone psychologically strong is bound to enter the realms of imagination and improvisation. The ability to create is really nothing to do with the class structure, but depends on internal qualities which are almost too basic to analyse. The destruction of the beautiful shared game is not an exit from the class system, but the exit from art into literalism and didacticism.

This "low" sector of the cultural spectrum seems to stand in a specific relationship to the hyperliterate, whom we discussed in an earlier chapter. The fact that the linguistic code is capable of infinite recombination is really the most basic fact about it. Not to realise this is a sign of a basic incompetence—not of simplicity, but of belonging to a terribly, artificially, underprivileged sector of society, in a site which is blocked and overshadowed. Perhaps we can associate this with an inadequate grasp of the rules of literacy, the product of terrible defects in the public education system. I suspect that people with a deep understanding of the code are better equipped to explain what is really going on across the whole system. The sceptical empirical approach is also a good fit to a capitalist economy, where we manufacture things through processes that can go wrong, and shop for products that may not be as desirable as they first seem. What is helpful in shopping, because it lets you cut through the temptations of advertising and packaging to a more modest and affordable reality, is disastrous in the field of poetry, and leads to something damaged and sub-artistic; excellent poetry needs a regression to the emotive, the speculative, the rhetorical, the passionate, the volatile, the exacerbated and specialised sensibility, the ambiguous, the artificial and speculative. While following this direction, poetry would link up with the currents in British academic life which, since 1968, have exerted their energies against the empirical, pessimistic, value-free, anti-theoretical, positivist mainstream. We have a set of co-located oppositions within verbal style:

dramatic	undemonstrative
un-English, Continental	conventional in describing feelings
	unemotive
egoistic	impersonal

like advertisements	flat drab noncommittal
aesthetic and poetic	the Movement
carrying significant information	light verse
innovative	conservative and populist
modernist	historicising
theoretical, conjectural	empirical

What does Tillich say:

> "Man is free, in so far as he has the power of deliberating and deciding, thus cutting through the mechanisms of stimulus and response. Man is free, in so far as he can play and build imaginary structures above the real structures to which he, like all beings, is bound. Man is free, in so far as he has the faculty of creating worlds above the given world, of creating the world of technical tools and products, the world of artistic expressions, the world of theoretical structures and practical organizations. Finally, man is free, in so far as he has the power of contradicting himself and his essential nature."[6]

Because the conscious action of humans is in these ways not prescribed by the behaviour of things, to describe a situation in terms of things only is to give an incomplete description. We do not apprehend situations in terms only of physical things, but in terms of living creatures, animals as well as humans, which are unpredictable to the extent that their brains and cognition are complex. Describing situations without a human, free, subjective dimension is therefore untrue to our daily experience of living, a false reduction.

If so many poets write poems without a subjective dimension, it is because of guilt and anxiety: all through their apprenticeship as writers, they wanted to be emotionally grand, they wrote selfishly and at too great length; and so, when they first wrote a poem that was about objects, firm things in the external world with boundaries, it was an emotional breakthrough and they wept for joy. If you go through a batch of bad poems (the litter of a magazine editor's desk), you can improve most of them by reducing the information about the poet's subjective state (boring!), and making the details about the object world more precise, more tangible. This is one of the schoolroom adages most popular, most devastating, in contemporary poetic thinking; *make it more external. Make it less internal. Your feelings are insignificant. Tell us more about the objects.* Unfortunately, you could also improve most of those poems by making the subjective element stronger and throwing out most of the objects.

The body is an object because it is subject to the laws of mechanics, for example gravity, friction, momentum. This objectness of the body is important in the way we talk about sexuality, in the boundary we draw between objective and subjective. The physical signs of excitement can controvert what is being said, if they do not support it. At this point the object (and its hydraulics) appear as objective truth, and words are tested against them. But in other situations, physical arousal is seen as a mark of insincerity: *you say you love me but you just want to go to bed with me.* These descriptions are inept, and a compositional rule of the poem should, perhaps, be that its texture must be complex enough to allow the evocation of a situation that is not banal. Writing about objects is a way of avoiding writing about feelings; feminism teaches us that an object-ridden view of the world is connected with an affectless, auto-gratificatory, view of sexuality. Because of this double surface where a body is simultaneously an object and a message communicating inner states and intentions, handling of objects gives away a lot about what a writer feels about his or her body, and about other people's bodies. Ejecting feelings into the object world can give that world a voice: when people write poems about stones, it is not coincidental that stones stay hard for a long time. The whole operation whereby a subjective state turns into a poem and so becomes permanent, and a tradable piece of property, detaches the sign from its referent: all brain states are transient. Someone might want to externalise their feelings as a way of excluding the possibility that they are false. This is dubious, because one of the abiding characteristics of feelings is that they are based on interpretations which can shift around. The impulse which makes you externalise your feelings in a poem might also make you exclude feelings from it, and exclude all the untestable interpretations which might weaken it, and all the rival interpretations of other people which compete with yours; so that you end up with mere descriptions of objects. Writing about objects can be a symptom of anxiety, of unresolved conflicts with the people around you. They apparently grant you power within the poem and over the poem, but in reality make the poem underspecified and vague; the reader is given no information about the subjective significance of the objects, and so they interpret the poem exactly as they wish. They will probably see you as anxious, inarticulate, and perplexed.

The body communicates internal states as a signifying surface; the fine movements of your facial muscles, or the way you walk, convey torrents of information which human observers are supremely, biologically, well qualified to read. But I spoke of being betrayed by the messages you send. What is this betrayal? A dislocation between the value it has for you, the emitter, and the one which it has for the receiver. You strip down the poem, destroying its information content, so that it cannot "betray" you. The key is distrust between you and the people around you whom you expect to receive the messages. Inarticulacy is a sign of lack of trust, and so of anxiety. If there is distrust within the situation which surrounds the poem in the silence before the first line is written, the poem will be minimal and inarticulate. Writing about objects is the poetic equivalent of staring at your shoes.

Reduction to objects is a form of violence, the rejection of language. Violence is the product of rage, typically male, gradually building up through levels of frustration in which symbolic mediation progressively fails as confidence in non-compulsory relationships with other people fades; one falls back on objects after giving up on the wishes of other people. In rage, one withdraws from the riches of the literary tradition, with its potential for suggestion and manipulation; from illusion and from shared illusions, and so from all shared games. Language is a game, art is a game; the regression to dumb objects is a recourse of terror, despair, and inarticulacy. Perhaps class problems make people ashamed to speak. If we draw an axis stretching between low shared-assumptions and high shared-assumptions, we will probably find poetry concentrated at the latter end, and can conjecture that the precursor of the poem is a distribution of sites of enriched sociality bringing about enriched speech; while awkward social situations are also found at predictable points. A party cannot take off when the majority of those present hold grudges against the social order, of attention and affection, animated by those present.

Why is there a rule about only talking about yourself? It is a defensive position adopted after accepting the belief that other people are unknowable. Better information comes from within than from empathy and "psychology". So how about the information carried outwards by language, in fact by poetry? Is this a belief that poetry cannot work? Literary fictions are a game which washes away the ownership of experiences to let all participate in them: for as many as will, like an old dance.

One of the speech rules I proposed above can be extended to read that "more refined description of inner psychological experience takes up more time and so is more egoistic". In application, this makes poetry, if it is more nuanced and more finely discriminated than everyday conversation, illegitimate because it is egoistic. Poetry which deals with experience in a hasty, banal, and conventional way is then morally advanced because it is bored by personal experience and finds it unimportant. Literariness and introspection are associates; the affects of withdrawal, contemplation, alienation, inability to communicate with the people around you, language pent up and locked, are a necessary part of the literary condition. If the writer has an inner world, it competes with the real one; but if the writer has no inner world, the book cannot come about.

The obsession with the sensuous which typifies culturally low and humble poetry derives from a commodity capitalist ideology and is an extension of handling goods to check their quality. Dismissal of speech as sales talk is radical pessimism, the collapse of mental functions, the breakdown of society. Such poetry is reduced to the exchange of objects; there is no shared interior in language any more, but only a shared exterior, the dead, calcified, exactly priced, emptied world of objects. There is no way out of the abyssal problem of interpreting other people's sign systems. 'Sensuous' writing, a refusal to listen based on fear of deceit, seems to accept and internalise the lack of the Holy Ghost.

Addressing the presentation of the self reveals the abyss of non-identification; it is not enough for someone to be evoked on the page, or to start talking on the radio, or to be there in a photograph, for me to become curious about what they are going to do next. Most of the time I am quite happy not to identify. In fact, what does appeal to me is what is appealing: an experience or set of experiences which, from the outside and the outset, are desirable. The whole project of representing a Self in symbolic form is misconceived, because what we want in art is the aesthetic. The project of self-presentation is less unmodified primitive egoism than helplessness in the face of an anxiety about doing anything else, i.e. being artistic.

The realism of language is misleading: everybody can judge a tune on its ability to appeal, but we are distracted from asking this question of a poem precisely because it appears to be a person, or part of a person. For the art critic David Sylvester: "The basic assumption of modern art (. . .) is that the first concern of a work of art is to present a configuration of shapes and colours and marks which in and of itself stimulates and satisfies, and that only after that condition has been fulfilled can the subtlety of observation, the depth of human feeling and insight, the moral grandeur, expressed in the work, have validity; before the work conveys reality it must achieve its own reality."[7] Even where a book of poems evokes a personality, that personality must possess a formal aesthetic appeal, or the book is an achievement of a quite secondary order. It may be that (popular) music has reached a hundred times the attainment of poetry just because music is not misled by realism, and that the popularity of music is due to the superior artistic insight of its adepts, and not to any other factor. The poet who abandons the project of being me in a me way has the inside track and can move a hundred times faster than others. It may even be that we can divide British poetry into two groups: art poetry, and bovine realism. It is, I would guess, because the vast majority belong to the latter group that the discourse of propaganda against the former is so prevalent, so well understood by everybody, and so much more common than an attempt to explain what they are doing. We can also observe that, when poetry is imported from abroad, it is almost inevitably the art poetry which is felt to be worth the costs of transport; and that British readers are much more likely to encounter art poetry from other countries than from Britain.

What we have been discussing is partly the Nonconformist heritage. I should confess an interest in this. My mother's family were Methodists;

in one concerted move, in the 1920s, they moved over to Anglicanism, because the music was better. This deprived the local Methodists of their organist and their best singers. My father's family were and are Presbyterians. Like other people in this country, I am unwilling to admit that my family were wrong about anything. So I find it hard to dislike Dissenters, and have always identified with the Puritans. Nonetheless, there are considerable problems with the Nonconformist heritage. Rejection of the Classical tradition because it was pagan, of the Mediterranean tradition in the visual arts because it was Catholic, of most aspects of the culture patronised by landowners because they were too Anglican, reduction of education to the most instrumental form in search of "improvement", paranoid imposition of morality on art, indifference to almost all forms of music and visual art, appalling dependence on Germans or Swiss for original theological work—this is a heritage which is written all over modern British culture, and which I simply cannot defend. However, as I have suggested in a chapter of *Origins of the Underground*, there is another strand of the radical Protestant heritage which we can be rather happier about. This is the heritage of Blake. As I suggested there, Britain did not know an avant-garde because the vital currents which produced it in a few European countries flowed, on this island, into a visionary and personal Protestantism which felt no need to secularise itself. The twentieth century was one of recovery of Blake rather than of advance into formalism. The diffuse nature of ecclesiastical authority in Britain did not invite radical revolt, and was benign towards personal religion. The problem of modern poetry has been less with monolithic conservative institutions and more with the weakness of the impulses telling poets to produce something public, clearly expressed, and adapted to collective enjoyment, rather than the occult potency of private enactment of myth.

I want to suggest that the cultural pattern is made up of a number of static arrays moving to an organic rhythm of waxing and waning. They do not replace each other but their relative size can change dramatically. A list of some entities which we can envisage as these arrays is in the map pages at the end of this book. These arrays have these features:

—they are focal, i.e. they have a zone of high intensity within a zone
  of lower intensity
—they are highly determined
—exercise powerful attractions (if they follow the determinations)
—isolated from other foci by intermundial spaces
—resolve fears of contamination
—belong to many people or can be reproduced by many people
—constitute territorial rules (to pass the determining limits)
—may occupy institutions or not

Perhaps they have a further history. We have said that the ideal Raine
plugged into had been recorded *in extenso* in the 1936 *Oxford Book of
Modern Verse*. It must have been old in 1936, it perhaps represented the
advanced wing of Western art as it was in the 1880s. You could write a
history of it.

Insofar as these norms are shared they allow an objective basis for
finding that a work of art is successful or unsuccessful, as the primary
readers are qualified to judge on this.

These arrays are not in direct competition with each other. In this model,
we could define the mainstream as functioning entirely within the zone of
minimal intensity. This can also be seen as deep orthodoxy. That would be
why no one wants poetry to be orthodox. The centre is therefore occupied
by vacuity and neatness, not by anything enthusiastic.

Poetry is regionalised into autonomous groups which ignore the centre
or wish there was none. We are not talking about 'shifts of sensibility',
but of a large culture where everything is happening simultaneously and
nothing decisive ever happens. This is not cultural collapse and mutual
incomprehension occurs at specific fault lines, not all over the place.
The schema of a Nonconformist and post-Protestant landscape which
evolves remorselessly from a dozen or so sects in 1644 into hundreds in
the 1960s is fascinating but surely wrong. People naturally learn from
each other and try to communicate with each other. They also imitate
each other. Literary practice therefore constantly develops towards shared
understanding even while the tendency to diverge also sweeps up bits of

the landscape and deposits them further away. It is surely true that many poets are the bearers of conventional ideas, helping the clarity of their works, but after all we are trying to increase clarity and must start where obscurity still lingers. Clearly, there are many poets who aim to tell the truth all the time, and whose ideal of clarity includes dispersing errors and phantom structures before the text starts.

We have seen two demanding literary imperatives, towards hyperliteracy and the death of abstraction, which we can recognise as complementary and opposite. Both are heretical at least in the sense that they are clearly not identical with good taste, i.e. that they command verbal behaviour which competes with and even drowns out pure artistic endeavour. Both are impelled by a strong sense of contamination or miasma - the poets concerned are very anxious to avoid certain qualities in their writing or image.

We can pause to consider how this relates to the theme described in the introduction of depolarising. The complexes described involve mighty imperatives which strongly resemble those followed by readers. As people pursue them, they penetrate and develop great cultural spaces which are, credibly, those in which the poetic experience takes place. It does not seem likely that people beset by these imperatives have an unconscious wish to give them up. The flight resolves their anxieties. Moreover, once having penetrated those great spaces they are used to living without the company of other groups and are out of earshot of what they say. We have said that the drives are opposites, and surely no writer could satisfy both of them at once. I suspect that the polarisation mentioned is the product of imperatives which are much more powerful than poetry because they draw their energy from social and emotional areas which are simply on a bigger scale than poetry. The anxiety mentioned is not the invention of an individual but is an adaptation to attitudes held by very large numbers of people.

This is one opposition in a cultural whole which exists on many planes simultaneously. It has taken a long time to describe but of course it does not describe all the stylistic divergence within poetry—its effects are overlaid by dozens of other oppositions.

These twin essays have an impersonal quality about them. They have this rather bleak quality because they represent poetic areas I have no identification with. That is, there is a huge space between these two extremes, and within that space is the poetry I want to write and the poetry I want to read.

Notes

[1] Lawrence Stone quoted from *Past and Present* (periodical, London), issue 18 (1960).

[2] Rowan Williams and Kenneth Leech (eds.) *Essays Catholic and Radical* (London: Bowerdean Press, 1983).

[3] *After Silent Centuries* (Oxford: Perpetua Press, 1994).

[4] An anthology edited by Rupert Loydell, culled from the first 33 issues of *Stride* magazine (Salzburg: Salzburg University Press, 1993). It is close to the poetry in the anthologies: *Completing the Picture: Exiles, Outsiders, and Independents*, ed. William Oxley (Exeter: Stride, 1995) and *Stumbling Dance*, ed. Rupert M. Loydell (Exeter: Stride, 1995).

[5] Discussed in *Fulfilling the Silent Rules*.

[6] from: *Systematic Theology*, excerpt in *Paul Tillich: Theologian of the Boundaries*, ed. Mark Kline Taylor. (London: Collins, 1987).

[7] David Sylvester *About Modern Art* (London: Chatto and Windus, 1996).

SHAMANISM IS NOT ANGLICANISM
Notes on shamanism as received in British culture

"Goblins, spirits, corpse candles and other unearthly visions have died a natural death and the country has been freed of the incubus of superstition. The 'wise man' who was consulted on all crucial points by our grandfathers, and even later, is as extinct as the dodo. There is no 'Cwrt y cadno' in Wales at present."
> (anonymous writer in the *Western Mail*, 1901;
> 'Cwrt y cadno' is 'the fox's court'.)[1]

"Of these contexts, the most all-embracing is that of 'primitivism' or 'neoprimitivism', accurately diagnosed by Lucy Lippard as '. . . nostalgia—not only for those periods we now [naively] imagine offered a social life simpler and more meaningful than our own, but also for any time when what people made—art—had a secure place in their daily lives.' A more specific category of nostalgia may be evoked here, that of 'Pastoral'. A pastoral yearning for an illusory Neolithic arcady underlies both the mawkish shamanistic posturings of numerous contemporary middle-class avant-garde artists, and their enthusiastic reception by audiences composed of bourgeois-bohemians and other urban sophisticates. The millenarian political and artistic primitivism of Beuys himself, far from being genuinely revolutionary, indicates on the contrary 'reactionary' fear of unpredictable change and anxiety about the future."[2]

Shamanism is now a vogue word. It was no doubt in the 1960s that it became fashionable. In poetry, we find that Ruth Fainlight's sequence 'Sibyls' is a covert version of shamanism; Alan Sillitoe wrote a poem called 'The Shaman' which was the title for a book published in 1968; Ted Hughes' *Crow* (1970) is based on shamanistic myths of the Koryaks and neighbouring north-east Siberian groups; J.H. Prynne's 'Aristeas: in seven years' (1968) recovers a shaman-tale from a Black Sea legend recorded by Herodotus; Eric Mottram's *Book of Herne* involves much knowledge of shamanistic lore; John Arden and Margaretta D'Arcy included an unmistakable Pictish shamaness in their play *The Island of the Mighty*; Maggie O'Sullivan has published a book called *House of the Shaman*; Michèle Roberts has published a poem based on the tale of Odin's nine-day ordeal, generally held to be shamanistic; Geraldine Monk's sequence about the Pendle Witches is a shamanistic poem in light disguise; Iain Sinclair has frequently evoked the idea to illuminate his favourite performance and fetish-artists; Elisabeth Bletsoe's poem 'The Oary Man'[3] uncovers a shaman figure in mediaeval Dorset; a poem in Francis Berry's *Ghosts of Greenland*[4] describes a Norse witch in terms we would relate to a shamaness. In fact, this kind of primitive animistic priest has become a topos in English poetry, part of the shared imaginary. Partly, it is exoticism: the lure of Shamans is a more extreme version of the lure of Celtic bards, discussed elsewhere in this volume; the shamans are the world-periphery, pristine and shadowy. Partly, it is an envy-formation; the poet does not consent to the desacralizing of poetry. In this guise, the shaman-poem is the successor to the belief in spirits which ran riot from the 1840s onward, peaking as a mass movement in the 1920s: Rupert Brooke joined the Society for Psychic Research, HD and Rosamund Lehmann fervently believed in spirit mediums; all this can be more conveniently dealt with in the persona of a Siberian wearing a necklace of bones. Our concept of shamans comes from prose texts, not from shamanistic poetry, which has been collected, but which has in no instance entered the general stream of available and widely read books; consequently, it is the attitude of the prose writers which has been picked up, not the ideas of the shamans themselves. The history of these attitudes among anthropologists remains to be written; it is hardly possible, however, that they were not influenced by a modern current of anti-imperialism, and so ethnographical poems can be seen either as a flight to the periphery, an imaginative attempt to leave imperialism behind: or as a kind of cultural tourism.

The first detailed description of Siberian shamanism to be published in Western Europe was in a book about the Russian Empire by Johann Gottlieb Georgi, in 1780. The word shaman derives from the Tunguz language of Manchuria, and was possibly first brought to the attention of Europeans by the traveller Pallas in his 1776 book, which included a chapter 'Von den Gaukeleyen des Schamanischen Aberglaubens, Zauberey und Weissagerey unter den Mongolischen Völkern' (Of the jugglery of the Shamanistic superstition, magic and soothsaying among the Mongolic peoples): this according to Herbert Risley in his *Native Races of North India*, (1903)[5], where he also points out that the word may have been used by the botanist Gmelin in his *Reise durch Siberien*[6] (Travels Through Siberia) . Risley suggested that it was derived from a Sanskrit word, *sraman* (priest), circulating in Central Asia in a Pali form *samana*; it would then be an Indo-European word echoed back. However, a contributor to Denis Sinor's *Cambridge History of Early Inner Asia*[6] suggests a local, Manchurian origin by citing an older form *shan-man* in early records of Tunguzic customs. If Manchuria is really a classic source of shamanistic practices, a place where they flourish, one is suspicious of their origins; because this is very close to the most ancient centres of Chinese culture, and the expectation is that anywhere on the Chinese periphery has Chinese cultural radiation; although it might be in simplified form, and might be of Chinese culture as it was several thousand years ago. Risley talks of spirit mediums, and percipiently points out that "spiritualism is little more than modernized Shamanism."

The word shaman in Russian signifies a charlatan; someone who performs extraordinary acts, who has magnetism, but is playing on the audience's suggestibility.

The idealization of the shaman is contradicted by another, older, and probably much stronger current of response to non-literate religion, which lays the stress on trickery and mummery. It is hard to read Paul Radin's *Primitive Religion*, and the field observations in Farley Mowat's *People of the Deer* and go on regarding shamans as harmless and benevolent. Radin treats them as part of the power structure, forerunners of the alliance between religion and chiefs or kings which we find in all early agricultural societies. People are afraid of the witch-doctor; he knows about poisons; people who ask awkward questions are smelt out as witches and perish. If literate religion is bad and preliterate religion is good, that is really a rewrite of the Fall. In contrast, we have Richard Dawkins' comment that communication arose as a form of deception: leading us to speculate that the invention of language, and of consciousness, were part of an 'arms race' within the species, in which the victors not only deceived the others but also successfully saw through the deceits of others. Art and religion are both based on illusion. The 'shared imaginary' does not merrily exist without any element of power. Already the unresolved complexities which give a work of art its depth coincide with those which make a religious dogma, or political propaganda, captious and convincing. Few means have not been used for both purposes.

In this theory, suggestibility and authority are closely related, as aspects of the same event of communication, which is also control. Religious discourse would be an example of logically bad language, which is impossible to test or analyse coherently, so that the listener is forced to respond on the basis of personal relationships instead. The message is wrapped up inside the archaic sub-rational signals that the messenger is wise and benevolent. The endless mythological narrative is merely an elaboration hiding the basic message of dependence.

The adulation of shamans is supported by a quite different ideology; including the notion that inequality and exploitation came into the world with the arrival of agriculture (or literacy?). This belief was particularly incredible after the work of the Fifties and Sixties (by Laing, Esterson, and various feminists) which frequently identified oppression in the family, and so in face to face relations; so that the Corporation and the State were merely extensions of fundamental types of human association, and not the origin of evil. If you know that the Innocence of hunter-gatherers on the score of violence, deceit, exploitation, extermination of prey species, etc., is only a moral fable, then the superiority of primitive art over Western art also becomes pale and tenuous. *Bingle bangle bungle I'm so happy in the jungle.* The primitivism of sophisticated, urban Westerners is a sophisticated game: we can do what we like because of our wealth. Boundless subjectivity (as we attribute it to witch doctors and their chants) is a form of the most modern thing, individualism, and is rather like the expansive urge which led to overseas settlement and to economic development. The release of what Freud calls unconscious processes is not really analogous to art which is primary in the chronological sense. Liberation is to be understood as a fight against the Christian framework which imprisoned European art until recent times. Free art neither resembles the art of Siberia and Borneo, nor can this become a bestseller and a staple of Western consumption. Shamaning has extended to become the intelligentsia's equivalent of yelling out *Baby let's go crazy apeshit yeah! Everybody freak out!* Shamanism in Western art has got about as much to do with Siberia and the Palaeoarctic as Aladdin has to do with China. But the exoticism, the supernatural, the fine song and dance, offer a superb opportunity for a *coup de théâtre*, as was pulled off by Nigel Kneale with his 1959 TV series *Quatermass and the Pit* (unexcelled in its way). Once such an idea is made to work (in cinema, television, or poetry), then its relationship to some notional reality in the Manchurian forest, or to elaborate pretences taking place in the forests of Manchuria, is no longer of interest. We do not take our witch doctor mythology from Eliade and Radin (on The Trickster), rather we re-interpret that data (itself of much interest) and fit it into pre-existing categories supplied by our own culture. The sources of such a legendary are easy to find in our own past. Take Tennyson's poem about Vivien, for example, with this evocation of Merlin's beard: 'He spoke in words part heard, in whispers part/ Half suffocated in the hoary fell/ And many-winter'd fleece of throat and chin'. Doesn't he sound a fabulous wise old magus figure? and the sexy witch, Vivien: 'There lay she all her length (...) a robe/ Of samite without price, that more exprest/ Than hid her, clung about her lissome limbs.' Is there any difference between a wizard and a shaman? Ah, but sorcerers have been eliminated from our art and forced into the realm of childhood. For us grownups, shamans are hip and sorcerers are uncool. The appeal of the shaman is the idea, smuggled in unconsciously, that the audience gives him total credulity, credulity shared by him or herself. Obviously, Western artists latch onto this because our culture is based on scepticism; our science and machines work because we are furiously sceptical, and therefore intercept a certain amount of the lies and propaganda on which society floats. Art suffers from this scepticism. We bring in magic, but only disguised as tourism, erudition, or (bizarrely) right-on Thirdy-Worldyness.

The first record of conscious primitivism in Western art is the *Bacchae* of Euripides (circa 406 BC), where the play's overt position against the ecstatic cult, and its *aposparagma* or 'tearing apart of live animals with bare hands' is betrayed by an unconscious admiration of their energy, if only in the way that a lion is admirable. So in fact the Choruses are the utterance of the Maenads (the name is cognate with *mania*). Euripides' evocation of these maniac women corresponds rather closely to some Westerners' use of 'shamanism', cloudily understood and evoked for exoticism and wildness. (Some fragments of the lost *Cretans* may point to Dionysiac passages slightly earlier; the survival of these texts allows us to interpret the Maenads in visual art, who may go back a century earlier.) Their god was Dionysus, and this led Nietzsche to make a famous distinction between Apollonian and Dionysiac in his 1872 work *Die Geburt der Tragödie*. Nietzsche's own, late, Dionysos Dithyrambs are the kind of ecstatic nature poetry which forms the ancestry of *House of the Shaman*. Van Tieghem points out that the first modern return to the Bacchae was a drama by the Swedish poet E.F. Stagnelius in 1822: this is an important date, but more important is the beginning of an understanding of Nietzsche in the 1890s.

Risley also remarks that Shamanism originates in Siberia; a preoccupation with the primitive, and with spiritual power, was influential between (say) 1900 and 1914; Theosophy placed its imaginary spiritual Masters in Tibet, not quite in Siberia but certainly pointing to a reservoir of spiritual power in Inner Asia, as Shambhala. This affect of envy was not new in Victorian times, but was part of their comprehension of Classical literature: all the greatness is right at the beginning, there is neither epic nor great poetic tragedy after the 4th century BC. What had gone wrong? There was a sense of guilt and inferiority felt about the thousand years after that: learning and reasoning were blamed, and this of course meant that Western poetry was under an even greater threat. Edward Thomas' review of the first *Georgian Book of Poetry*, in 1912, said: 'it brings out with great cleverness many sides of the modern love of the simple and primitive, as seen in children, peasants, savages, early men, animals, and Nature in general.' An attempt to get poetry back to the body led to a preoccupation with dance, and also to the adoption of free verse, seen as a more authentic rendition of speech and other physical rhythms than strict metre. Part of the importance of Tragedy is that the Choruses are written in a kind of free verse, and in a Greek dialect felt to be primitive; Nietzsche's Dithyrambs are in free verse. They are also a kind of dance. William Ridgeway's 1915 work on *The Dramas and Dramatic Dances of Non-European Races* is related to reforms of theatre in Edwardian times. At around this time, Ridgeway was influential in founding the first Cambridge Chair of Anthropology; his interest was that he saw anthropology as a key to the Classics, especially the origins of drama. His work on early Greece, on the transition from barbarism to our Classical Age, is frequently cited by Jane Ellen Harrison in her Dionysiac and anti-classical *Prolegomena to the Study of Greek Religion* (1903). We should also compare literal magic: the actress Florence Farr, part of the new theatre, and a member of T.E. Hulme's original poetry discussion group in 1908 (the proto-Imagists), was also the secretary of the Order of the Golden Dawn. Magic and dance are both significant action, an attempt to reverse the fatal abstractness of language; by conjuring up demons to chase away phantoms. Plays in the Georgian Books by Gordon Bottomley and Lascelles Abercrombie show a mutinous primitivism; Bottomley's search for a "spiritual reservoir" in Dark Age Britain foreshadows a thousand modern poems; Thomas and Abercrombie located the reservoir in "peasant speech", Lawrence located it in parts of the nervous system and of the psyche. All this is not really illuminating poetry with the solid results of anthropology, but instead the reading of anthropology, archaeology, etc., in a wholly text-based tradition of scholarship, to solve the problem of poetry—and especially poetic drama—ceasing to be great. Hughes, Fainlight, etc. presumably thought they were solving this problem too.

Shamanistic elements among North European farming peoples

Siberian influences are possibly not a new thing in Northern European culture. De Vries, writing about Old Norse religion, quotes a 1935 book by one Strömbäck: "Strömbäck has brought in his informative investigation the proof that *seiðr* is a process which resembles the magical practice of Lappish (and general Altaic) shamans." This magic (other words are used for other sorts of magic) is, says Strömbäck, an influence coming in from the Ural-Altaic world, from the cultural complex which includes Siberia and so also the *locus classicus* of shamanism, but which reaches as far as Northern Russia and Northern Scandinavia. It would certainly be interesting if those chronically poor and scattered cultures had produced something potent enough to influence European peasants and then leave traces in a European literature. "The singing of the retinue is supposed to put the *seiðkona* (magic woman) into an ecstatic state, so that her soul leaves her body and goes elsewhere. (…) These resemblances to Lappish practices are based on cultural links which go back deep into prehistory; one can presumably regard shamanism as a trait of North-Eurasian primitive cultures (*Urkulturen*)." This last remark agrees with what Eliade said; Findeisen's opinion is that "the hunting culture of the North Asians is an uninterrupted continuation of the common culture of the hunting Old Stone Age into the present." Farming was preceded, in Northern Europe, by Mesolithic hunter-gatherer-fisher cultures. The repertoire of religion, without technically advanced scenography, is finite. This native stock probably did include seers going into trances, spells to make rivers and woods replenish with game, etc., without then being a copy of the religion of the Tunguz or the Eskimo. The arrival of farming was rather late in areas such as Scandinavia. It is difficult to tell apart a possible borrowing of Altaic themes, from Lapps migrating into Scandinavia from the north-east, from a local retention of Mesolithic shamanism, either by existing hunter-gatherers, or even by peasants. In any case the many traits defined as 'shamanistic' by Eliade do not appear in Norse records as a coherent whole, rather we have half a dozen separate traits appearing in isolation.

The word *seiðkona* appears already in Thomas Gray's Notes to his poem, 'The Descent of Odin', where he quotes a description of her:

> "She had on a blue vest spangled all over with stones, a necklace of glass beads, and a cap made of the skin of a black lamb lined with white cat-skin. She leaned on a staff adorned with brass, with a round head set with stones; and was girt with an Hunlandish belt, at which hung her pouch full of magical instruments."

The reference to Hunland, to be identified with the western end of the Steppe world, alerts us to another possible reservoir of shamanistic practices; Wolfram interprets, in his *History of the Goths*, a certain passage of Jordanes as a record of conflict in South Russia between local shamanistic cults and the traditional Gothic religion, circa 200 AD.

The Norse sources point to an alien origin of this type of magic. De Vries also says:

"Namentlich die Lappen sind als zauberkundig bekannt und gefürchtet gewesen. Wenn fremde, auf einer niedrigeren Kulturstufe stehenden Volkselemente mit anderen zusammen-wohnen, so werden sie oft als wohlbewandert in der Magie betrachtet; der Schamanismus und das Verfahren mit der Zaubertrommel haben wohlbesonders dazu beigetragen, den Lappen den Ruf der Zauberei zu verschaffen. Die Beispiele für 'finnische' Zauberer sind in der Literatur ausserordentlich zahlreich, sogar so häufig, dass man dem Wort *finn* eine erweiterte Bedeutung hat beilegen wollen: es soll nicht nur der Name des lappischen Volkes, sondern eine allgemeine Bezeichnung für einen Zauberer gewesen sein. Daneben gibt es aber jedenfalls zweifellos Beispiele für Lappen, die besonders zauberkundig waren (…)."

[Especially the Lapps were known and feared as expert in magic. When alien folk elements, standing on a lower cultural level, live together with others, they are often regarded as familiar with magic; shamanism and the handling of the shaman's drum probably contributed in particular to giving the Lapps the reputation of magic. The examples of Finnish magicians in the literature are extraordinarily frequent, so frequent indeed that it has been suggested that we should attribute a wider meaning to the word: supposing that it is not only the name of the Lapp people, but a general term for a magician. In contrast to this, there are nonetheless undoubted examples of Lapps who were specially good at magic (...)]

(The word Finn in old Scandinavian texts means Lapp, or so we are led to believe; but the people in North Norway in 1,000 AD may have been different from the Lapps we know about.) So already in 13th century Norse texts we have an admiration for primitive magic. We have two cultural nostalgias here: the thirteenth century Christian composers of the antiquarian type of Icelandic saga were nostalgic for the pagan era of Norse culture, i.e. before AD 1,000; and the pagan Norse of the heroic era were in awe of the non-agricultural peoples in the interior parts of Scandinavia. This sentiment clearly anticipates the nostalgia for magic and shamanism of twentieth-century poets. These practices appear in the sagas only as literary devices, not as current belief: study of dates indicates that we don't have any texts composed by practicing pagans, or which could have been used in genuine rituals. This of course resembles the case in the Mediterranean, where what we know of mythology comes largely from texts composed by sophisticated and syncretistic literati who were non-believers. It's hard for us to get back to a stratum of genuinely credulous, pious, utterance; which is perhaps one of the reasons why anthropology aroused so much interest, about a century ago, when it could present people who really believed in the supernatural. Anthropology, though, had to compete with theosophy. Francis Berry's poem uses the same source as Gray; he shows the aged witch using the female narrator as a medium:

> Of the seal, of the floe, of the ice,
> About her eyes which spin glass,
> About a fish, about a tusk, about the walrus,
> About a special peg, or bone, which dances
> Both in and out, about the grass, about a flap
> A bleeding flap, or wound, and in it plunges,
> > Winces, prances,
> A thudding sire, a bull, a thing, a fire,
> About the bull, about the calf, about the eyes
> > Of spirits' wild glass.
> Seal, floe, ice, eyes, fish, tusk, bone, flap.

Any attack on "ethnographical forgery" has to deal with the awkward literary-historical fact of the mass of writing which uses mythology and cosmology without believing in it. Greek drama of the 5th century BC presumably already belongs to this type. Surely the analogy between modern poets using myth, and the *fornaldra* sagas and the Classical writers such as Homer and Ovid, is rather striking.

The results of studying the Norse tradition are rather disappointing in the sense that they don't identify features of Anglo-Saxon religion for us: if the magic in question came in from mobile, non-farming people of Finno-Ugrian speech, it might have circulated in Scandinavia only, and not in the homeland of the Angles and Saxons. Perhaps it doesn't matter so much about the historical truth; perhaps what matters is the way poets have felt legitimized, by the legends about shamans, to depart into a world of the eschatological and supernatural and still be culturally acceptable. English poetry has undergone a mythical renewal; the themes of Ted Hughes,

Peter Redgrove, Iain Sinclair, Maggie O'Sullivan, and Brian Catling would have been simply impossible in the nineteenth century. The mythical cycles of Christianity and Classical antiquity, which have sustained English poetry right from its origins, are exhausted; if we rule out an alternative mythology, it is probable that English poetry would become exhausted and cease.

In the early period of Christianisation, in a still transitional society, certain practices of pagan origin survived at the level of magic; we have some Anglo-Saxon spells which incredibly survived the Christian Middle Ages. Also, there probably were witches during the period of large-scale witch-trials and burnings, in the sixteenth and seventeenth centuries. Books by Margaret Murray (criticized, importantly, by Norman Cohn in *Europe's Inner Demons*) put these facts in connection, and uphold the theory of an underground religion which flourished in secret from Christianity, survived (perhaps) until the present day, and preserves Germanic paganism in a pristine and folk form. You can even, today, join covens whose spokesmen will claim that their knowledge and tradition is thousands of years old. Some of it may really go back as far as the 1950s. My attention was drawn to this while wandering round the Small Presses Book Fair, which certainly had a good many more stalls dedicated to occultism than it did to poetry. The witch industry has by now caught the bandwagon, and claims that "we are your shamans". It also claims—and why not?—to stand for the liberation of women, sexual liberation, freedom from nasty foreign ideas, greenness and love of the earth, decentralisation, satisfying concreteness, and so forth.

What is artistically useful is the conventionality and predictability of our common image of the Primitive and the World of the Spirits. A poet could not produce free associating poetry, and poetry set in the world of a Tunguz or Koryak, unless we were thoroughly familiar with the scene and could catch most of the bits as they fly past us. Only at this point does the opposite quality of unpredictability become a virtue. Our Petit Trianon, Doctor Who, British Museum primitivism offers educated poets a way out of realism into a mythic world. Unexpectedly, it becomes the poetic equivalent of Jackson Pollock, Clyfford Still, and Asger Jorn, a boundless subjectivity when all forms have been burst. At the juncture of the retrievable and the unknown, we find the sublime.

NOTES

General sources: Paul Radin, *Primitive Religion* (London: Hamish Hamilton, 1938); Farley Mowat, *People of the Deer* (London: Michael Joseph, 1952); Alfred, Lord Tennyson, in 'Vivien'; Philippe Van Tieghem, *L'ère romantique. Le romantisme dans la littérature européenne* (Paris, 1948, publisher uncredited); William Ridgeway, *The Dramas and Dramatic Dances of Non-European Races*, (Cambridge: Cambridge University Press 1915); Jane Ellen Harrison, *Prolegomena to the Study of Greek Religion* (Cambridge: Cambridge University Press, 1903); Jan De Vries, *Altgermanische Religionsgeschichte* (Berlin: Walter de Gruyter, 2 vols, 1956–7); Dag Strömbäck, *Sejd. Textstudier i nordisk religionshistoria* (Stockholm, 1935); Hans Findeisen, *Schamanentum* (Stuttgart: W Kohlhammer, 1957); Wolfram Herwig, *History of the Goths* (Berkeley: University of California Press, 1988); Norman Cohn, *Europe's Inner Demons* (London: Chatto, 1975).

[1] *Cwrt y cadno*: Dai Smith, ed., *A People and a Proletariat* (London: Pluto, 1980).
[2] Tom Gibbons 'Occultism', in *Modern Painters* (periodical: London), volume 2, number 3, (reviewing a book by John Moffitt).
[3] The poem 'Oary man' appears on Elisabeth Bletsoe, *Direction Poetry* Volume One (tape; Pentraeth: Direction, 1994).
[4] Francis Berry *Ghosts of Greenland* (London: Routledge, 1966).
[5] Herbert Risley, *The People of India* (Calcutta and Simla: Thacker, Spink & Co., 1915).
[6] as cited by Risley, *op.cit.*
[7] Denis Sinor, ed., *Cambridge History of Early Inner Asia*, vol. 1 (at p.419, in a chapter by Herbert Franke; Cambridge: Cambridge University Press, 1990).

JUJU! MAGOG! HOBGOB! DABRA! : MAGGIE O'SULLIVAN[1]

The failure of the Apocalyptic or New Romantic poetry of the 1940s was, it seems to me, due to their moderation; their flights of imagination are nailed down by orthodox diction and metrical formalism. Staidness of language stifled the energies yearningly evoked. Even mythographically, they failed to break out of the Christian framework. Twenty years were to pass before an effective solution was found to these problems. The appeal of that group was their passion and the visionary state from which they wrote; their language contradicted these claims at every step. They must have thought that this losing strategy was 'passion contained with discipline and skill'. In fact such extreme states of mind could only be captured by coordinating all aspects of the linguistic object: metrical, syntactic, logical, lexical. It is in this light that we have to consider O'Sullivan:

> nailed Eagles   beryl   alter vasish
> Owls, Blood-bed
> Bird-gear   turbulent
> Ruled
>
> it,
>
> Raven
>
> blue acquiescing tar
>   thread
> the.air.it.will.be.tinned.
>   pull —
> feather against call —
>
> Crow-Shade
> plumb, true

(*from* 'Hill Figures')

Because every element of the signifying complex is mimetic, this is a zenith of technique. The imagery is neo-Apocalyptic but the other parts of the verse fabric have been burnt away, found wanting. At the same time, the inventory of relations between verbal entities has been impoverished.

    In the history of Western anthropological writing, the word shaman has replaced witch doctor, medicine man, juju man. The reality has, of course, remained the same. (The phrase "Toyz Iz uz magician", p.45, appears to combine a local sorcerer concept with a well-known chain of toyshops.) The title comes I believe from a work by Joseph Beuys, one for all kinds of sham antics. More interestingly, an associate recently described Maggie O'Sullivan as "a cross between Gerard Manley Hopkins and Ian Hamilton Finlay".

Looking back at the publicity of concrete and sound poets reminds us of the odd fact that extreme subjectivity and wildness has always been claimed for them; the most academic of artists, those who work completely from theory. Leaving aside the self-deception implicit in this, we grasp that the justifying ideology of this avant-garde wasn't so far from that other liberatory current of the 1960s, which began as hippiedom and was later renamed New Age. A broad sector of contemporary Creative Persons doesn't at all mind dressing up as witches and wizards and proclaiming their closeness to Primal Magic. How far is it from sha-persons to sword-and-sworcery novels? or from *Lud Heat* to *The Shadow of the Torturer*? or even from *Crow* to *In the House of the Shaman*?[2]

The second to last poem in the book is a Lorica. This is a Latin word for a leather breastplate, also for a kind of poem in the form of a protective charm. We know two examples, both by fifth- or sixth-century Romano-Britons: Gildas and Patrick. The transition from literature back to apotropaic magic is also the transition from ordered speech to arbitrary strings of words, turning back to things and grouped in a visual pattern. The piece by Gildas (especially) is a bizarre piece of rhetoric and exoticism, which one can well imagine as following up some tradition of spells. This would not, however, have been an Insular tradition, given the illiteracy of the Celts, but a practice from the Babylon-Syrian-Coptic region, the heartland of magic. My bet is that most of 'shamanism' is a radiation-diffusion from the advanced agricultural and literate civilizations. The undated, but perhaps also sixth-century and British, Leiden Fragment is unmistakably a pagan love charm disguised as a Christian hymn: 'descendat meus amor super illam, eascrutentur membra illius pro amore meo'. The Gildas Lorica has 49 lines of body parts, the Leiden charm has 18 lines of them. The cataloguing of body parts is that element which binds Christian texts (chiefly curses) most closely to their pagan antecedents; in the case of the loricas, it ties them to a type of love charm or curse (*may the named person's parts wither until she gives herself to me*), widespread in the Roman world, but well known in Roman Britain; so that, to our amazement, we find identical structures present in the sixth-century lorica, a ninth-century Anglo-Saxon ritual curse printed by Liebermann, and third-century Romano-British incantation scrolls.

It was G. S. Kirk who pointed out, in *The Nature of Greek Myths*[3], that the priests, as well as being responsible for philosophy and lofty ethical judgements, were also the slaughtermen, there at the consecration, up to their elbows in reeking blood; having much to do with the insides of animals' bodies. As if the invisible realm were inside the body. But at least they had the good manners to use a knife.

To a certain extent, our excitement in consuming art is limited by the excitement of the artist. If the artist seems bored, phobic, laborious, following routine, we can only enjoy the art to a limited extent. This is the basis for wanting the artist to be as entranced and involved as possible, and so for admiring the Shaman, in the form in which Westerners imagine him, as the culminating artist. This makes it possible for the artist to develop along the path of subjectivity, strengthening and training the forces of the personality as an alternative to technical fluency. It is not coincidental that the re-assertion of the irrational forces which helped form Greek art should have just come just before the rejection of the Classical—and Apollonian—visual ideal, which had been unchallenged in Western art since before the Renaissance. Nietzsche's distinction is also the line between freedom and structure, as it has appeared in Western art over the past century. Look at this passage:

> lilac tea latin silk copper fuse turba velours
> > bantam dimensions
> sunrise durrus emerald chanceries
> > raised
>
> the land is in rises
> fully with sable corridor

> (*from* 'Lorica for Zoe')

This is free in metre, vocabulary, syntax, and in the sequence of ideas. The attainments of Apollo scarcely feature. The issue is not, for example, whether Eskimo shaman songs are written in strict metre and to strict tunes. The freedom is supposed to indicate an excited state of mind. It is a radical departure from the ironic, domesticated realism of common bad English poetry: it asks a drastic psychological departure of the reader. The poem as it were shakes the patterns of language apart to impose its own more urgent line. I was going to compare O'Sullivan's work to free jazz (which can reach extraordinary peaks, and dissolves the memory of ordinary life in a few minutes) when I noticed this passage: 'Shake, Two, Three, Four! / Kick! Vanilla! / giddy feathered/ Crinkle- / gown.' Vanilla? Surely we have here a reworking of Joey Dee's classic *Peppermint Twist*: 'Round and round and up and down and / One two three kick! / One two three jump!' As one of the gogo dancers at the fabulous Peppermint Lounge recalled recently, "The fringes on our fannies were *clocked* as going at 80 miles an hour."

This kind of thing has been theorized a lot in connection with abstract art; as Peter Fuller remarks, "In twentieth-century 'expressionism', objectively perceived anatomy becomes less and less important: the bodily basis of much painting is rather the unseen body of the artist, which is revealed through such phenomena as scale, rhythm, and simulation of somatic processes" (in 'David Bomberg'[4]). To gain insight into other people's intentions (a sophisticated faculty), we need insight into their somatic processes, their drive structures; that which remains most intact from pre-human ancestors. When discussing shared subjectivity, we need to remember what the unit structures of subjectivity might be. We could clarify much of modern art by studying the basis of meaning in memory and physical experience; formal creativity pushes us into altered states by means of hyperassociation, but the array of symbols must be based on stored experience (i.e. old states) or else there would be no stored associations for them to set off. Much modern art is, I am afraid, hypo-associative. One would expect the forfeiture of reason to raise physiological experience to a new prominence. O'Sullivan's work is, frequently or even normally, about plants and animals: drawing on unconscious fantasies about occupying a different body, which, because of their rooting in the physical grounds of our experience, are common and direct, but also creative and in conflict with reason.

> Median Sagittal Plain
> Salts Mirror
> Outer Poises Opaler Too.
> Tear-low slaughter
> Steady on Horror
> Crackly
>
> Laddery
>
> Triply Hooves
> pounded stomach on string
> (. . .)
> Trance
> Orbiting
> 2 Horns, scalded, misspelt. Approximal
> membraneous shadow plaiting, the
> Letter Missing, Missingly
>
> Climates end, Spans —
>
> of the Jar, Want Conductors, Want Light —
> Want as a province of sheer retinal Directory
>
> (. . .)
> Embryonic lassing
> ARTILLERY
> Crosses. Crisscross, Crossings gone
> Carapace
> Cutaway Iambic
> Cloaca documents, Octaves of the Kidney

(from 'Giant Yellow')

All of this is a kind of dreamed anatomy, if it can be retrieved at all. Perhaps we could regard it as a mnemonic map to guide shamans in treating internal illnesses without killing the patient. *In the House of the Shaman* is divided into three books, but all of them contain the same themes: 'Kinship with

Animals' could describe the whole. Landscape hardly features, only warm bodies. Median sagittal proximal retinal are technical anatomical terms. A couple of pages later we find: 'Gived Contortionist: / Sylla / bled Garjey, / auric fin spun key skins / Boundary between (...)—acro pleural petal fugal / thick fat spat fast (...) shimmer gifts meant / hoofmarks / hairsbreadth / Winged Antimony / Entered / Lacerations / risen / earth tr. Yellow Tooks / birds & their habits—jump the channels / call the visions in', with even more Modified Anatomy. If cerebral activity is a recombination of data from the senses, we would need a special sensory map to imagine the physical states of other humans (and perhaps animals) as a way of reading their intentions; and this is perhaps one of the ways in which the imagination arose. The stress here is not on actual inner-body sensations, but on imagined, and fantastic, alien inner-body sensations.

Curiously enough, this anatomical discourse does remind me of shamanism: the Eskimo *angakoq* who goes to the bottom of the sea and there pleads with the Old Lady to replenish the sea with seals and walruses so that the Eskimo can eat them. As someone (I know not who) pointed out, the process by which the spirit takes over and rides the human seer in a possession ceremony (disembodied soul) mirrors the process of eating caught animals to acquire strength (dis-animate bodies). Communication with the spirit world has mostly been associated with the sacrifice—an act of slaughter. The shaman who wields the knife to cut the hole through which life escapes is logically enough the first surgeon. Myth has to involve losing a body or acquiring one; the Old Lady was a mortal woman who on having hands and feet cut off (a family quarrel) became the first seal and supplied the Sea Eskimo with their food ever after. O'Sullivan's poetry has to do with fertility—the formation of new bodies (of animals) as looked after by a Mistress of the Wild Things in a widespread Eurasian myth. She describes animals partway through the regeneration process, caught in mid-transformation; their geometry still capable of transforms into quite different body plans; rendered always, not as dead anatomies of tissues and limbs, but as maps of sensation.

The anatomy of the poem has been modified, too. There has been a shift of scale: rhythm is now no longer concerned with the definition of long acoustic units (a decasyllabic line or even a cluster of lines) but with the alternation of noise and silence within much smaller autonomous units. There are no lines in this book, nor is it clear how a line can come about where there are no sentences. The reduction of scale gives a more affective and spiritual quality. The focus on stress as a physiological event has led to the word *pulse*[5] as a description of how the poet gives way to a rhythmic flow of beats; this has important implications for the relation between intimate subjective awareness and measured organized knowledge as the source of the information of which the poem is made up. It is not impossible that the rushing simple structures of O'Sullivan's work (and of Ulli Freer, Adrian Clarke, Robert Sheppard, cris cheek, for example) are a rejection of the discourse of government and corporations—and academics, I suppose—in favour of some kind of anarchism. Evidently syntax is part of ordering relations between individuals in a functioning group—the exchange of information is related to decisions being made. This gesture can also be seen as the abandonment of politics in favour of innerness.

O'Sullivan's project incorporates all kinds of linguistic patterns from babble through counting-out rhymes and shouted dance instructions. It is integrative and inclusive; it might be an 'experimental area' but it has not been starved of diversity. It is stuffed full of interesting structures; unlike texts whose rule that nothing familiar be included is the opposite of freedom. Along with its hypotaxis and polysyllables, formal English noticeably lacks the diminutives which are a part of informal speech. There are a number of word coinages in *House*, many of which I cannot interpret; but the use of '-y' to form diminutives is common; in the passage

> Uppies! Downies! Jumpies!
> Fire-Sinuses!
> Moonjies!
> Playsies!

we find a formative, now almost confined to children's speech, being applied in adult poetry. The sequence sounds like instructions for a game or a song with actions. So a loss of structure on one side (no conjunctions, no prepositions, very few verbs, no lines of poetry) goes along with a greater permissiveness to other kinds of structure. Free poetry tends to be terribly unpermissive. This sequence reminds me of a counting-out rhyme: *Ippy-dippy-dation, My operation, How many people at the station?* A lot that is going on falls under this formula of applying existing rules of word formation and connection in new contexts. Another rule states that primary stresses must be as frequent as possible, so that most words are nouns and most are short (cf. Pulse). The words flow along a structure which is not linguistic but contextual: atomistic phrases go together because they are part of some larger context, a scene. Words are piled up, not linked analytically: SCALDERY AXE ACCELERATIONS UTTERBLUE OX, or FERN LASH LARGED OCTAVES   BLACKENING SEPTIC RUSSULA/ ICON OX TALL THUNDERER   SAID SEEN STRANG SINEWS. As I said, the catalogue of relationships between entities has been emptied. You grasp the whole by intuition, or not at all. There is no name for this noun-string construction, although it is familiar to partisans of Mr Nicholas Cave (BIG-JESUS-TRASH-CAN) and Ms Elisabeth Fraser ('Froufrou foxes in midsummer fires')[6]. What the scene in question might be is harder to say, although the allusion to Siberian religion in the title offers a whole range of programmes or orders of service as candidates. It becomes useful here to know what shamanism is.

One could imagine the scenario to be the priest carefully laying out the bones of a prey animal already caught and eaten, ritually assuring that new animals will be born so that they too can be eaten. Twice (in the book 'Another Weather System', part 1 of this volume) the poet refers to Blood Month (*blotmonath*), i.e. November, when the pagan Anglo-Saxons made many sacrifices (*blot*). The ritual to ensure the rebirth of the year probably also aimed to ensure the multiplication of animals. If the service corresponds to Norse *disablot*, it was dedicated to a kind of minor goddess. So the cluster 'the year, drawn/ white, its NORTH BLACK WINTERING/ drapes pitch' may refer to this winter ritual. When the poet refers to 'Skull & Bone & comb / breathe & / river, the crow / is in time / thinned, stirred / stabbing / souther/ impings— / / all the greater multiplying', we can imagine that multiplying is being assured. 'Imps' are grafts (of plants) in Anglo-Saxon, but to my surprise the *Concise Oxford Dictionary* gives "imp the wings of (bird), strengthen its flight; (rare) enlarge, eke out". The situation points forward to the Christian graveyard, where bones are carefully laid in order, in expectation of a similar miracle of resurrection.

Well, there is little call for the theology of religions which nobody believes in. The theology only enters the realm of poetry as a system of subjectivity—as I've said, the pursuit of extreme states in art falls down when it comes to sharing them. This problem struck rock musicians, who thought that all it took to make great records was a capacious supply of drugs. Even as you throw away the contents of the workaday world as too tedious, you discover that a poem is made out of information. How can you turn subjectivity into information? Some kind of shared structures are necessary—even if they originate in fantasy. Objectivity is blocked off by the problem of scepticism and academic expertise; poetry has to expel fact or be engulfed by an alien power. *In the House of the Shaman* works because it is not based in theology or in anthropological field reports, but in physical experiences of growth, recuperation, fertility, and emotional shifts. Subjective experience may be a translation of these physical events. The problem is turning a personal language into a shared one. In painting, the expulsion of the object brought a greater concentration on the body, as a set of sensory maps which could be translated into an external, painted, object by direct action; no doubt the same is true of this poetry, violently shaped by sensations too rapid to amount to knowledge. The opposition between true and untrue has been eliminated. There is no point trying to work out what these staccato phrases mean; the reader either grasps the feel from the overall way the text is organized, and starts fantasizing about the same thing the writer is fantasizing about, or the whole thing is like a dry harbour. I think on the whole this is what I want poetry to be like; domestic realists, up against the wall! This has the same crazed intensity that rock music used to have. *Tackety! Tantivy! Nanjivy! Glug!*

NOTES

[1] This essay concentrates on the volume *In the House of the Shaman* (London: Reality Street Editions, 1993), from which all the O'Sullivan quotations are drawn.

[2] The references are to: Iain Sinclair, *Lud Heat: A Book of the Dead Hamlets* (London: Albion Village Press, 1975)—since reissued in *Lud Heat and Suicide Bridge* (London: Granta Books, 2002); Gene Wolfe, *The Shadow of the Torturer* (first volume of *The Book of the New Sun* (London: Legend, 1981); Ted Hughes, *From the Life and Songs of the Crow* (London: Faber, 1971).

[3] G.S. Kirk: *The Nature of Greek Myths* (Harmondsworth: Penguin, 1974).

[4] Peter Fuller: 'David Bomberg' in *Beyond the Crisis in Art* (London: Artists' and Writers' Collective Publishing, 1980).

[5] *pulse*: defined on previous page. See also 262–7 of FCon.

[6] Mr Nicholas Cave and Ms Elisabeth Fraser: recording with the Birthday Party and the Cocteau Twins, respectively.

Deep Politics

> Parapolitics is the unavowed level of political action. Deep politics
> is the level of system assumptions which never gets recorded in
> the documents at all.
> — Peter Dale Scott, *Deep Politics II: The Death of JFK*

Do we perceive a whole landscape of poetry? Surely, reading a poem involves intimacy between two people, an intense experience of projective identification, as you gaze into each other's eyes. The poet is happy for other poets not to interrupt and the reader possibly feels the same way. Both sides explore individuality, even narcissism. However, there is also a sort of infrastructure of poetry—a public equipment of reviewing, reputation, printing, retailing, which plays a role in mediating this intimacy and exalted solitude. Although everything is happening inside the poem, there is also an outside to the poem, recorded in a dense mythology of malice, exclusion, frustration. We can ask, I think, whether this infrastructure is well managed. In itself, it is roughly as interesting as the diagram of a ventilation duct. However, someone wondering why the visible world of poetry is designed so as to hide the significant poets and obscure the real processes at work may be helped by a discussion of institutions, managers, and process.

The story which Peter Barry tells in *Poetry Wars*[1] is about the progressive past in 1971–7 of the flagship *Poetry Review*, which because of its huge subscription list was a public arena, seen by all sectors of public opinion. He tells how a radical slate was elected to the Council of the Poetry Society, and how Eric Mottram edited *Poetry Review* for six years and excluded the mainstream, how opposition polarised and burst out into a public row, how the Arts Council as major funder raised questions about the management of the Society, and how climactically fourteen Council members resigned at one meeting in March 1977. New editors took over, and the Underground went underground again. There followed a period of calm and prosperity for the magazine and the Society.

There are several ways of reading this story. One is of a heroic band of brothers to whom destiny had imparted a special charge of bringing about The Future, being absurdly betrayed and snagged by cultural reactionaries, with the consequence that an avid audience was deprived of real poetry forever after. Another is of hopeful and innocent poetry fans baffled by the obscurity and apparent blankness of the poetry on offer, or alienated by the arrogance and narrowness being upheld. These fans were saved by the graceful exit of the culprits and were very happy with the cleaned-up landscape, which was The Future and filled with hundreds of other poets. We don't have to swallow either of these stories.

Eric Homberger describes the English poetry scene since 1974 or so as balkanized—the landscape is split by horizons, beyond which no light, no sound, flows. Barry is making visible the line of invisibility between the 'British Poetry Revival' (BPR), a wave of poets who rejected English convention, and the conventional or mainstream poets. He presents this as still the major division within English poetry. The rows were caused by deep artistic disagreements which, therefore, existed before the rows. We are not given reasons to think that the rows altered the landscape. The reasons for the balkanisation of poetry must be sought elsewhere. You may well ask if this boardroom struggle for control of an institution is part of the history of poetry. The fascination of the event is that through all the noise poetic ideals became visible. It simultaneously produced disinformation, where the fear of losing was a fear of being shut out of the future.

My artistic breakthrough was happening just at the time of these events, in 1977. They meant nothing to me. But they turned up the volume on loyalty and loathing. After a painful lag, I realised that some moves within the poem made some people write me off as a 'rebel and loser', while others made other people reject me as 'bourgeois and compromised'. Any social ideal is likely to involve a diet—eliminating certain *people*. Aesthetic experience prefers an ideal state of harmony. Someone who dissents is likely to be expelled. Collusion makes the invisible mightier than the visible, and thrives on exclusion. Most people in the poetry world have a strong sense of where they shouldn't be. If you have that feeling, you should probably do what it says. But if we are trying to explain the scene we have to *see* the divisions.

Group boundaries may seize stylistic markers, entering the way the poem is written; they become loyalty tests, affecting the way it is read. The poem stops being a functional lump of information and is taken over by gestures towards ideals—of freedom, or orderliness—or towards a group and its ideal group process. So the poem becomes much richer in data—which may be trapped in the pipes of the code. How would you go about reconciliation? video'd decommissioning of ten 60s sound poets? controlled detonation of Don Paterson?

Relations with the Arts Council (actually, one officer) broke down in 1973. Almost four years of insecurity and tension followed, making routine decisions stressful. Resignation was a reasonable way out, although what felt like martyrdom was banal, the everyday lot of the arts worker. "But you don't love me like I love myself!" That's right.

If it was a war, the weapon of choice was character assassination. Dead light seeps through the horizon and gives rise to poisoned information. Disagreement on basic facts has made discussion of the events fruitless and contentious. The book is presented as based on the documents and reprints eleven pages of them as evidence. The allure of a public debate over a common event is that, for once, the parties may talk about the same thing, rather than sticking to areas chosen to suit their attitudes. Where hostility is fed by fantasy, recovering the truth can bring the small but riven poetry world closer together. The open disputes could have produced clear and valuable statements of prejudice, or even of principle, but in fact it seems they didn't. The personal abuse was colourful but never reached any archives. It may be that the story of poems being imagined and imaginatively read is not in the documents. One has to ask: what documents? whose voice? whose archive? Barry's decision not to do any interviews for information gathering is baffling. However, as a former insider in one faction who no longer shares their opinions on everything he is a first-rate witness.

Something he sheds light on is the alleged unpopularity of Eric's *Poetry Review*. Actually, it seems that sales did not crash. The disaster of the modern poets was after that—and due to the failure of the talent around Mottram to organise a successor magazine. Annoying large swathes of the poetry audience is not the same as being unpopular.

Professor Barry was a student of Mottram, edited a magazine (*Alembic*) which ran on exclusively Mottramite lines, and has close associations with many of the protagonists within that camp. The Arts Council's version is that their interest in the internal affairs of this major client was aroused by the noise of protest against the policy of the committee, and of *Poetry Review*, emanating from groups formed specially to make those protests. Hmmm. How badly do you have to offend readers in order to make them form groups to protest against you? Maybe most of the audience *like* conventional poems? Although this was a clash of ideals, only the ideas of one side get discussed. Further, the focal area is cut to leave out the artistic goals being pursued by Literature Officer Charles Osborne—since, as we are told, Osborne has his version of events on record. Thus the winners are not allowed on stage. While limiting himself to a brief account of the artistic side of the BPR, Barry says even less about the mainstream. Has any notable poet emerged from the mainstream in the past 25 (*alt.* 50) years? His book is not about the clash of ideals. The taxonomy of the 'British Poetry Revival' offered is not persuasive. In poetry as in a city, points on the periphery are further away from each other than each is from the centre. The 'movement' suggested began in 1960 and includes probably more than 500 published poets by now. They diverged but did not converge. The poets selected to highlight are Carlyle Reedy and Robert Sheppard—surely a tactical error. This work will not sway the uncommitted.

Thinking of an ideal poem is close to writing an ideal poem. The gap is small. Consequently, thinking about an ideal poem is benign for all of us. If you have 1,000 poets writing at one time, they can't all write the same poem. Consequently, speculation about new kinds of poem is benign and *reduces* rivalry.

A chapter analyses the creative ideas of Mottram. He had a genius for persuading people they could live in these ideals without starving to death. Moving in this new territory is terrifying because you are walking on thin air. These were the keys to a new world for poetry and you can live there—the books now exist. The frontier is where the great fortunes are made. You go into the high state to bring something back which can be read back by other people.

Nobody would claim that the future Mottram foresaw was interchangeable with the future *as it actually happened*. Over the years, each side can claim to have a legacy in the poetry of 1977–2005. The old English society died, and to escape the big chill poets apparently had to choose one of 3 (or 5, or 9?) paths, and move out of sight of poets on other orbits. The loss of communications brought about the utterly fragmented poetic landscape which we now see around us. And leaders claim to *own* those paths. Whose future is the one we have? This is vital, because most of the readers of the 70s, and most of the excelling poets, could be claimed by both sides. If Cobbing could *own* everything radical, the opera fan Charles Osborne could *own* everything lucid, melodic and lyric. Poetry has thrived in the atmosphere, freer and richer in ideas after the changes of 1967–77, while the Mottram group has been almost invisible. Maybe the 1977 fuss had no influence on the way poetry has been written over the 25 years? has no explanatory value at all?

One of the irritations was that Mottram, a prose writer of genius, got rid of book reviews. This proud rejection of explanation may explain why so few people know anything about modern-style British poetry. *Poetry Review* had previously been rather good at reviews of new poetry. Is there any link between total group solidarity and writing poetry which is incomprehensible to anyone except the poet's fellow-travellers? And, upholding theories on the basis of illuministic inspiration rather than the collection of evidence or discussion with independent judges?

Behind the barren history of committees we perceive a middle tier of human habits and desires behind which grand ideas can be dimly detected. This middle tier is filled with people, rather than ideas, and impulses too concrete and personal to be ideas, such as loyalty, envy, attraction. Projective identification naturalises any role and makes the cultural field invisible to those caught inside it. This most controversial row in modern poetic history offered an opportunity to expose the unconscious structure of this field. These are not free individual choices but follow the silent rules of which all cultural acts are fulfilments, which are highly structured, which belong to no individual. The rules preset, for example, why you think someone less intelligent than you is limited, local, and boring, and someone more intelligent than you is cold, detached, paradoxical, inauthentic, but you don't think you are either limited or inauthentic. These rules changed very rapidly in the 1970s and the idea of continuity and legacy from then to now is questionable. The field is bigger than any of the individuals within it, but any moves can be seen as related to the whole field. We may well think that the stimulus of rejection is what brings about the wonderful energies of self-consciousness and exploration inside great modern poetry. One of the silent rules seems to be that great poets cannot be popular. Another seems to be that great editors end up not having anything to edit.

That staggering belief that "we are the future and we're here now" can provoke astounding over-achievement, breathtaking arrogance, devastating loss of proportion, inhibition of normal artistic impulses, colonialist condescension towards less privileged poetic groups, outright denial of the evidence, greatness against all odds and records. It may be incompatible with managing a national society with a broad range, by age and artistic inclination, of members. Into which the Arts Council can pour money.

Postscript

I tried to interview Peter Barry after writing this, and he explained how the research was tightly planned around the time he had spare from teaching; he studied all the archives, but had no time to do interviews as well. The interview came to nothing—I think he was too busy. I'm glad he had time to finish the book so well.

I have defined balkanisation as something which developed rapidly during the period. Evidently then the landscape of 1997 is different from the landscape of 1960. It is easy to find a succession of styles in the area of reflexive poetry, where conscious innovation is at a premium. This satisfying time series becomes less so when we look at a larger area of the poetic field, where visibly most writers have nothing to do with innovation and very little to do with reflexivity.

Historians, conventionally, study events and use them to uncover larger dispositions of forces, and with the aid of serial events go on to find temporal shifts in those dispositions. Historians of politics rely on overt disputes, causes where different factions made their reactions public and further engaged in criticisms and refutations of each other. The only public event I can find over the 40 years this study covers is the wars at the Poetry Society in roughly 1973–7. Even then, no one can agree on the significance of the events. The record of public debate about that cause is meagre. It is questionable whether a structural change in poetry occurred as a result of it. Perhaps we have to decline to the level of individual books as events. Take a copy of *Poetry Review* which I have just bought in an Oxfam shop. Vol. 57, summer 1966, price three shillings and sixpence. Combing the reviews and the advertisements, we find books by Robert Armstrong, J.C. Hall, Ruth Pitter, Charles Tomlinson, Brian Higgins, George Barker. All of these are events. Maybe they sum up what was happening in that quarter of 1966. But a list of them is completely frustrating; no one could read it without wanting to know what the cultural meaning of the books was. You ask who the poets were and the answer can only be given in terms of a view of the cultural field. What is the pattern?

Due process and the Ammonite or, The Imagined Village

The events of 1973–7 which led to the removal of a radically innovative editor from *Poetry Review* seem to have been repeated in the unexpected departure of two brilliant editors from the magazine in 2004. I wonder how much has changed in the conservative alliance in the intervening decades. The most talked-about process in the poetry world, over a period of several years, was the installation of an editorial team who had restored *Poetry Review* to greatness, and their unexpected removal. Although this was not really an event in the public domain, people who watch the flight of birds will have guessed that Influential People rang up certain office-holders, off the record, and ordered an assassination. *The country won't stand for it. They have to go.* The offence was praising and publishing modernist poetry. There is a continuing opposition between the Mainstream—filled today with unambitious pop poetry—and the underground world of artistic and intelligent poetry, published sporadically and by small concerns.

It is convenient to talk about two sides. A bit of probing suggests that eight or even eleven factions, more or less completely sealed off from each other, exist within the British cultural sphere.

The poetry scene is a small world run by the nastiest and most territorial people and where the public realm has shrivelled away—the key decisions are anonymous, unaccountable, and unrecorded. But, believe me, someone messed up the landscape—it didn't get this way on its own.

I think the background is of the poetry editors of the big publishing houses watching funded publications such as *Poetry Review* like hawks to see that their string of poets gets published a lot and reviewed favourably, and when that doesn't happen they pick up the phone and engage in character assassination. Arts policy has been shaped by the seedy preoccupations of small businessmen, unchecked and unredeemed. I've always assumed that was the story, but the evidence will never be made public. To the extent that the poetry world is dominated by conservatism, and that this is unconsciousness, a sludge of vast blind impulses that resist verbalisation, a verbal account of what happens is impossible in principle. I have grave doubts about writing some kind of history of poetry—I mean of shared events, of institutions, of A and B lists, etc.—when none of the evidence is in the public domain. If there is no credible historical account on its way, there is no tribunal which judges of the validity of public actions—and this is terrifying, because it implies that the feeling of acting validly is all there is.

I don't agree that you can just do what you like. This loss of evidence would argue in favour of dramatic and unanalysed, projective versions of events, which are not literally true but which pull up the non-verbal into consciousness. They may be as close as we can get to the truth. The whole incident reminds us of a regime change at *Stand*, in the late 1990s.

We are still living in the shadow of the Utopian future which people glimpsed in the 1970s. The Utopia involved humans behaving perfectly—and the indefinite delay of this state has left us in the lurch, in a permanent interim where people have no standards at all. Someone promises to do something for you and four years later they still haven't done it. But they don't see this as bad behaviour—in their heads they are part of that

Utopia, and after it comes they will behave perfectly. Wouldn't it be better to behave decently towards real people in real situations? Sometimes I have the impression that the small press world has been winding down for 25 years—from an initial state of fantastically high energy and commitment, through stages that sink ever lower into apathy, indifference, and bad faith.

I think there is an ethical vacuum in the cultural world. The question is about operative ethics—applied to real decisions rather than ones in an idealised distant situation. We need an ethics suited to the world we actually live in. I would propose that the cultural managers recognise the magnitude of the suppression that has taken place under their reign. As for the dwellers in what used to be called the Underground, they should give up their belief in their own automatic superiority and freedom from normal ethical standards. I think a credible account of modern poetic history—of the last 40 years—can only emerge slowly, and only after an ethical breakthrough which would mean that a wide variety of people would testify honestly.

So many varieties of damaged language come out of a damaged relationship between self and society. I don't want to read a poem that needs to be reached by a recovery vehicle before I can get anywhere near it.

If there is a politics of poetry, it rotates around niches vested as public offices, and about judging whether individuals are fit and proper to occupy those niches. The act which bears the political strain is then the act of assessing character. This may appear secret and internal, but it is the central ethical act (in this dispensation), and may not remain secret for long. It may help to apply this to editors: the firing of editors is all related to their judgements of poets, which are made public by every issue. What is made public arouses puce lumps of rage in some quarters—and feelings of loyalty and love in others. The central dogma of our society is possessive individualism—the predominance of *amour-propre* and private passions as guides to conduct. Such judgements are where ideas from the deep territory of the privately owned, a place close to the core of the ego, cross over into a realm where they are shared and criticised—and where they can be considered as someone else's property. That is—most poets regard their reputation as their property. That is—your internal reactions belong to them (and they claim jurisdiction over them and may claim damages if you disobey them). All this is unsustainable—which is why it is so hard to set cultural politics on a rational basis.

It's clear that decisions within a poem don't belong to an autonomous world. The poet is asking to be judged, and writes in such a way as to influence those judgements. At some levels, reading is an act of inspection; to a certain extent, the poet can supply the answers but the reader asks the questions. A poem opens a situation and satisfies by answering the questions we are asking about the situation. A poet signals morality, signals modernity, signals tribal affiliation, and so on. Because much of the argument around poetry is dedicated to these signals, it seems likely that they are a central part of reading it. It goes so much better if you both want the same thing.

The formula would be:

— individual liberty at the level of thematic and stylistic choice;
— restraint and painstaking accuracy at the level of talking and writing about poetry;
— conditional liberty at the level of portraying other people's states of mind in poems.

Reactions to a poem belong to you, not to the poet. It is a problem pushing your deep inner reactions outwards, into words, where other people can criticise them. After this process has taken place, your reactions change—they become less spontaneous, more complicated, more anxious. However, this socialisation process is not all bad. Anyway, it is something that happens to you as you live more years on the planet, whether you write reviews or not. Other people's reactions get more and more important. Deep identification, taking place as you read poems for example, makes you less egoistic and more complicated. I am quite happy to say that there is lots of poetry which possesses this complication and which I didn't understand when I was a teenager, and which is the only kind I want to read now. I am sure this is the main difference between the poetry I like and the poetry which I find trivial, irritating, and shallow—mainstream poetry, in fact. But this generalisation doesn't hold good everywhere, since after all radical simplification is also a feature of some very good poetry, and it is arguable that this is a *defining* feature of lyric poetry.

We can't use the word blacklist because when I used it in the office someone complained, later, that the equation of being black with being unimportant was painful for her. It's possible to hurt people without knowing it but you *don't have to go on doing it*. But let's talk about A B and C lists instead, and admit that culture has a great deal to do with lists. There are never going to be enough places on the boat for everyone. Deuteronomy 23:3 says: *An Ammonite or Moabite shall not enter into the congregation of the LORD; even to their tenth generation shall they not enter into the congregation of the LORD for ever.*

Because culture is based on distinctions and classifications, it is possible that intensifying cultural activity—as a priest or a writer—makes you draw distinctions more intensively. The more literate you are, the more enthusiastic you are about imposing these stupid rules on the Ammonites. The dark side of beautiful language: that the beauty is reached by selectivity, and that in social life this sort of beauty means removing certain kinds of people.

To purge intellectuals (and everything they stood for) from the sacred realm of culture was one of the main campaigns in English culture during the 20th century. Restoring it, probably, to the farmer drawing his plough down the furrows in close touch with the sensuous realities of life; or, digging the potatoes. Or flirting with sheep. Whatever. So that making the landscape more beautiful actually meant, when you look at it, erasing intellectuals, and anything they said, their poetry, their ideas, the books they read. Anything that wasn't already around in 1500 AD is inherently unaesthetic. Pylons spoil the view. Intellectuals must be kept away from the sacred precincts of poetry. Abstract words are unpoetic. The poem is to the world of ideas what the countryside is to the city. The abstract word is to the poetic idyll what the rusting carcass of a car is to a rustic idyllic spot. In this way . . . you decide that an editor who even mentions Prynne favourably has to be eliminated. The idyll has trees and lakes but is curiously free of people.

We can look at Georgina Boyes' study *The Imagined Village* for the cultural background to this mid-century preoccupation[2]. To a significant extent, the New Age took over this cultural fantasy, with writers like Paul Screeton fantasizing about Neolithic technology because that is when the Village was invented: he is attacking all culture and technology which postdates the Neolithic, and in this is taking up earlier ruralist-archaeological writers like H.J. Massingham.

One way of making the ground clean for one set of children is by physically annihilating other sets of children. That is, the benevolent acts of a cultural manager towards his pet poets are acts of malevolence towards other poets, who are being chopped out and burnt on the bonfire. The cultural managers don't feel guilty because all their wickedness and folly has been aimed at defending the market share of their clients—acts of protection and patronage. They feel justified in burning out modernism without any due process, and they regard this as proof that they are good people. As usual in England, people making claims about morality are really thinking about money. In this case, people claiming to clean up the landscape were really thinking about market share.

I was talking about ethics. I think this Bad Father model of behaviour is incompatible with public office. If you're going to hold public office, you have to have more scope, more breadth, than that. There should be a tier—of reviewers, anthologists, historians—who give a fair hearing to what comes along, and don't conspire to help their favourites.

There are recognition codes on the cellular surface of poems which display people also as Ammonites, Amalekites, maybe even Adornoites. They allow you to make decisions instantaneously—which is utterly the wrong way of making decisions. Public discourse about poetry is not based on artistic values, but on loyalties. It's also ignorant, because neither side has read any books published by the other one for the last 30 years. In fact— very few people have the faintest idea what the shape of the poetry world is. They're all too busy thinking about the people in the bar they drink in. People may behave as intellectuals in realms distant from their own interests, but when it comes to cultural politics they function at rodent level. Small, furry egos with very poor eyesight. And a strong sense of territoriality. There is a small rat realm beyond self-projection. You don't hear from it very much. When you renounce all loyalties, temporarily, the first result may be guilt at having treated all the other parts of the scene so unfairly.

The avant-garde vanished over the horizon, and they're invisible now. Which of course makes the rejection of them spooky and unreal—it's like an inherited memory from an interaction that took place in 1930 but which is still seared into someone's brain. The reaction to fear of contamination is a deep, reptile-brain, thing; mainstream poets know that reflexive poets will hate them, this kind of knowledge is like someone gay being able to work out from a glance at 1,000 yards that someone is anti-gay, it's like an actor's sense of the audience, it's like a rabbit knowing it has to run. It's rapid, totally egocentric, but not very accurate. Obviously anyone who is going to be engaged as an editor, reviewer, critic, etc. has to venture into the more adult part of their brains and start to appreciate social geometry as opposed to egocentric reactions of panic and lust. It's always a good time to replace inherited traumas with well-lit, recent, intelligently framed and sequenced, evidence. (Let me point, for instance, to the recent (2003) Prynne Symposium on *Jacket* issue 24 at www.jacketmagazine.com.)

It's hard to reprogramme these rodent responses, but maybe we can do some work to make them conscious and public. I also think we need something like a peace process. It amazes me that so far none of the squad leaders of the poetic right wing have owned up and repented of their actions in repressing the innovative and creative wing for so long. I think forgiveness is likely to follow on from an admission that terrible things were done in order to produce an idyll of conformity and consent.

NOTES

[1] Peter Barry *Poetry Wars* (Cambridge: Salt Publishing, 2006).
[2] Georgina Boyes, *The imagined village: culture, ideology and the English Folk Revival* (Manchester: Manchester University Press, 1993).

[3] If you want to form an opinion on what Osborne was trying to repress, there is no alternative to reading the original 22 issues of *Poetry Review* in which the evidence is recorded. An issue of *Poetry Information* (periodical, Newcastle upon Tyne) has an index of all the poets shown in those issues. Since the fight was about innovation and the future, the record of what those hundred or so poets did after the mid-70s is also important. But most people have formed opinions on the matter which are wholly independent from the evidence. Mottram's manifestoes are indispensable to forming a view:

— 'The British Poetry Revival 1960–74' (in *Catalogue of the Polytechnic of Central London Poetry Conference*, 1974).
— *The Triumph of the Mobile: The Structure of information, the Language of Computers and Contemporary Poetry* (London: Writers Forum, 2004).

The Assizes of Conceit: Afterword

Keen readers will have noticed that the feared sentence of heresy has not actually been pronounced, and I have gone through the entire book as if no one was guilty of pernicious aesthetic error. This may suggest that the whole process has been unfair from the start, and that—since in fact I picked poets whose work I admire—there was no fair chance of a thrilling negative verdict and a thumping act of execration. That is, like a detective story in which no crime was committed.

I have to admit that some poetry is uninteresting. Perhaps we could return to the heresy, described at the start, of overrating your own talent—imitating the Creator by creating a delusory world. Let us agree that more than one young poet has actually dwelt in such a delusion. The context is something which Freud defined as the infantile hallucination of omnipotence, an all-encompassing state, from an early phase of psychic development, in which someone believes in a "magical" world in which no obstacles exist, and especially that their own abilities are boundless. Although this is dissipated by interaction with the world and with other people as childhood really gets under way, it unmistakably recurs in the idealistic stage of adolescence, when fantasies predominate and in them ideals are formed which point to the perfectibility of society and of daily life. Hardly less certainly, the state recurs as the basis for fantasy and idealism in art. We wish someone who is going to drive a car, or build a house for us, or carry out a role within a public authority, to be free of such vagaries. There is another mental phase, of realism, which coincides with the world as it actually is and even with the wishes of other people as they actually are. The most naive of poets are also the most arrogant and the most dominated by the hallucination of omnipotence, as they believe that their every gesture carries cosmic significance, and they can write hundreds of pages of poetry all of which must be preserved. It is not rare to encounter scripts from poets who think they are Jesus, or Rimbaud, or Lenin, or Quentin Tarantino. The more ignorant they are, the more omnipotent they feel.

However, we have to consider that the energy which drives art is substantially drawn from this state of idealising the self and the universe, that the condition of freedom is the most precious thing in art, and that if we grind down art until it is co-extensive with the physical universe of constraint it will not work any more. That is, that art depends on the smuggling in of the hallucination of omnipotence in more or less scarce and complicated forms.

If this is really the case, then simply purging young poets of their confidence in their own ability, in the potential of art, in the possibilities of other people, and in the potential of the universe is not going to set them on the steep path to excellence, but to prepare them for abandoning poetry and becoming efficient clerks in some well-run institution. Further, the young poets who are going to achieve the most are precisely the ones with the strength to hang on to the most primitive inner state, with its unrecuperated optimism and belief in creativity, freedom, transformation. At a personal level, these are the most provocative—the most arrogant, if you wish, because also the most ambitious.

We could use archaeology as a comparison. The basic event is a miracle—resurrection, the transcendence of time, patterns greater than the individual, the finding of treasures. Archaeology as a job is mostly digging and sieving and not finding. Fake archaeologists are the ones who never criticise any discovery—the miracles happen all the time, and the infantile taste of omnipotence prevails without resistance. You can dig anywhere, in fact, and find ancient and highly patterned things. This is cloying and nauseating. However, you can't eliminate these buried-treasure events as the emotional basis of archaeology, and in fact the events which are the most exciting to read about, the ones which animate the whole undertaking, are the ones which are the closest recreation of the miracle state—where treasures are uncovered and patterns supporting grand theory form, new and yet clear. To return to poetry, maybe the most successful poetry is one in which the poet's ego-illusion is the least damaged and the reader is the most generously drawn inside it. The happy core of poetry may be simply the state of buoyancy, happiness, high rate of associations without censorship, of the poet. Yet these are the most archaic features, the ones most obstinately linked to childhood.

The question of politics is especially prone to bring about a lack of understanding. It's irritating when someone of very small talent lays claim to a very large idea. In the dream of omnipotence, they think that changing the sign means changing the reality. They disqualify all real-life politicians because they cannot do this. A young poet wheels on a film of the world completely changing, the existing niches, such as the one the reviewer lives in, being dissolved, and a new order being saved from perils by attending to the Poet's instructions. I can see that critics are indignant about young poets, whom they regard as insolent and unimportant, daring to invoke ideas about politics, on such a scale as to engulf the existence of the critics and the future of society. The critic encircles the poet and the poet encircles the critic. The poet uses their ignorance as a mighty symbol of the unknowable aspects of the future. Objectively, the future will bring about the dissolution of the world we are familiar with. This is the nature of time, and the poet is not wrong about this.

We seem to have reached the brink of another topic, that of critics (attached to the status quo) forming bad judgements of young poets which are delusory and so a form of heresy. The limbs of this heresy are these: judgement of unwritten poetry as if it were knowable; judgement of new political ideas without waiting for practical test; judgement of new artistic methods without waiting for them to reach maturity. But ideas which cannot be evaluated cannot be known to be without value. They therefore deserve close attention until they lose that status—coinciding with the attention seeking of young poets in a pivotal movement which may, perfectly well, end up with close attention being abidingly given to both ideas and poets. The politics of poetry takes place in the delay before this uncertainty has stabilised.

All the scenes and devices from great poems appear endlessly in bad poems. This has to do with the ego illusion: anything which happens to you seems more vivid than what happens to other people, and if you're naive you think your own experiences are super-vivid for other people. So any inexperienced poet uses lots of stock footage—like the footage of an octopus which Ed Wood is so pleased with in *The Ed Wood Story*. Of course the stock footage is interesting—that's why we know it so well.

The landscape a critic of new poetry moves through vitally includes a swathe, dominating the visual field or tucked away in a corner, of undefined forms: without colour or line, unstable, shimmering constantly between different half resolutions, bursting with potential, charged with error, forever about to yield to some brilliant stroke of imagination and linguistic reason. The urge for premature definition sweeps aside vagueness at the cost of introducing fundamental error.

All those salvation fantasies, trips around the world one mile high in the air, attempts to be as incomprehensible as Prynne, projects for transforming Near Eastern politics, lecture courses in the finer details of their own personality, leave stately rolls of fat in the ego paunch or *omentum selfaticum.*

There is in fact no great allegorical painting of the Mannerist era showing the weighing of the egos of young writers. One imagines a huge dusky hall with seats for austere Judges and a large set of scales, like ones used for weighing cattle at prize shows, with the poet's ego in one of the platters, held in place by a leather strap. The judges have birds' heads and their attention is on the long spire which is the needle of the scales. It leans dully, faithfully, in one direction. Scattered over the receding dimness of the hall, muscular servitors run to and fro bringing engraved iron discs, piles of bricks, lumps of scrap metal, tanks of water, in order to reach an exact counterweight to the grandiose bulk of the ego and so measure its exact ponderousness. They are experts in their field and with time even the ego of a Cambridge poet can be neutralised. Of course anything heavier than an orange is too heavy. But the exact weight must be recorded in the register with its patient brindled calfskin binding. Towards the foreground of the picture is a youthful poet, gesturing recklessly and saying "I stole all these images from T.S. Eliot so how can you still say he's a better poet than me! I am the paradigm shift! You don't understand me!" At last one platter would rise into the air and both would hang in counterpoise. The egomania of poets is not boundless. It is merely large when compared with houses, ships, hills, etc. And such self-esteem is an intellectual error as well as a vice. We can rightly call it a heresy.

At this moment, our time has run out. I have to stop talking. We can look back at the preface and at the plan of a virtuous database, in which true information about all the poets of period worth considering is stored. This is a plan based on ignorance: where is the database of all poets published in the period which we could scan to make a valid determination of which ones were worth considering? And, without the selective database of 500 or so poets 'with reputations', how was I able to decide who to write about? In the upshot, only thirteen poets are separately discussed in this book. I hope all the same that light has been shed on key problems, and that the truth process will be carried forward by other people. The lack of overlap between Raine, Benveniste, and O'Sullivan suggests that the documentation I have collected may not be helpful when we look at other poets. The message is that once you shatter an orthodoxy—for us, locally, Anglican, patriotic, committed to the rule of law, to regular metre, etc.—a thousand variants emerge, and these do not form a new orthodoxy.

What do we expect from depolarisation? A large number of poets would see it simply as the proportion of the market which favours their own poetry expanding from two percent to ninety-eight percent. This is banal, and by the way unlikely. It seems like a fantasy project, and is not the right answer. We might mean an abandonment of stylistic research, so that the poets who do not write like everyone else give up and start writing like everyone else, with a convulsive collapse of a differentiated landscape into one without features. This is heavily undesirable. In sum, no one expects the diversity of poetry to decrease, which would be at odds with the whole western way of life. When we spoke earlier of balkanisation, the problem there was not that poetry has become so much more diverse since 1960, but that groups (or perhaps just vocal individuals?) were spreading disinformation, no doubt as a result of misunderstanding—and of malice. Depolarisation is therefore most significant when we are talking about the instruments which provide access to poetry—for example reviews, publication in books, selection for anthologies, selection for magazines, mention in surveys. Just behind these, we find a very small number of people, a rather homogeneous group called cultural managers. Few people would disagree that in Britain modernity has been rejected and driven underground in poetry, whereas in visual arts it has strode to the forefront—in the same country, in the same period. Most probably, then, the occlusion of modernity is a debt we owe to the cultural managers. I am arguing that the poetry infrastructure has structural failings. Certainly some people who like modern poetry have also reached managerial positions; the story of how editors were dramatically removed from those positions at *Stand*, and at *Poetry Review* (in 2004 and 1977, respectively) may well explain why the others conform, and the story is the most important one to understand even though it is not in the public domain. I said the managers were homogenous; this is apparently less because of a shared artistic sensibility than because of the need for alliance with each other. The absence of accountability or media interest in poetry leaves a vacuum in which these alliances become unnaturally important—and the ability of a clique to subvert and exclude deviants such as innovators is unchallenged. When we speak of depolarisation as a force that could shift the landscape what we essentially mean is the collapse of the ability of the conservative cultural managers to exclude anything but the mainstream from visibility in shops or the media. The proposal involves a second stage in which the same people are still in charge but are the cultural officers for a diverse and modern offering of poetic styles—with no more trouble than other officials experience at the Tate Britain or the Whitechapel Gallery.

The corollary, of the intellectuals reading mainstream poetry, is less important because the intellectuals cannot block the mainstream from access to the market, and never have had such a capability. It is a desirable corollary but would not change the landscape. The further shifts in the multipolar geometry which the end of balkanisation would imply—Scottish poets reading English poetry, to mention one of the unlikely ones—are also desirable, but do not have revolutionary potential.

One topic for research is the curve of mainstream decline.

The whole underground movement was impelled by the idea that official poetry had run helplessly aground. This was a convulsive, animal-brain, panic reaction, rather than a finding of exact philological science. However, not only this, but also the counter-reaction against innovative poetry, are dominant features in the history of poetry—if you fail to understand them, you fail to understand the history.

The growth of British poetic activity during the 1960s, or perhaps more precisely 1965–75, was of such a scale that an oversight ceased to be possible. This profusion is good for the reader, but of course implies that the belief that the mainstream is devoid of good poetry ceased to be verifiable.

Research could test the accuracy of this hypothetical curve:

— the mainstream was in a terrible disarray in the 1950s and 1960s;
— the current of Pop poetry was initially rejected by the academic/ educated tier but this opposition became completely blurred and the two streams merged, gradually from the later 70s;
— the Underground split into Pop and experimental streams in the mid-70s;
— the experimental Underground was invisible to the public from 1977, having lost the Poetry Wars, and had terrible recruitment problems;
— the mainstream was revived, under these conditions, and its mighty inhibitions were sapped and weakened by the flow of postmodernism; so that from a certain point, perhaps circa 1990, good mainstream poets began to turn up;
— the phantom of a cultural revolution drawing with it a Marxist republic produced a peculiar bitterness of oppositions during the 1970s; the evident stabilisation of cultural authority and the property system during the 1980s has dissolved the bitterness, but the consequences within the poetry realm have not quite disappeared;
— the present era therefore is seeing simultaneous depolarisation and diversification (with differences evolving and getting more pronounced with time).

I am not in a position to do this research, and the amount of books being published will make any research slow. However, I can admit that in the past couple of years I have spent a lot of time reading Thwaite and Levi, mainstream Christian poets of (or, debuting in) the 1950s who scaled the artistic heights.

The effect of the sheer volume of poetry getting published at present, and of the lack of reviews, is that selecting poetry is too difficult: a response of radical selectivity, based on stylistic generalisations, is almost inevitable. One way of describing this is as increased polarisation.

The term poetry wars may be misguided—there were, at any rate, no casualties of these engagements. One moment which caused an especial sense of panic and rage was a theoretical discussion which claimed to eliminate the work of individuals from above, without inspection of individual works. I think that experts have withdrawn from this sort of ripping sheets off the map. I don't think you get (to use an analogy) people sounding off any more that any figurative painting is hysterical and out of date, or that only communists and drug addicts would make an abstract painting. I think the price of peace has been a withdrawal from theoretical activity and from the generalisations which make abstract and speculative thought possible. This is a familiar compromise in English life, and in its historical form may go back to the settlement, political and ecclesiastical, after 1660, when people for the most part realised that avoiding clear intellectual positions was the price of avoiding any more civil wars. Notoriously, this prejudice led to an intensive development of empirical accumulation of data—and would leave a space open for hundreds of accurate assessments of individuals, which as we've said is missing from the media. This looks like a good way to go. In fact, I would suggest that an appreciation of the full range of good poetry would make generalisations difficult.

PAGES FROM THE ORTHODOX MAP

Prosopography

There is admittedly a shortage of terms for modern poetry. Also, poets have a sense of their own promethean uniqueness which makes them challenge classification. However, some listing may make the meaning of the terms easier to follow and check up on. This is elementary information aimed to help people without endless knowledge of the scene.

Surrealists
Philip O'Connor	Hugh Sykes Davies

New Romantics
Patrick Anderson	George Barker	Francis Berry
Dorian Cooke	David Gascoyne	W.S. Graham
J.F. Hendry	Nigel Heseltine	Glyn Jones
Roland Mathias	Nicholas Moore	Hubert Nicholson
Kathleen Raine	Herbert Read	Edith Sitwell
Dylan Thomas	Henry Treece	Vernon Watkins
Peter Yates		

Forerunners of the 'British Poetry Revival':
W.S. Graham	Charles Madge	Joseph Macleod
Lynette Roberts		

Oxford Poets of the 1950s
John Fuller	Geoffrey Hill	Peter Levi
George MacBeth	Adrian Mitchell	Anthony Thwaite

Sixties Poetry of direct address
David Chaloner	Lee Harwood	John James
Christopher Logue	Barry MacSweeney	Tom Pickard
Tom Raworth	Ken Smith	

The 'British Poetry Revival' (as defined by Eric Mottram in 1974):
Basil Bunting	Jim Burns	Bob Cobbing
David Chaloner	Andrew Crozier	Elaine Feinstein
Ian Hamilton Finlay	Allen Fisher	Roy Fisher
Harry Guest	John Hall	Lee Harwood
Jeremy Hilton	Anselm Hollo	Michael Horovitz

Dom Silvester Houédard	Ted Hughes	John James
David Jones	Christopher Logue	Hugh MacDiarmid
Barry MacSweeney	Matthew Mead	Christopher Middleton
Stuart Montgomery	Edwin Morgan	Jeff Nuttall
Tom Pickard	Tom Raworth	Peter Redgrove
Peter Riley	Ken Smith	Nathaniel Tarn
Charles Tomlinson	Chris Torrance	Gael Turnbull

Obviously, some of these were persistent rather than a revival!

Concrete poetry

Ian Hamilton Finlay	Dom Silvester Houédard

Anthropologist-poets

Tom Lowenstein	Martin Thom	David Wevill

Neo-gothic

B Catling	David Harsent	Ted Hughes
Iain Sinclair		

Poets involved in performance art

B Catling	Ulli Freer	Khaled Hakim
Jeff Nuttall		

Avant-garde oral poetry

Peter Finch	Edwin Morgan

Conceptual and process poetry

Allen Fisher	Peter Finch	Giles Goodland
Nic Laight	Nick Macias	Edwin Morgan
Christopher Middleton	Niall Quinn	

Jungian and mythic

David Barnett	D.M. Black	Elisabeth Bletsoe
Michael Haslam	Maggie O'Sullivan	Peter Redgrove
Penelope Shuttle	Pauline Stainer	Vittoria Vaughan

Neo-Platonist

Gerard Casey	Edwin Muir	Kathleen Raine
Vernon Watkins		

Feminist poets

Elizabeth Bartlett	Alison Fell	Grace Lake
Denise Riley	Michèle Roberts	

The Ferry-Grosseteste School:

Anthony Barnett	David Chaloner	Andrew Crozier
Roy Fisher	John Hall	Michael Haslam
Ralph Hawkins	John James	Grace Lake
R.F. Langley	Tom Lowenstein	Helen Macdonald
Kevin Nolan	J.H. Prynne	Denise Riley
John Riley	Peter Riley	John Seed
Iain Sinclair	Martin Thom	Nigel Wheale

The Epistemological line

Anthony Barnett	Roy Fisher	W.S. Graham
J.H. Prynne		

Objectivists

Basil Bunting	Andrew Crozier	John Seed
Colin Simms		

Influenced by Olson and geography

Allen Fisher	Eric Mottram	Colin Simms

The London school:

cris cheek	Adrian Clarke	Bob Cobbing
Allen Fisher	Ulli Freer	Bill Griffiths
Eric Mottram	Jeff Nuttall	Maggie O'Sullivan
Gavin Selerie	Robert Sheppard	

Some Other Underground Poets:

Tim Atkins	Michael Ayres	Chris Bendon
Asa Benveniste	Sean Bonney	Kelvin Corcoran
Paul Gogarty	David Greenslade	Jeff Hilson
Paul Holman	Philip Jenkins	Tony Lopez
Rob MacKenzie	Peter Manson	Brian Marley
D.S. Marriott	Jeremy Reed	Simon Smith
Steve Sneyd	Karlien van den Beukel	Ben Watson
		(a.k.a. Out to Lunch)

Informationists
Robert Crawford   W.N. Herbert   Edwin Morgan
Richard Price

Poets influenced by John Ashbery
John Ash   Lee Harwood

Conservative post-modern
James Fenton   Glyn Maxwell   Andrew Motion
Paul Muldoon

Uninhibited post-modern
Edwin Morgan   John Hartley Williams

Some acceptable mainstream books, 1960–2006
Peter Abbs, *For Man and Islands* (1978)
Moniza Alvi, *Carrying My Wife* (2000)
Elizabeth Bartlett, *Two Women Dancing* (1995)
Alison Brackenbury, *1829* (1995)
John Burnside *Swimming in the Flood* (1995)
Robert Crawford, *Spirit Machines* (1999)
Peter Didsbury, *The Butchers of Hull* (1982)
Jane Draycott and Lesley Saunders, *Christina the Astonishing* (1998)
Ian Duhig, *The Bradford Count* (1991)
Harry Guest, *Elegies* (1980)
Peter Levi, *Collected Poems 1955–75 (1976)*
Carola Luther, *Walking the Animals* (2004)
Norman MacCaig, *Selected Poems* (1971)
Jamie McKendrick, *Sky Nails* (2000)
Alice Oswald, *Dart* (2002)
Jeremy Over *A little bit of bread and no Cheese* (2001)
F.T. Prince, *Collected Poems* (1993)
Kathleen Raine, *The Hollow Hill* (1966)
Tom Rawling, *The Names of a Sea-trout* (1993)
Alan Ross, *Poems 1942–67* (1968)
Robert Saxton, *Manganese* (2003)
Jo Shapcott, *My Life Asleep* (1998)
Penelope Shuttle, *The Orchard Upstairs* (1980)
Pauline Stainer, *The Ice-pilot Speaks* (1994); *The Lady and the Hare* (2004)

Anthony Thwaite, *New Confessions; Inscriptions; Victorian Voices*
Jeffrey Wainwright, *Heart's Desire* (1978)
John Hartley Williams, *Canada* (1997)

Balkan Gazetteer for the Period 1945–97

Advent of a new Underground since 1980. This process is not clear to me. There is a lack of credible anthologies. Proper evaluation has yet to take place. A new term would have to be invented for them—after a revival, maybe 'British poetry goes on breathing'. Generalisations about the 'British Poetry Revival' (BPR) will probably not apply.

Anthropological narrative. Marked by the discipline of social anthropology, especially by the Archaeology and Anthropology tripos at Cambridge. These poets do not necessarily have anything else to do with each other. Breaks with the 20th century convention that poetry is not narrative. Uses the stories to reveal entire semantic structures and to 'defamiliarise' modern European civilisation. Martin Thom, Ted Hughes, David Barnett, Tom Lowenstein.

Avant-garde pastoral. Poems fitting for inscriptions on garden furniture, yet linked to the avant-garde. Peter Larkin, Ian Hamilton Finlay.

Balkanization. In a balkan geography, there are twelve different stories about every event, each book, and every story can be disproved. Readers need elementally simple guides to the terrain. And what your enemies think of you is the description which is closest to consensus.

Banal classifications. because poets share almost every level of language, they are unhealthily preoccupied with the stratum-ette which makes them distinctive, if indeed one exists. For this reason, classifications identifying common elements make them very angry.

Betjeman / Auden. British poetry was generally being dumbed down in the 1960s. It is easy to link this to 'mass culture'. However, elsewhere Betjeman was the best-selling poet of the entire post-war era. Auden, the most prestigious literary poet, systematically imitated Betjeman in the last 20 years of his life. It is reasonable to link dumbing down to these two and the commercial success of 'middle class light verse'.

Auden has been the key figure for conservative English verse of the past 45 years; but the late, Betjemanised, Auden was the model which was picked up. The fusion of 'Pop poetry' and 'conservative light verse' is fundamental to the mainstream of the last 20 years, chirpy but vacuous.

British Poetry Revival. The classic description is by Eric Mottram, with the subtitle '1960–74', which makes it clear that several hundred poets were involved. From 1960, there was an explosion of poetic activity. The idea that only a few people could write proper poetry was forgotten. This was part of the wider optimism and left-wing radicalism of 1960s culture. No claim to a common style could be made for this group defined by the rejection of the conservative establishment. If there was a key idea it was immediacy, direct address, the present moment. The appeal was largely to do with lifestyle, and the avant-garde was only a fraction of the scene. A considerable hangover set in in the mid-70s, also for Mottram. This brought a mutual rejection between avant-garde and Pop elements.

Conservative postmodernism. A new mainstream of the 1980s which picks up qualities from Pop, shedding moralistic and authoritarian planks. Identified with a denial that the era of radicalism had happened; and seen as the return of conservatism with the smallest possible adjunct of modernity. Smooth and depoliticised. Examples: Glyn Maxwell, Andrew Motion, James Fenton.

Confessional poetry. This is something which happened in the USA, and which Al Alvarez predicted in 1960 would be very important in Britain. It never actually got written. Associated with Sylvia Plath. 30 years later, Barry MacSweeney did use this style.

Counter-culture and New Age. In the era of radical "counter-culture" which began, or at least took off, in 1968, the relations between New Age spirituality and a rejuvenated, anti-Soviet Marxism are a matter of great controversy. Similarly the relations in revived English poetry between Jungian personal myth and critical experimentation are a source of disputes. The Counter-culture represents an attack on structures of knowledge, on rationality, on alienating social structures generally.

Domestic anecdote. A classic essay by Andrew Crozier associates the mainstream with the poetry of domestic anecdote. The events in the poem are not felt to be important. The domestic setting is a refuge from disturbing ideas and the public realm. The reader is supposed to go along with the poem because to reject it is to reject themselves. The more banal the poem is, the more you are expected to like it.

Dumbing down. One version is that the Anglican Church responded to the crisis of the 1950s by a wide-ranging update which included the abandoning of Anglican literary traditions in favour of something like guitar songs at the youth club. Communications had to be relevant, existential, speak to urban youth, be classless, involve dialogue. This could mean that protest poetry and Pop poetry were ripples from the Anglican aggiornamento.

Someone who denies that dumbing down is taking place on a big scale is obviously a participant in the process. The process is often described as 'democratic'. Strangely enough, simplified and didactic poetry featuring naive and appealing characters is a feature of all dictatorial regimes. Giving someone less information is a way of abridging their civil rights.

The emptying of tradition. Since the past of English poetry is so overwhelming, and English people are so in love with the past, it would seem logical that there should be a lot of English poetry in traditional manners. It is a matter for surprise that there is no good poetry of this kind. English people are good at re-enactment—pageant and pastiche. The incongruity of traditional means is a central theoretical puzzle.

Mid-century British cultural theory frequently discussed the collapse of a shared conceptual and ethical framework, and it seems beyond doubt that they were right. The sterility of the inherited forms is presumably an effect of this. Where orthodoxy has collapsed, only heresies are fit to stand.

Another version is that Auden was the legitimate heir and he migrated into middle-class light verse and domestic anecdote. Aesthetically sterile, these nonetheless make up the standard style of the era.

Ferry-Grosseteste School (also known as the Cambridge School). A group crystallising in the mid-60s and dispersing in the late 70s, immortalised in the anthology *A Various Art*. Features include an interest in the structures of everyday life, reflexivity, sophistication. Ex.: J.H. Prynne, R.F. Langley, Andrew Crozier.

Folklore, folksong. A sort of 'universal minimum' which can either be seen as a great source of legendary themes and rhythms or as what poets slump into if they stop trying. Used to impose guilt on original poets by people who reject the development of individualism over the past 400 years. There was a 'folk boom' in around 1958–65. The style was essentially used up by Kipling and Housman. Main example in modern printed poetry is George Mackay Brown.

Historicism. Hegel, following Winckelmann, developed a system in which styles were rigidly bound to historical eras and inexorably faded away. Marxism was based on Hegel. A common mid-century interpretation of technical innovation in art was a rigorous succession—in which, really, only modernism counts. This pretty much wipes out British art. In Britain, people instinctively do not believe in a 'time-line' and do not create theories out of which art springs. However, it is common for people to write, paint, etc. in a traditional fashion and to find after 40 or 50 years that they have been wasting their time and that they did not find a credible style. Oh No! maybe History exists after all!

Imitation. If we chuck out the totalising Hegelian model, we can redefine style time as the set of models which it is valid to imitate. A great deal of effort has been expended finding out that models do not work. Certainly you have to start out from the point that you can't either write in a traditional Anglican literary style or in a Classical (Graeco-Roman) style. The 19th Century was devoted to finding that you can't write like Shakespeare any more, and the mid 20th century was spent finding that you can't write like Blake any more. Maybe the late 20th Century has been spent finding that you can't write like Prynne?

Informationism Scottish school of the early 1980s under the influence of Edwin Morgan, preoccupied with mental maps, the vagaries of virtual data including consciousness, subverting legacy narratives, and the position of Scotland. Examples: Robert Crawford, W.N. Herbert.

Jungian/mythic school. Sets aside the precepts both of realism and of the puritan avant-garde to focus on self-expression. Has a strong view on writing beautifully and on the benefits of working through personal symbols. A neglected group. Ex.: Elisabeth Bletsoe, Peter Redgrove, D.M. Black, Tom Lowenstein.

Late Marxism, 1968, Adornoism. The Communist Party had a history of crushing gifted writers and minimising their possible contribution to the cause they believed in. The Soviet invasion of Hungary in 1956 caused a mass exodus from the Party, and in the new freelance Marxism, the 'New Left', an intellectual approach was possible.

The student movement of 1968 had at least some sources in fringe Marxism, and certainly had a major impact on poetry.

The contrast within the Left between common sense realism based on sentiment and a theoretical, abstractly based, untraditional and virally mutating poetry of intellectuals is one of the features of the era.

Theodor Adorno has been one of the key figures for intellectual poets in this country, representing uncompromising rejection of existing culture from a position of superiority.

London School. Pool of avant-garde poets associated with Writers Forum. Their evolution from the 1960s to the present day is unclear. The main axis of the group is non-discursive and unreflexive, which means they have a low profile with the intellectual audience. However, many poets associated with the milieu have transcended the commitment to dirt, noise, and spontaneity. Examples: Maggie O'Sullivan, Ulli Freer, Adrian Clarke.

Ludic (lit. 'playful'.) Starts with the dispersal of the mature self to make way for multiple and fantastic voices. Preoccupation with early stages of language and unrealised or uncoded possibilities. Linked also to regional dislike of standard English. While this has historic links with Pop poetry, it was also branded as 'postmodernism' at the appropriate time. Surrealism had a line of inventing games that generated imaginary worlds in language, and whenever realism weakens this line crops up again. Examples: Edwin Morgan, Peter Finch, George MacBeth.

Mainstream. The mainstream denies that there is a mainstream. One definition is that everything which is not the BPR is mainstream. Another is that there is a dead centre of used-up images, tropes and events, and that anything which fails to get more than a few millimetres from this centre is mainstream. The poets believe that banal feelings and experiences are vivid because they really happened to them: such poetry is completely egocentric. They have no originality they can point to, but they have a strong sense of self. To infect the reader with this, the poet makes much of sentimental family nostalgia, places, household objects. Yet the linguistic means of expressing personality in poetry are abandoned. An anxiety confines them to the interior of a narrow perimeter. There is no point naming individuals in this context, since the point is loss of individuality.

Meta-Gothic. involves basic distortions of the body image in explorations of the classic "Gothic" style which may either be narrations of the process by which the human body came into being or a variation on the supernatural elements of religion. Examples: Ted Hughes, David Harsent, Iain Sinclair, B Catling.

Middle-aged Pop. The increasing age and decreasing excitability of the poets and their readers led to a vein of writing which had lost the surrealist brilliance of classic Pop but kept the shallowness. This is a departure from 1950s norms but has long since become intellectually timid and a new conformism. Ex.: Carol Ann Duffy, Liz Lochhead.

Neo-Objectivism. Poets linked to Pound via the refraction of a Thirties school of US poets such as Oppen and Niedecker. Ex.: Basil Bunting, Colin Simms, John Seed.

Peripheral nationalist poets. Large number of Welsh and Scottish poets writing in diverse styles (although less diverse than in other countries). The largest stock of brilliant and neglected poets. Uninfluenced by English fashions. Ex.: Norman MacCaig, Tony Conran, Euros Bowen, T.S. Law. As a generalisation, the Left and experimental upsurge in English poetry after 1968 corresponded to a nationalist upsurge in Scotland and Wales, which artistically promoted folk forms and formal *cynghanedd* verse rather than an avant-garde.

Pop lyrics are very very popular while poetry is very, very unpopular. But pop lyrics are poems. Could repay study but generally defeats thought. Owes much to folk song.

Pop poetry. Very simple poetry of direct address, linked especially to the second half of the Sixties. Examples: Brian Patten, Adrian Mitchell, Roger McGough, Adrian Henri. Its historic fate was to be massively popular and irritate the bourgeois guardians, who indeed had a pre-existing image of themselves as defending Culture against falling standards. The audience saw it predominantly in terms of lifestyle—Swinging London, or Liverpool, and liberated youth culture. Most amateur poets today write informal, self-centred, 'spontaneous' poems—the Pop heritage. Pop was directly inspired by Jacques Prévert, and at its origins had a distinct avant-garde component, its minimalism and surrealism forcing the poet to abandon the traditional sounds of the English poem. One trajectory out of Pop followed this component to develop a new avant garde, of which Raworth, Edwin Morgan, and Peter Finch are good examples. The main line of Pop abandoned the early rigour and regressed rapidly back towards sentiment, realism, etc.

Protest poetry. Not formally very distinct from other styles but did represent a notion of popular sovereignty and of the poet as spokesman/advocate. Much influenced by attempts to make Christianity "relevant" and "youthful", it flourished in pacifist/marxist campaigns of the 1950s, such as the Ban the Bomb movement, and its simplicity paved the way for Pop. It also stimulated more complex political poetry. T.S. Law, Christopher Logue, Adrian Mitchell, Ewart Milne.

Rule and Energy. John Press's 1963 account of poetry since the war identifies two rival streams, one similar to the Movement and one which represents energy, the irrational, the visionary. He emphasises poets in the latter stream such as Kathleen Raine, Vernon Watkins, Ted Hughes, Gascoyne, Barker. This counter-element in the academic and conservative Fifties is a version of the New Romanticism of the 1940s but also, if we look at Press' careful analysis, an anticipation of the New Age and its personal myths.

Sinfield. Alan Sinfield's essay in a 1983 book tells of the decline of Christianity (in 1945–70) as a communal, public religion and of the devastating sense of loss of Christian writers. Privatisation, internalisation, arbitrary gestures, and the search for a heresy which would restore the sense of communion are all symptoms of this disarray. If there is an explanatory theory for mid-century poetry, this is probably it.

Socialist realism. A coherent anti-capitalist style marked by optimism, populism, and a stress on technology, as the creation of working people. These techniques were influential on other political poets. The rejection of the prevailing social order led on to great imaginative acts and most of the other schools here.

Suavity/ Toughness. One division of the mainstream of the 1950s is between suave and tough—incompatible lines. The suave current eventually become conservative postmodernism, with a line roughly Auden–John Fuller–Glyn Maxwell. The 'tough' academic-Christian line set out to save civilisation by frustrating the wishes, large and small, of everyone around them. A phenomenon of the 1950s which still controlled institutions and patronage into the 1980s. More remembered for their repressive hegemony than for their poems.

Surviving Neo-Romantics. Since the New Romantic school consisted of poets born between 1910 and 1920, their disappearance from view after 1950 is baffling. In occlusion, they constituted the first Underground. George Barker, Glyn Jones, Roland Mathias, Kathleen Raine, Eithne Wilkins.

Geoffrey Thurley. In Thurley's classic work *The Ironic Harvest* he traces the history of detachment (the ironic harvest) as it affected the course of modern English poetry, suggesting that this overriding teleology was accepted uncritically and needs much deeper examination to recognise its full impact. What we guess from Thurley is no less than that the goal of irony, detachment, and non-commitment is favoured by the professional classes because they are going to sell their analytical skills to the highest bidder and so cannot afford to have opinions. If you have opinions, your employment opportunities are restricted. He provides an underpinning for a traditional Left position, that the educated were supercilious, incapable of artistic creation because they distrusted emotional commitment and regarded it as "provincial". He writes the history of existential poetry, fragile because the forces in play were so much greater than the powers of the poets to affect Fate. His real strength is in analysing the weaknesses of the mid-century English tradition, but the chapter on the sixties is fragrant with new hope and spontaneity.

Women's poetry. Using a profusion of styles, a newly self-conscious uptake of personal experience into a critique of the social order, linked to a political movement. has grown progressively more diverse as external pressures weakened. Early forms were continuous with protest poetry. Michèle Roberts, Alison Fell, Elizabeth Bartlett.

Lightning Source UK Ltd.
Milton Keynes UK
15 June 2010

155657UK00001B/51/P